HELPING AT-RISK STUDENTS

Helping At-Risk Students

A Group Counseling Approach for Grades 6–9

Second Edition

Jill Waterman
Elizabeth Walker

The Guilford Press
New York   London

63/63/642

© 2009 The Guilford Press
A Division of Guilford Publications, Inc.
72 Spring Street, New York, NY 10012
www.guilford.com

Printed in Canada

This book is printed on acid-free paper.

Last digit is print number: 9   8   7   6   5   4   3   2   1

Library of Congress Cataloging-in-Publication Data
Waterman, Jill, 1945–
   Helping at-risk students : a group counseling approach for grades 6–9 / Jill Waterman, Elizabeth
Walker. — 2nd ed.
      p. cm.
   Includes bibliographical references and index.
   ISBN 978-1-60623-002-2 (pbk. : alk. paper)
   1. Counseling in middle school education.   2. Counseling in secondary education.   3. Group
counseling for children.   4. Group counseling for teenagers.   5. Problem children—Counseling of.
6. Interpersonal communication in children.   7. Social skills in children—Study and teaching.
I. Walker, Elizabeth, 1973–   II. Title.
   LB1027.5.W29 2009
   373.14—dc22

                                                                   2008037879

373.14
.W29
2009

To my sons, Justy and Aaron, who experienced the 6th through 10th grades during the continuing evolution of the counseling program, frequently giving me insights, inspiring me, setting me straight, and often humbling me. They are terrific! And as the second edition of the book is published, I can report that we all survived to their adulthood.

—J. W.

To my parents, whose love and support have made me who I am. And to my husband, Ryan, whose goodness and wisdom are a constant reminder of the person I would like to be. And, given that the past few years have been especially productive, I would also like to dedicate this second edition to my four wonderful children: Luke, Bridget, Sara, and Jacob.

—E. W.

To the many wonderful young people who have participated in our groups. Their energy, enthusiasm, and love of life, as well as their pain, have touched our minds and our hearts in so many ways.

—J. W. and E. W.

About the Authors

Jill Waterman, PhD, is Adjunct Professor of Psychology at the University of California, Los Angeles, and coordinator of the UCLA Psychology Clinic, the training clinic for UCLA's top-ranked PhD program in clinical psychology. In addition to numerous articles on aspects of child trauma, she is the coauthor of *Sexual Abuse of Young Children: Evaluation and Treatment* and *Behind the Playground Walls: Sexual Abuse in Preschools*. Her research focuses on various aspects of child trauma and on developing and evaluating interventions aimed at helping our most vulnerable children. Dr. Waterman is also a practicing psychotherapist in the Los Angeles area and has 24-year-old twin sons.

Elizabeth Walker, PhD, received her doctorate in clinical psychology from the University of California, Los Angeles, in 2000. As a graduate student, she spent several years working with inner-city students in the Los Angeles area, and she currently works with economically disadvantaged, ethnically diverse high school students in Denver. Additionally, she is especially interested in integrating religion and spirituality into the therapeutic process. Dr. Walker lives in the Denver area with her husband and four children.

Preface

Aimed at helping our most vulnerable young adolescents, this book attempts to provide tools and techniques for practitioners working with youth at risk for academic, behavioral, and emotional difficulties that result from such factors as difficult family situations, learning problems, or socioeconomic disadvantage. The curriculum, which we call SPARK, combines a group process model aimed at developing interpersonal skills and a psychoeducational model focused on building competence by development of specific skills needed by all youth, and particularly needed by at-risk youth. The goals are to provide a trusting, supportive environment that facilitates discussion and disclosure regarding, for example, educational goals, aggression and violence, ethnic identity and discrimination, and interpersonal relationships, and to teach specific skills such as anger management, emotion regulation, effective study skills, communication tools, and peer pressure resistance.

The SPARK curriculum has eight modules, each with several sessions. Each of the modules addresses issues salient for at-risk youth (Trust-Building and Communication Skills; Anger Management and Emotion Regulation Skills; Ethnic Identity and Anti-Prejudice; Educational Aspirations; Peer Pressure, Bullying, and Gangs; Male–Female Relationships; Exposure to Violence and Posttraumatic Stress Reactions; and Family Relationships). The modules can be expanded to fit the needs of a particular school or group. For example, if a group includes several very aggressive students, the Anger Management and Emotion Regulation Skills module can be extended as needed. Similarly, modules that do not seem relevant for a particular school or group can be dropped. For example, the Male–Female Relationships module might not be used with a group of immature sixth graders. Designed to help students who may be turned off by school, SPARK groups are activity based, engaging, and interactive. The curriculum can be helpful for students who are already experiencing problems and can be used as a tool to prevent problems from developing.

The program can be utilized in a variety of settings. We have focused primarily on the school setting in accordance with the trend for mental health and social services for children to be increasingly school based. The school provides an important location for programs such as SPARK, which are aimed at high-risk students who often would not otherwise have access to such prevention and intervention services because of a lack of community resources or family difficulties. The curriculum was developed in a small-group setting; however, most of the activities in the curriculum can easily be adapted for use with whole classrooms. The activities come with discussion questions and major points that can easily be used by classroom teachers. Specific ideas for whole classroom use are presented in Chapter One. Within the school setting, the curriculum can be implemented successfully by a wide range of school-based practitioners, including school psychologists, guidance counselors, school social workers, school nurses, other administrative school personnel, and interested teachers. Graduate students in education, social work, and psychology can also implement the curriculum in collaboration with school personnel.

In addition to school professionals, the curriculum has been used successfully by social workers, psychologists, and other allied health personnel in mental health settings, including outpatient groups and day treatment settings for adolescents. Some of the activities require a small- or large-group setting, but some can be utilized in individual counseling within both school and clinic settings. The program can also be used by university-based trainers working with students preparing for careers in education, psychology, and social work.

In the years since publication of the first edition, we have further refined the curriculum and addressed gaps in the first edition through work with other SPARK groups in school and housing project contexts. For the second edition, we have made many revisions and additions. In Chapter One, we have added a section on adapting the curriculum for full classroom use; we present five basic principles for adaptation and detail which activities and modules translate easily for classroom use and how to modify others for whole classroom use. In addition, we suggest use of a binder for each student, with

sections for handouts, assignments, and points and rewards, and discuss how to set up a simple reward system for bringing back homework assignments and positive participation.

In the actual SPARK curriculum, we have added a new three-session module called Male–Female Relationships to address students' often skewed view of gender and dating relationships. New sessions have also been added to several modules. In the Trust-Building and Communication Skills module, we have developed a new session to help students develop good listening skills (including interpreting body language and empathic responding) and improved speaking skills (using I-statements, being assertive without being aggressive). We have also added a session on dealing with relational aggression (bullying, gossiping, etc.) and renamed the appropriate module Peer Pressure, Bullying, and Gangs. The original anger management module has been revised extensively to include a focus on emotion regulation skills as well as use of a thermometer analogy to help identify triggers and body sensations associated with a rise in one's "emotional" temperature, and more emphasis on coping thoughts and coping actions when angry. For the Educational Aspirations module, we have replaced the third session with a session that uses the movie *Rudy* to illustrate how reaching a goal takes hard work; in addition, specific "Student Strategies for Success" in the areas of in-class preparation, organization, and homework are presented and discussed. The session on posttraumatic stress has been expanded to cover more coping strategies. In addition, we have added more handouts throughout the curriculum to help with retention and generalization. Several significant changes have also been made to the pre- and posttreatment interview; for example, we have replaced our unstandardized measure of anger and aggression with a standardized, well-documented measure of anger and positive and negative coping strategies and reduced the number of response scales needed by half. We feel that the new content, the use of notebooks for the students, and the increased number of handouts will significantly add to the value and effectiveness of the curriculum.

SPARK evolved over a period of years but began with a few groups meeting after school in housing projects in Los Angeles. In these settings we saw very vividly some of the issues faced daily by at-risk youth. The playgrounds and sandboxes were strewn with broken glass and even spent bullet casings, and gang members hung out beside the buildings and occasionally menaced passersby. Once an adult resident burst into the room where our group was being held and asked if he could stay because he was being chased by a man with a gun who was trying to kill him. Many of the children often heard gunfire when home, had parents dealing with drug addiction or in jail, and had heavy responsibilities such as caring for younger children. Through such experiences, we realized the level of fear and uncertainty, the chronic exposure to violence, and the lack of supportive resources that confronted these young adolescents every day of their lives. We discovered that any curriculum we developed would have to address issues of anger management, exposure to violence, and family relationships.

When presented with the opportunity to move the program to selected public schools, we were glad to proceed, because we felt we could reach a larger group of students. We developed our first informal curriculum in 1992 and spent 7½ years refining the activities and the format, based on work and field testing with over 375 adolescents in the sixth through the ninth grades. Activities were revised both to increase the interest level for students and to teach each skill as effectively as possible. We found that the groups were more successful when we gave the participants handouts and when we reinforced the major points made at the end of each session. In addition, we generated information about how to select members and start groups, counseling techniques useful in working with children in this stage of development, and ideas for handling possible trouble spots or dilemmas. After many refinements over several years, we decided that it was time to stop revising and start disseminating.

Through working in challenging settings, we have found implementation of the program to be very rewarding. Each time a student learns nonviolent ways of responding to aggression and actually uses these new skills; resists peer pressure to join a gang or have sex; develops greater understanding and tolerance for those who are ethnically different; is able to support another group member, friend, or classmate in crisis; or comes to terms with a past traumatic violent event is an affirmation of the importance of reaching out to these young and very vulnerable students. We envision SPARK being utilized in schools across the country to help today's troubled and vulnerable youth cope with the stresses they face in their families and communities. We hope that you will find utilization of the curriculum and the book to be a powerful and rewarding experience as you work to touch and positively impact the lives of at-risk youth.

Acknowledgments

This project has been a collaborative one, involving many people during the 15 years since it began. The program originally started in the housing projects of Los Angeles when we were working with John Pusey of the 4-H Urban Youth program of the University of California Cooperative Extension. Two years later, the project moved into the schools and became part of CUES (Community–University Enrichment in the Schools), a multifaceted project involving the UCLA Department of Psychology and several schools in the Los Angeles Unified School District. CUES was funded for 3 years by the U.S. Department of Education, National Institute of Education (DOED P252A20055-94). The overall CUES project was headed by Seymour Feshbach, PhD, with Jennifer Abe-Kim, PhD, and then Curtiss Rooks serving very effectively as project directors. When the funding ended in 1994, only the group counseling project survived; it continued on a shoestring budget with help from the Los Angeles Unified School District and the volunteer work of many UCLA students and school staff.

We give our heartfelt thanks to the many students in the UCLA PhD program in clinical psychology who served as project coordinators for the CUES group counseling component, which formed the basis for the SPARK program: Jacqueline Raia, PhD, Sukey Egger, PhD, David Watt, PhD, Rose Corona, PhD, Liza Suarez, PhD, Anatasia Kim, PhD, Antonio Polo, PhD, Erika Van Buren, PhD, and Jason Lang, PhD. In addition to serving as project coordinators, all of these team members also co-led multiple counseling groups. Also co-leading multiple groups over several years were Jennifer Wood, PhD, Kimberly King, PhD, Nangel Lindberg, PhD, Silvia Gutierrez, PhD, and Tene Lewis, PhD. Sukey Egger and David Watt were instrumental in organizing and expanding the manual content to make it easier for new leaders to lead groups. In addition to her other valuable roles, Liza Suarez translated the curriculum materials, handouts, and supporting materials into Spanish; helped format all the appendices; and provided useful suggestions in statistical analyses of the data. Silvia Gutierrez contributed some ideas for the Male–Female Relationships module that has been incorporated years later in the second edition. Omar Gudino, MA, graciously translated the new Spanish appendices for the second edition. These graduate students who made up our staff were nothing short of fantastic, working long hours without pay for the joy of helping at-risk minority students. Our undergraduate students carried out post-group interviews and coded and entered data. They too were dedicated and cared very much for the middle school and high school students who participated in the project. In fact, as a result of their experiences, several of the undergraduates decided to go into school counseling or administration. Pam Marks, Administrative Officer for the clinical psychology program, was helpful in many small ways that meant so much in crisis situations. Jill Waterman's son Justy Burdick was invaluable in helping with manuscript preparation and formatting the appendices for the first edition, and her other son, Aaron Burdick, performed the same tasks for the second edition.

In the schools, we were fortunate to work with dedicated principals, administrative staff, and counselors, who provided space for the groups to meet, photocopying, and other administrative help, and who made and coordinated referrals to the groups. Above all, our school liaisons believed that all at-risk students, regardless of their backgrounds and hardships, could succeed if given needed assistance.

Last and most important, we thank the approximately 650 students who have participated in groups. They are inspiring, lovable, energetic, fun, and completely awesome, and we hope their futures will be brighter as a result of their participation.

Contents

HELPING AT-RISK STUDENTS

CHAPTER ONE

Guidelines for Setting Up and Leading Groups

The structured psychoeducational group counseling approach for at-risk youth presented here was developed at UCLA in conjunction with Los Angeles–area schools over a period of 9 years, and has been revised significantly for this second edition. Intended to address issues salient to middle school and high school students who are struggling with academic, behavioral, and emotional difficulties, the curriculum is a 15- to 20-week program meant to span a school semester. This chapter covers the goals of the program, how to get groups started, structure of the groups, group counseling techniques, and dilemmas for group leaders. In Chapter Two, the curriculum is presented, with detailed instructions on how to conduct each session. Chapter Three gives information on group participants and on the effectiveness of the program and is followed by appendices with curriculum materials available in Spanish and English for reproduction and use, as well as a reference section. Most activities can be adapted easily for use in the classroom. We have called the program SPARK because it is meant to spark increases in student achievement, social-emotional growth, and nonviolent responding. Having a name helps to uniquely identify the program within the school and allows students to feel connected to the program. Therefore, we have referred to the program as SPARK throughout the book; however, if another name seems more appropriate in a particular school or setting, it can be substituted.

Goals of the SPARK Program

The goals of the program are as follows:

1. To provide a trusting, supportive group environment that facilitates discussion and disclosure with peers.
2. To build competence by teaching specific skills, such as anger management, empathic responding, interpersonal problem resolution, peer pressure resistance, and communication skills.
3. To provide activities and discussion to facilitate exploration of issues of concern to youth, including educational goals, aggression and violence, ethnic identity, prejudice and discrimination, family relationships, and dating relationships.

Getting Started

Selecting Group Members

SPARK groups are intended for preadolescents and adolescents who are experiencing or are at risk for a variety of academic, behavioral, and emotional problems. Examples of common referral problems are: "Johnny's grades have dropped from B's to D's and F's in the last year"; "Isobel saw her brother get shot in a drive-by shooting last month and has been in a fog ever since"; "Michael seems angry all the time and gets into fights when waiting for the bus after school"; "Fernando cries at the drop of a hat and says he doesn't care if he lives or dies." Other common reasons for student referrals include anxiety, depression, angry outbursts, exposure to family or community violence, family conflict, and loss of a family member. The groups seem to be most successful when there is a balance between members who are more outgoing and those who are quieter. If all members are very quiet, it is difficult to develop lively discussions, while if most members need to be the center of attention, it is difficult to accomplish the tasks for each session.

When recruiting group members, it is important to consider characteristics of potential members that are likely to help rather than hinder the group process. Extremely disruptive youth should be excluded because they prevent other members from benefiting from the group; these students' needs may best be met through individual counseling. It is best to exclude children who are frequently absent, since such students generally miss many sessions and retard development of group cohesion. However, we occasionally have had participants who are chronically truant but come to school only to attend the counseling groups.

If there are major long-standing interpersonal conflicts between two potential group members (e.g., gang vendetta), it is best to place them in separate groups. Although the program has been successfully run with children in special day schools and in self-contained programs for emotionally disturbed children, it is mainly intended for at-risk youth in regular middle and high schools. When it is run with special needs children, we have found it helpful to plan for the curriculum to take almost twice as long to cover as it would with students in regular classes. The curriculum has been developed for use in ethnically diverse urban schools; however, most of the modules are appropriate for use in any secondary school setting.

Teachers, counselors, and administrators are asked to refer children for possible inclusion in the program. They are asked to specify the reason for referral and to include any information that would be useful for group leaders to know. Often the same child is referred by several different sources. A sample referral form is provided in Appendix A-1 and may be reproduced as is or modified to meet the needs of a particular school.

Gender and Ethnic Composition

The specifics of the composition of the groups are decided by the group leader(s), based on the needs of the students. In general, our groups have been composed of both boys and girls. There should be at least two or three members of each gender in a particular group, as it is very difficult (especially for middle school students) to be the only girl or only boy in a group. Students who are the sole representative of their gender in a particular session have seemed ill at ease and have commented on their discomfort. More boys tend to be referred than girls, and occasionally a single-gender group may be necessary. Groups composed only of boys, especially at the early middle school level, tend to be very high energy and sometimes difficult to manage.

With regard to ethnic composition, there are pros and cons to groups containing all participants of one ethnicity. In general, groups with members of a single ethnicity, especially ethnic minorities, tend to develop trust more quickly and to disclose more deep and meaningful material earlier in the process. Drawn together by a common bond, they often share background characteristics and similar experiences that lead to greater understanding and empathy. However, some of the major elements of the program, such as discussions of ethnic pride, discrimination, and prejudice, are much more meaningful in the context of multiethnic groups. Groups with mixed ethnicity provide the opportunity for members to develop close relationships with members of other ethnic groups with whom they ordinarily might not even interact. Developed primarily in schools with significant African American and Latino populations, the SPARK groups have generally been multiethnic.

Spanish-language materials for leading groups are available in Appendices C and D. When conducting groups in Spanish, it is important to consider the amount of student exposure to English and Spanish. For example, some students may be more comfortable speaking Spanish as they do at home, while at the same time be more familiar with written English, which they use at school. Therefore, it is important for the written material to be available in both Spanish and English, demonstrating flexibility to meet the needs of individual students. In addition, during the Ethnic Identity and Anti-Prejudice module (Module Three), Spanish-speaking groups should include discussion about students' experiences with immigration and acculturation.

Grade Level

Depending on the size of the school and the number of possible group members, grade-level distribution in the groups may vary. The smaller the range of grade levels in a particular group, the better. Developmentally, groups of 6th graders are very different from groups of 9th or 10th graders. The disparities among maturity levels can be staggering, especially in middle school as children go through puberty. We recommend that no more than two consecutive grades be lumped together. Ideally, the entry level at middle school (typically sixth grade) and at high school (usually ninth grade) would have their own groups to ease transition, and other groups could be more mixed with regard to grade level. Particularly in middle school, gender and grade need to be considered together. For example, one group with mostly seventh-grade girls and sixth-grade boys was characterized by almost no interaction between the less mature, often silly boys and the more sophisticated girls, who would not deign to relate to such "children."

Group Size

The ideal group size is between 7 and 10 members. Smaller groups do not allow for as much diversity of opinion and discussion, while larger groups do not allow time to accommodate all group members. It is best to recruit a few more group members than desired, as several may not be able to continue with the group for a variety of reasons. Common reasons for leaving the group include moving to a different district, getting expelled, not wanting to miss a class (generally physical education), and discomfort in a group setting. Especially in inner-city schools, children frequently transfer in and out of schools. Families who have been victims of community violence frequently cope by moving out of the area. Although such moves may provide more safety, they also prevent students from utilizing the support of the group to cope with their reactions and feelings. New members can be added during the Trust-Building and Communication Skills module if necessary (generally the first three sessions), but should not be added after that point, as it disrupts trust and group cohesion.

Structure of the Groups

Generally conforming to a school semester, SPARK groups are based on a 15- to 20-session model, allowing a week or two at the beginning of each semester to recruit and interview members. The curriculum consists of eight modules. While all of the modules are usually presented, it is possible to pick and choose among them to fit the particular needs of a group or school. Similarly, the number of sessions devoted to any of the modules can be reduced or expanded to deal with hot topics or issues for a specific group of children. It is also possible to rearrange the order of the modules when appropriate. If, for example, a topic such as racial discrimination or gang involvement comes up naturally, it may be more powerful to present the module at that time, even if it is out of order. However, beginning all groups with the Trust-Building and Communication Skills module (Module One) is highly recommended, since the development of a safe environment for disclosure and skills to respond empathically will facilitate the meaning and effect of the remaining modules.

Typically, groups are held during school hours and students are pulled out of a regularly scheduled class. Groups meet for one class period (generally 50 to 60 minutes) each week. In order to minimize the time away from a particular class, group sessions can alternate between two class periods. In other words, a group might meet during first period one week, during second period the next week, during first second period the third week, and during second period the following week. Other means of minimizing missed class time can be worked out by individual schools. SPARK groups can be run after school as well; however, attendance tends to be much poorer, as students have other after-school activities, such as sports, and sometimes have responsibilities caring for younger siblings.

Groups have usually been held in unused classrooms or lounges. It is important for the space to be private, so that students can be assured that disclosures will remain within the group. Generally, chairs are moved to form a circle to facilitate open communication and sharing. It is helpful to have the same space for all the group sessions, if possible.

Designed to help students who may be turned off by school, SPARK groups are activity based and interactive. Sessions begin with Check-in, where each student has the opportunity to share experiences or feelings that have occurred in the last week. Then the leader introduces the module, the goal, and the activity for the week. At the end, students participate in Check-out, where they are asked to tell what they learned from the activity to reinforce the curriculum goal, and to share their feelings about the group session.

At the end of the first session, students are given a three-ring binder with dividers, in which they are encouraged to keep handouts from the group and the few homework assignments that are given. The dividers should be labeled "Handouts," "Assignments," and "Points and Rewards." A sample title page for the binder is available in Appendix A-8. Especially for younger students, we have found it very useful to allow them to earn points each session that can be cashed in at the end of a session for small pieces of candy or held until the end of the group, when they can be redeemed for small prizes if there is a budget available for things such as CDs, student store gift certificates, or other small items that may be popular among the particular group of students. While leaders can set up the point system in whatever way they wish, one suggested way is for students to be able to earn one point each session for each of the following: (1) bringing their notebook to group each week; (2) not getting any warnings or time-outs; (3) completing a homework assignment and bringing it to group if relevant. In addition, they might also be able to earn one point each for bringing back their consent form for the field trip to a university on the first day and missing no more than one group session. The number of points, what earns points, and the particular prizes can be modified as appropriate for a particular school or group. The group leader(s) need to keep track of the points earned and whether the student gets the candy or holds on to the points. A tracking log for this is available in Appendix A-9.

Group Leaders

The most successful group leaders have the following qualities:

1. They really like preadolescents and adolescents.
2. They are liked by preadolescents and adolescents.
3. They can follow the curriculum but are flexible enough to accommodate a particular student's burning issue.
4. They are interested in group dynamics.
5. They are comfortable with and respect different cultures.
6. They can maintain confidentiality except where disclosure is required by law.

Group leaders who have utilized the program have generally come from within school or university settings. Leaders within school settings have generally been counselors, although interested and committed teachers can also carry out the program successfully. It is most effective if teachers who plan to utilize the curriculum in the full classroom format have some mental health background. Leaders of other groups have been graduate students from local university training programs in clinical or educational psychology and social work.

The program works best with co-leaders, although this may not always be logistically possible. Suggested combinations would be two counselors or teachers, a counselor and a teacher, a counselor and a graduate student, or two graduate students. There are many advantages to having co-leaders. The leaders can divide such tasks as recruiting members, conducting individual pregroup (and postgroup) interviews, and getting materials photocopied and organized. Having co-leaders also provides for backup if one leader is stymied about where to take the group or if one leader is busy dealing with a difficult member. Additionally, discussing the group process with another leader often helps clarify direction and group dynamics. Co-leaders also provide more opportunity for students to bond with someone with whom they are comfortable.

Presenting the Groups to Prospective Members

Over the course of conducting groups in the past, we have found the following procedures to be most effective. They should be modified as necessary to fit the needs of a particular school and group. Students who have been referred are summoned from class in groups of about 10. To minimize stigma and address fears that they may be in trouble, students are told that teachers or counselors have identified them as students who have a lot of potential and who could work well in a group setting. The structure of the SPARK program is explained, and examples of different modules are given (see the sample script in Appendix A-2). Students who express interest are given a parent consent form, a sample of which is shown in Appendix A-3. At the end of the meeting, students are told where to return the consent forms (most commonly the counselor's office). As an incentive, they are told that they will receive a small treat, such as candy or a special pencil, when they return their consent form, regardless of whether the form has been signed. Students who have not returned their consent forms should be contacted a few days later to see if they are still interested. If they are, they should receive another consent form. Students are told that the parent(s) can call with any questions they may have, or that the group leader will call the parent(s) if the student prefers. If a student seems interested but is not sure about the parent's response, the group leader can explicitly offer to call the parent. It is important for the person who calls to speak the same language as the parent.

Pregroup Individual Interviews and/or Questionnaires

Once parent consent forms are returned, we strongly suggest interviewing each potential group member individually if at all possible. Students who have problems in school often find completing questionnaires particularly difficult, and the results are likely to be incomplete and/or inaccurate. However, if the only practical

way to gather the information in a particular school is in questionnaire form, it is better than not gathering the information at all. The pregroup interview serves several purposes:

1. *To obtain student assent.* It is important for the student to formally agree to participate in the group. It is also important to make sure students understand the exceptions to confidentiality (if they are in danger, if they feel they may hurt themselves or someone else). A sample student assent form is included in Appendix A-4.
2. *To gather information about the student that is important for group leaders to know.* Awareness of the student's current living situation, recent stressors, feelings about education, anger, current symptoms, exposure to violence, peer support, and feelings about gangs will greatly facilitate an understanding of what the student brings to the group. The interview also allows the leader to assess suicidality, a significant issue for some referred students that will be discussed in detail later in this chapter.
3. *To build a bond and connection with the student.* If the student connects with the leader on a one-on-one basis, it helps with development of rapport in the group and helps the students feel that the leader understands them.
4. *To assess whether the groups have been helpful.* Gathering information about students prior to beginning the group and after it has ended allows evaluation of whether the group has been helpful.

A sample interview guide is given in Appendix A-5. Some topics covered in the interview may be irrelevant for a particular group, and leaders are urged to use only topics that seem important to assess for their own groups. Response scales that accompany the interview are in Appendix A-6. Detailed information about the interview can be found in Appendix A-7. Spanish versions of the parent consent, student assent, interview guide, and response scales are available in Appendix C.

Group Counseling Techniques

Developing Trust and Understanding Confidentiality

At the heart of any successful group intervention is the establishment of trust. This is the first task of the SPARK program and is covered in detail in Module One. At the beginning of the first session, members are asked to rate how much they trust other group members on a 5-point scale (see Appendix B-la). This tells leaders how much of an issue trust will be in the group. Trust is often a major concern in school-based groups, since members are likely to see at least some other members in classes or on campus, may be friends (or enemies), or may have connections in the neighborhood outside of school. The Trust-Building and Communication Skills module is detailed in Chapter Two.

Understanding and agreeing to confidentiality is crucial to the program. Students disclose a great deal of personal information in the groups. It is important to provide a safe environment in which to do so and to ensure that students respect each person's right to privacy. It is a requirement of group participation that students sign the Confidentiality Contract (see Appendix B-lb) by the end of the second session. Only if members feel that what they say will be protected will they be able to make the disclosures necessary to commit to the group and its members and to receive maximum benefit from participation. To reinforce the specifics

of confidentiality, members are asked to explain it in detail to latecomers or new members. It is extremely important that members sign the Confidentiality Contract. For example, before we began using formal confidentiality contracts, a girl in one group revealed that she had had an abortion. When she realized the next week that half the school now knew what she considered shameful information, she not only dropped out of the group but also felt it necessary to change schools.

Building Group Cohesion

In addition to building trust, the program uses several other mechanisms to develop a sense of group cohesion. Specific methods for implementing the following are given in Chapter Two in the Trust-Building and Communication Skills module.

Group Name

In the first session, a list of possible group names is generated by the group and voted on. Having a mutually agreed-upon name, no matter how strange, allows for a sense of belonging. Names have included "Yo Mama," "Killer Bees," "The Confidentiality Club," and "Bruins [UCLA team name] and Buttheads."

Group-Generated Rules and Consequences

Group rules are generated by members when they become necessary, both to enhance group cohesion and to set a procedure for keeping order that works for youth who may frequently rebel against rules and authority. The younger the group members, the sooner group rules may need to be developed. They are almost always necessary in middle school groups by Session Two, but they may not be needed until quite late in the curriculum (or not at all) for older high school students. Group leaders write down all suggested rules, whether appropriate or not (some interesting initial suggestions have been "Bring gum to share with all members" and "Everyone must wear black shoes"), ask for opinions and discussion, and then have members vote on each one. If the leader feels that a particular rule is needed after the group generates their list or at another time, he or she can ask, for example, "Do we need a rule about hitting other people?" Generally, the group will agree, but the leader will not impose a rule unilaterally, except under extreme circumstances.

Some typical rules a group might develop include:

1. Don't touch anyone else or their things.
2. No name calling.
3. Don't interrupt when someone else is talking.
4. Respect other people's feelings.
5. No eating unless you share with all the group members.

After the rules are generated, the group also generates the consequences for not following the rules. Leaders ask, "What should happen if one of these rules is broken?" Members generate a list of possible consequences, and leaders again write down all suggestions for later discussion. If a really inappropriate consequence is suggested (e.g., beat up the rule violator), members will usually nix it during the discussion period. If they do not, the leader can ask, "Does anyone see any possible problems with this one?" After full discussion, consequences are voted on. Ideal consequences are usually a warning, followed by one or two time-outs (for a

specified period of time) in the room, and then by sending the student back to class for the rest of the session. Groups do not always generate these ideal consequences, but the ones they develop almost always work as long as they are clearly enforced. Some of the more unique consequences that groups have developed include doing push-ups, writing standards (e.g., I will not hit anyone in group.), and sitting in the corner facing the wall. The final list of group rules and consequences should be posted so that it is available during all future group sessions.

In addition to being developed by the group, rules and consequences are also enforced by the group. If no one calls a rule that is being broken, the leader will ask, "Does anyone see a rule being broken?" Almost always, a member will identify the rule. If not, the leader can say, for example, "What about the 'no interrupting' rule?" Allowing group members to generate and enforce the rules gives them a sense of ownership and cohesion with regard to the group process, and it facilitates the internalization of limits and consequences for their behavior.

Emphasizing Commonalities and Eliciting Support

Another avenue for building group cohesion is helping members see commonalities among their lives and their troublesome issues. The first Trust-Building and Communication Skills session involves an exercise for pointing out similarities among group members (the Me Too game in Session One). In addition, group leaders comment on areas where group members may have interests or situations in common. One way to accomplish this is by asking questions—for example, "Has anyone else's parents gone through a divorce?" or "Are there others who have to take care of their younger brothers or sisters?" Another technique is to bring up previously disclosed statements that relate to the current discussion—for instance, "Jose, you told us a few weeks ago about your cousin being shot. Did you have some of the same feelings that Gina is describing?"

Empathic Responding and Reflections

In order for group members to feel comfortable and free to talk about difficult things, an atmosphere where such sensitive disclosures are treated with respect is needed. The first step, building trust, was discussed previously. However, once trust is established and disclosures begin, the manner in which they are handled will determine whether the process of self-disclosure is enhanced or diminished. Deep disclosures about topics such as the student's family or inner feelings make most adolescents uncomfortable, and some almost instinctively respond by making a joke out of it, changing the subject, or belittling or doubting the disclosure. We use four ways to help group members develop an empathic and respectful way of responding to the sensitive disclosures of other members. First, group leaders model understanding and empathic responses to members' sensitive disclosures, mainly using reflection of feelings—for example, "You must have felt devastated when you learned that your sister had run away" or "Sounds like you were really mad when he threw the ball directly at your face."

Second, as part of the Trust-Building and Communication Skills module, group members participate in one activity to help them recognize and label feelings (Feelings Grab Bag), one that helps students learn clear communication techniques (Listening and Speaking Skills), and another, optional activity that gives them the

opportunity to respond with empathy to the anonymous disclosures of other group members (Secret Pooling). Third, the Good Listening Skills handout in Session Three of the Trust-Building and Communication Skills module gives explicit instructions about responding in helpful ways to others' disclosures. Fourth, leaders ask members to tell how they think another feels ("What do you think Sarah might be feeling in response to the insult from her teacher?") or how they would feel if it happened to them ("How do you think you would feel if a teacher said that to you?"). Usually, not all members fully reach the goal of empathic responding; however, if most group members learn to treat sensitive disclosures with respect, an atmosphere of trust can be maintained even if one or two members continue to respond somewhat inappropriately.

Group Process

Reflections of Group Process

In a manner similar to that discussed above for reflecting the feelings of group members, leaders also reflect the tenor or tone of the entire group. This is particularly helpful when feelings in the group are intense, when strong feelings may have developed between group members, or when there is a breakdown in the group process. Examples of group process reflections are: "I notice that everyone got silly and giggly when John mentioned sex with his girlfriend"; "Group members seem to be feeling a lot of rage about Jessica's being beaten up by a gang"; "Right now, it seems as if people's race is motivating which side they are on, rather than being able to work things out as a group"; or "What Sammy said was so heavy that it's hard for people to respond, even though I can see from your faces that you have lots of reactions."

Pointing Out Verbal versus Nonverbal Communication

It is also useful to note instances in which what the student says does not match how he or she says it. For example, if a student talks about having a great time with his friends but does so in a low voice with no expression, the leader might say, "Your words say that you had a fantastic time, but your voice and how you are sitting say something very different." The issue of how body language may contradict the verbal message and how the intent of a communication may not be the same as its impact are explicitly discussed in the third session of the Trust-Building and Communication Skills module. This commonly comes up when a member is nervous about talking about something upsetting. A student might disclose that she was betrayed by her best friend in a hurtful way, but she may smile and laugh as she discloses the betrayal. The leader can point out the discrepancy between the verbal and nonverbal communication by saying something like "You are telling us about something that seems hurtful and sad, yet you are smiling and laughing. Maybe it's really painful to actually feel the sad feelings." Sometimes group members will point out such discrepancies, although they may do it in nonsupportive ways. For example, a student may say, "Oh, you're not bothered by being jumped after school—you're laughing about it. Maybe it didn't even really happen." The group leader can help by pointing out the discrepancy: "You're wondering if Maria could have been jumped because you think she would be feeling upset and she's telling us about it while laughing. Maria, maybe it's easier to share what happened if you put away your sad and mad feelings and make a joke about it."

Processing Interpersonal Issues between Group Members

If interpersonal issues arise between two group members based on interactions in the group, students are encouraged to share their feelings with each other and to state what they would like from the other person. For example, a student might say, "I was really pissed when you called me a fat pig, and I'd like you to stop calling me names." If a student is unable to share feelings or state what he or she would like, other group members are asked to help. The group leader might ask, "Who thinks they know how Joe might be feeling now?" or "What could Tony do to help Gina feel better right now?" or "What can we say to Gina or to Tony to let them know we understand how they feel?"

Because the program is generally school based, some of the members often have other relationships (friends, enemies, neighbors, etc.) that predate the start of the group. That they could continue to interact with each other provides the possibility of ongoing support after the end of the SPARK program, but it also has the potential of creating difficulties in the group. Over the years, we have found that it is best not to spend too much group time trying to process and deal with anger or rivalry between group members that developed long before the group began meeting. Doing so can take time away from important material in the curriculum. In our experience, these long-standing issues are not easily resolved. In addition, focusing much group time and energy on two students may be detrimental to the other group members. Generally, it is helpful to briefly air the issues to see if any solution is immediately apparent. If not, we have found it best to physically separate enemies so that they do not sit near each other, and to suggest that they deal with their outside issues away from the group.

Occasionally one group member will start to like another group member romantically. If the student's ardor is not returned, the leader may need to help the other student tell the Lothario to back off. For example, if a student looks uncomfortable when the admirer sits too close or physically touches him or her, the leader can ask the student if he or she is comfortable with Pat sitting so close, and if the answer is no, the student can be encouraged to ask Pat to move back. Sometimes the attraction is mutual. If there is overt affection or if the talking between the two becomes distracting to the group, the rules can be invoked or the students can be asked to separate so that everyone can concentrate on the group.

Developmental Considerations

Maturity level and relevant issues vary greatly over the secondary school age range. Younger children are affected differently by exposure to family and community violence than older teens. They show more fear, more intrusive and disturbing thoughts, and fewer coping skills than older victims and witnesses. Older teens exposed to violence tend to be more flat in their affect, and it sometimes seems as if they have become numb as a defense against their horrific experiences. One 10th grader exposed to both community and family violence described how he felt nothing most of the time; the only time he really felt alive was when he and his friends lobbed cherry bombs at cars and watched the explosions. So while younger children need help learning how to contain and appropriately channel their

affect, some older teens need to focus on exploration and expression of feelings. It can also help to normalize these reactions in the group, stressing that what may seem like an insensitive reaction or an overreaction to a particular event may represent a useful coping mechanism in the face of repeated exposure to adversity.

Preteens and young teens need more structure in their groups than do older teens. Middle school group leaders need to stick closely to the curriculum and the activities, develop rules, and make sure the group enforces the rules strictly. In contrast, in most older high school groups, leaders can allow a discussion relevant to the topic that is not in the curriculum and then easily relate it back to the main curricular points.

Maintaining Order and Leader Sanity

The generation of group rules and consequences provides the basis for maintaining enough order for students to profit from the curriculum (see Chapter Two, Module One, Session Two for an in-depth discussion about establishing group rules). Many of the children referred for groups, particularly in inner-city schools, have strong negative feelings about authority figures and actively seek to undermine them. Putting the onus of developing and enforcing the group rules on the group members helps the students take ownership of the group and reduces disruption. However, the leaders must provide the parameters to allow this approach to be successful. The two most common leader errors in maintaining order are (1) enforcing the rules themselves, which sets up an "us–them" relationship similar to that which many students experience with their parents or teachers, and (2) wanting to be "nice guys" and therefore ignoring or glossing over minor rule violations, which often results in things getting out of hand very quickly.

The most effective leader stance is to be clear and firm in *facilitating* enforcement of the rules. That means that if members do not call a rule that is being broken, the leader asks if anyone sees a rule being broken. If no one answers (which is rare), the leader wonders aloud about the particular rule—for example, "What about number 3, no name calling?" Similarly, the leader must make sure that the consequence ensues, but the leader does not directly impose it. Instead the leader asks, "What is the consequence?" and group members state the consequence for the rule violator—for example, "Shanika, you need to sit in the corner for 5 minutes without saying anything." It is extremely important to establish an expectation that the rules and consequences, once devised by the group, will be followed.

In general, expect younger adolescent groups to require more management, earlier rule generation, and more rule enforcement than older groups. Sixth-grade boys usually require the most containment. In younger groups and in the occasional older group with management issues, leaders have found it helpful to use a group reward at the end of the session. Members usually get one small piece of candy if they have had no more than one warning and two pieces if they have not had any warnings.

Uses and Parameters of Check-In and Check-Out

Check-in occurs at the beginning of every group after the first meeting, and each student is encouraged to contribute. It is meant to help members reconnect and to give them an opportunity to bring up things that are happening in their lives that might need to be discussed in the group. For example, if a family member has been hurt, a girlfriend or boyfriend is seeing someone else, or a fight is brewing in the school, students have an opportunity to share and to receive support from the other members. Leaders both model empathic reflections and positively comment on the empathic statements or self-disclosures of others. In addition, leaders may have to cut off some students who feel compelled to share every detail of their weekend, as well as deal with inappropriate laughter or comments that may not help the discloser feel safe. This is usually done either by asking if a rule is being broken (such as "respecting others" or "no interrupting") or by using group process techniques. The leader can ask other members how they would feel if they were talking about something very difficult and people laughed or made fun of them, or can comment on how uncomfortable the student must have been that he or she needed to put down the discloser.

Similarly, Check-out occurs at the end of each meeting. There are three purposes to Check-out. First, it allows group members to share how they felt about the activity and the topic of the day's group. Second, it allows members to give feedback to each other (e.g., "I sure hope your brother is OK" or "I hope you find your backpack"). Third, it allows the leader to make sure that the point of the activity and lesson were learned. The leader asks: "What was the point of the activity today? What did you learn? How might you apply this in your life this week?" This reinforces the lesson and encourages generalization. Specific questions are given in the Check-out section for each session of the curriculum.

Check-in and Check-out can also be utilized by group leaders to reinforce points made in previous sessions. This is probably most commonly done with hot-headed and cool-headed responses (from the Anger Management and Emotion Regulation Skills module) when students bring up incidents involving aggression or violence. However, it is helpful to use relevant information from any previous module in Check-in or Check-out to emphasize transfer and generalization of points discussed.

Issues in Ending the Groups

Many students grow attached to the leaders and other members of their group. Therefore, it is important to let them know when the end of the group is approaching to allow members to talk about their feelings about ending. Feelings of sadness or abandonment, which may be intensified by the students' own previous personal experiences with loss, need to be expressed and discussed. We suggest bringing it up when there are about four sessions left, at first simply pointing out the number of sessions remaining. In the next 3 weeks, it is important to mention the number of sessions remaining and elicit the feelings that members have about the group ending. Check-in and Check-out provide the best mechanism for discussing these feelings. Specific ways of bringing up and discussing the end of the group are given in the curriculum in the relevant sessions.

The importance of dealing with students' feelings about ending the groups was most poignantly brought home by our most difficult experience with ending a group. When we were first doing SPARK groups, we worked with a very needy group of students, many of whom did not

live with their own parents. At that point, we were running 10-week groups, and the leaders were not focused on how important they had become to these children or how termination might affect the members. However, when it was time to leave after the 10th session, several children ran out to the street and lay down in front of the leaders' car to prevent them from leaving. The leaders were terribly upset and felt distressed for the students.

Often, group leaders also experience sadness in anticipation of finishing the group, and we encourage the leaders to share these feelings with the group. In addition to modeling expressing in-group emotions, it also provides the opportunity to genuinely express feelings. Of course, occasionally there are groups that are so difficult to manage that the leaders may welcome the end. In general, the amount of emotional connection between leaders and students determines how strong the leaders' feelings about ending the groups will be.

Specific activities for the last session are detailed in the curriculum. A party with snacks is held. Members are asked to reflect back on what was covered in the group meetings and what they will take from the groups to help them in their lives. In addition, students participate in a group feedback exercise (What I Like about You, see Appendix B-8a) where each person tells what he or she values in each of the other group members, and the group leader writes these down for the students to take with them. Each member also receives a certificate of achievement for completing the SPARK program (an example of this certificate appears in Appendix B-8b).

Sometimes groups may want to continue or to have reunions after the sessions have ended. In our program, we have not been able to continue because other students are waiting to participate in SPARK groups. However, if the school has the resources to continue the groups with a less structured format, and if the leaders feel it would be productive, continuing could be highly beneficial. We have occasionally held reunions (usually toward the end of the next semester or at the beginning of the next school year), which students have enjoyed. This provides the chance to reinforce curricular points (often relating to anger management or conflict resolution) in addition to allowing students to renew relationships and catch up on each other's lives.

Dilemmas for Group Leaders

Handling Issues of Child Abuse and Suicidality

Child abuse and suicidality are difficult issues. We have found that they come up with some frequency for at-risk adolescents. They can arise either in the pregroup interviews or during the group sessions themselves. The first and basic principle is to discuss exceptions to confidentiality right at the beginning of the pregroup interview and to cover this in detail as part of the confidentiality discussion in the first group session. Adolescents who then choose to share such experiences and feelings are aware that the material cannot be kept confidential. We focus these initial discussions on the need to keep the child safe.

Child Abuse

When physical or sexual abuse is disclosed by adolescents, it must be reported to the appropriate authorities (generally the department of children's services if the perpetrator is a family member, or

the local police if the perpetrator is not a family member, although specific procedures may vary from state to state). We have found it most useful for the group leader to stay with the student throughout the reporting process, even if the leader is not typically the person who makes child abuse reports in a particular school or setting. The leader's role is to offer support to the student and to explore his or her feelings about disclosure, including fear of consequences or reprisal. We suggest that whoever typically makes child abuse reports in the school make any reports that come up in the context of the program; this arrangement and specific procedures should be clarified before the beginning of groups. When groups have been led by university graduate students, the university student has taken the adolescent to the appropriate school reporter and remained with the student throughout the reporting procedure.

It is helpful and supportive to check with the student within the next day or so after the report has been made. The leader should elicit and process the student's feelings, discuss what may have happened with the social service agency or police, and help the student cope with any consequences he or she may have experienced with regard to the family's reaction. Sometimes it is helpful to offer to meet with the student and the student's family.

Suicidality

Suicidal thoughts are reported even more frequently than child abuse by adolescents referred for SPARK groups. In our pregroup interview, we ask students to rate how often a variety of things happen to them. When a student answers "sometimes," "lots of times," or "all the time" to "wanting to hurt yourself" or "wanting to kill yourself," we follow up at the end of the interview to assess the seriousness of the statement. There is more reason for concern if (1) the student has made a previous suicide attempt or (2) the child has a well-formulated plan and the means to carry out that plan (e.g., it would be much more serious for a student to plan to jump off a tall building if the student lived in Manhattan than if he or she lived in a small rural community). For a student who has suicidal thoughts but is not judged a significant risk, the group leader contracts with the student not to take any action before the two of them have talked first and lets the student know how to reach him or her if the student feels suicidal. Often this provides an opportunity for a student to talk about a significant life crisis or circumstance. Additionally, we encourage students to use available social support by helping them identify at least one person with whom they can talk if they are feeling distressed. Students can also be given the numbers of crisis hotlines such as 1-800-SUICIDE or 1-800-273-TALK in case they cannot reach the group leader.

If the student is unable to make such a contract or if the risk of suicide is seen as substantial, the parent or guardian is contacted by the leader (or other appropriate school personnel). The leader should be able to recommend resources for individual counseling to the parent, and if a suicide attempt seems imminent, the leader should advise the parent to take the child to an emergency room. It should be explained to the student that contacting the parent is necessary in order to keep the student safe. Sometimes students express fear that they will get into trouble if their parents find out about their suicidal feelings. Sometimes they also feel shame or guilt about their suicidal feelings. The group leader should take care in address-ing these concerns. It can help to explain to both students and parents that it is not uncommon for adolescents to have suicidal thoughts or feelings sometimes, and to praise the students for sharing these feelings so they can be safe and get help.

Balancing the Needs of Individual Group Members with the Requirements of the Psychoeducational Curriculum

A common problem that arises is how to balance presenting the information and activities in the curriculum with the needs of individual group members. If, for example, a problem that a student brings up in Check-in takes more than half the session to discuss, the activity for the day may not be completed, and the important points in that session may not be made. If the leader has the luxury of extending the number of sessions of the group, this is a less serious issue than when the group needs to be finished at a certain time. This has been most problematic at schools that operate year round. In these schools, semesters may be shorter and may be followed by long breaks, making it imperative to follow the curriculum closely so that all relevant modules can be presented in a timely fashion.

One way of dealing with this dilemma is to develop a sense of what types of student issues are important enough to warrant time that would otherwise go to the curriculum. One such issue is current loss. If a student has lost someone in the last month through death or if a loved one has been seriously injured or ill, the student needs the support of the group. Similarly, if the student has been seriously hurt or has experienced a traumatic event in the last month, or if a serious fight or disruption at the school has occurred, significant discussion in the group is warranted.

There are several types of situations about which students may want to talk at length at Check-in, but the discussion needs to be contained so that the group can proceed with the curricular activities. Some group members like to share every detail of their weekend or may want to talk about teachers and other students who bother them. These issues do not deserve attention to the detriment of the curriculum, and students should be politely discouraged from talking too much. For example, the group leader might say, "Thanks for sharing about your weekend, Hakim. Let's move on to Cindy."

Another situation that can cause concern for the leader occurs when a very troubled student makes long and disturbing disclosures week after week. If, for example, a suicidal student with many family problems talks for a long time in every group about these issues, the other members can become focused on helping the student, making it a therapy group for that student, or they may begin to ostracize the student as weird or engage in teasing. If it becomes clear that this is a pattern in the group, it is helpful for the leader to meet individually with the student and make a referral for individual or family counseling. In this case, the student's issues are too major to be resolved in the group, and they take time that is needed to help all the students with the shared issues raised in the curriculum.

Dealing with Members Who Do Not Participate

Students who do not participate pose a dilemma for leaders. If students are not encouraged to participate, they will not receive maximum benefit. On the other hand, if students are pushed too hard, they may feel uncomfortable and drop out. We use multiple approaches to help such students become part of the group. First, we actively encourage them to engage in the activities. For example, in the first session, if a student is not participating in the Me Too game, the leader will name something he or she has in common with the student that should make the student stand up (e.g., "I'm wearing black shoes" or "I have brown eyes."). In later sessions, this would involve asking the student, if appropriate, "Has this ever happened to you?"

Second, group leaders make comments that convey group interest, support, and acceptance. Examples include: "You don't have to talk about this now, but when you're ready, we'd really like to hear about your experience" and "I bet everyone here has had times when they felt like nobody could possibly understand how they felt and when they didn't want to talk about something, but sometimes it really can help to share and talk." The goal is to convey support without pushing the student.

Third, if conveying support does not elicit participation after several sessions, we wonder aloud whether something is making it hard for the student to participate. If the student in question does not answer, the other group members can be asked if they have any ideas about why it might be hard for the student to participate. Sometimes other students can give very insightful answers, such as "I don't think he feels comfortable speaking English"; "Terry and Bruce make fun of him whenever he opens his mouth, so I understand why he wouldn't feel safe to talk here"; or "He doesn't ever talk in class either, but he talks fine when he's with his friends." Such answers may provide the basis for making adjustments in the group so that the member feels safe.

Fourth, if the student continues to be withdrawn and noncommunicative by the end of the third session, the leader may need to speak with the student individually about whether he or she wants to continue coming to the group. If the student does want to continue, he or she is encouraged to participate in the activities at least minimally. In other words, if each member is to take a turn in an activity, the member should be willing to speak, even if only short or minimal answers are given and no information is volunteered. The leader continues to encourage participation but does not force it. Occasionally, the group leader may ask the student whether he or she would like to share feelings about the topic, but the student's refusal should be accepted. If the student feels so uncomfortable about sharing that he or she does not wish to remain in the group, the group leader should accept the decision and help the student feel comfortable about stopping.

Dealing with Chronically Disruptive Members

Occasionally, a group will have a charismatic student who is highly disruptive during a number of sessions. Such members have the potential to ruin a group, but they can also be a positive force and a source of great energy. First, the student's behavior is dealt with, using the rules and consequences. If this is unsuccessful in ending the student's disruption of the group, the student may be a candidate for the "leader talk," which can result in channeling the student's energy for the

benefit of the group process. In addition to being disruptive, candidates for the leader talk must be well liked or respected by other students. Strange or universally disliked students are not candidates. In the leader talk, a group leader meets individually with the disruptive student with the following goals:

1. To acknowledge how powerful the student is—the leader might say, "The other group members look up to you and want to be like you."
2. To note the difficulties the group is experiencing—"You know things haven't been going too smoothly in the group, with people interrupting while others are talking. We're not able to do the activities, and everyone ends up frustrated."
3. To enlist the student's help in getting the group under control—"I was wondering if you might be able to help, since you are a natural leader and the kids listen to you and think you're cool. You could act like kind of a co-leader and help keep the group focused on the activities and not be so rowdy. What do you think?"

Generally, the student is flattered, puffs up with pride, and agrees to help out. Then at the beginning of the next group session, the leader reminds the student privately, "So you're going to help out today, right?" If the student is less disruptive, the leader thanks the student privately for the help at the end of the session and expresses hope that the student will be willing to continue helping, since the group went so much better today. This manner of dealing with chronically disruptive members has generally been very successful.

Parameters of the Group Leader Role

Participation in Activities

The leader begins the first activity, the Me Too game, and needs to participate in order to model disclosure and encourage participation by all group members. How much the group leader participates in the other activities depends on the tenor of the particular group and the group leader's comfort level. In some groups, members will press the group leaders to participate in activities such as Feelings Grab Bag, Labeling, and Hot-Head Cool-Head role play. In these cases, it is helpful for the group leader to participate, as the members may be asking the leader to take the same risks they are taking. This tends to increase trust in the group. However, if there is an activity that the leader does not feel comfortable participating in, then the leader should tell the group. A stream of questions asking why and cajoling may follow. For other groups, leader participation may not be an issue at all, and leaders will not be asked to participate if they do not naturally do so.

Self-Disclosure by Leaders

Similarly, groups vary in the degree to which they press leaders to disclose details of their lives or their feelings or opinions, and leaders vary in their comfort in sharing such information. As discussed above, sometimes pressing leaders to tell about themselves is a test of trust. Leaders are asking members to share difficult feelings and events—will the leaders be willing to do the same? Most frequently, leaders are asked about whether they have a boyfriend, girlfriend, husband, or wife. Other common questions involve children,

what the leaders did last weekend or last summer, and where they went to college. The most difficult questions that leaders are frequently asked relate to sex and drug use. For example, leaders have been asked, "Do you and your boyfriend have sex?" "Have you ever smoked pot?" and "What drugs did you do in high school and college?" The rule of thumb about leader comfort in answering applies here as well, but the issues are more complex.

In general, leaders have to decide whether they are willing to honestly disclose their own experiences when they may run counter to what they are hoping to teach the students. The three possible responses a leader has to such questions are to (1) honestly disclose his or her experiences; (2) say that it is personal or that he or she doesn't feel comfortable talking about it; or (3) lie and give the answer that reflects the value he or she is trying to communicate to the group. Each of these options is fraught with possible negative consequences. If a leader is honest and, for example, discloses that he or she smoked pot, the leader may gain the trust of group members but could be at risk if members violate the Confidentiality Contract and let other school personnel or their parents know that the leader used illegal drugs. If a leader lets the group know that he or she is not comfortable sharing with them, the leader is being honest but may be sending the message that it is not safe to disclose in the group, and the level of openness may drop. If the leader lies about experiences, he or she communicates the desired message to the group but may feel dishonest and may be perceived as such by group members. Obviously, there are no easy answers; leaders should be prepared for such dilemmas and think about their feelings prior to starting work with the group. It is important not to do so much disclosure that the leader becomes a group member rather than the group leader and facilitator.

Dealing with One's Own Feelings

As leaders come to know the group members intimately and in depth, a variety of feelings may be evoked. In our experience, the most common feelings that cause leaders distress are rescue fantasies and frustration. Certain students with negative past experiences elicit strong empathic feelings in therapists—for example, a student witnessed his father shoot and kill his mother; other students have lost relatives to community violence; and many students relate instances of emotional abuse or neglect by parents or other caregivers. It is helpful to make referrals for individual or family counseling where appropriate and to be empathic, available, and understanding with the student. But it is also important to recognize limits. The leader cannot take the student home or become a substitute parent.

The other common distressing feeling of group leaders is frustration. A common source of frustration is not being able to reach a student. This happens most frequently when students appear to have great potential but keep sabotaging themselves, for example by not studying for a test or by fighting after committing to avoid fights. The other common source of frustration is students who undermine or disrupt the group. Techniques for handling such students are discussed above, but leaders also need to deal with their own feelings of anger and irritation at such students. Frequently, disruptive students have had major losses and painful experiences in their lives. It can be helpful for the leader to reinterpret the student's behavior as an expression of underlying

distress, which generally allows the leader to feel more connected and less angry.

In general, the feelings of group leaders toward most members become positive and deepen over the course of the group. Leaders have generally found the SPARK group counseling experience to be challenging, enriching, exciting, and meaningful as they affect the lives of youth.

Adapting the Curriculum for Full Classroom Use

While the curriculum and activities were designed for small group use, many of the modules and activities can be adapted for use with the full class. If the program is run by teachers rather than counselors, it is helpful for the teacher to have some mental health background and to be cognizant of the sensitive nature of some of the topics. We will give several general principles for adaptation as well as examples of which activities and modules translate well for full classroom use, and which may be problematic in the classroom setting.

First, confidentiality is a much greater problem in the full classroom setting and it is not reasonable to expect a whole classroom to be able to keep a confidentiality contract, especially since the child cannot really choose not to participate in a full classroom activity. Therefore, while there is an emphasis on respecting other's disclosures and not sharing them with others, confidentiality contracts are not used.

Second, a basic principle of adaptation is to break activities into small groups and have the leader (and aides if available) circulate among the groups. Thus, role-playing activities or other activities in which two or three students participate together are easily adaptable to the classroom format. Examples that are well suited to this format are the Listening Skills role play of the Trust-Building and Communication Skills module; the Hot-Head Cool-Head role play of the Anger Management and Emotion Regulation skills module; the Ethnic Identity poster activity from the Ethnic Identity and Anti-Prejudice module; and the Aggressor, Victim, Bystander activity from the Peer Pressure, Bullying, and Gangs module.

Third, some activities that involve the whole smaller group translate well to the full classroom setting. Activities that each student does individually and then shares with the whole group adapt well, with the caveat that only some and not all of the students will get a chance to share with the whole class. Examples might be the Scary Art Gallery activity from Module Seven, on violence exposure and post-traumatic stress, or Developing Your Own Calming Image from the Anger Management and Emotion Regulation Skills module. Additionally, activities that involve relaxation or imagery (e.g., muscle relaxation in the Anger Management and Emotion Regulation Skills module) or involve viewing a movie (e.g., the movie *Rudy* in the Educational Aspirations module) also adapt easily to the larger classroom format.

Fourth, activities that involve each group member presenting to the group need to be modified (or in some instances dropped) when using the whole-classroom format. For example, one activity that would need modification is the Feelings Grab Bag from Trust-Building and Communication Skills, where each student

draws a feeling from a bag, acts it out to be guessed as in charades, and tells about a time he or she felt like that, and then all the other members tell about a time they felt that way. Eight to ten students could each act out a feeling, and then a few responses could be elicited from other class members about times when they felt that feeling. Another example is the Personality Family Album activity from the Family Relationships module. Rather than having each student tell about one quality they have in common with a family member that they like and one quality they have in common with a family member that they don't like, students could write these down on a piece of paper, and then a few students could share these with the rest of the class. The optional Secret Pooling activity in the Trust-Building and Communication Skills module should not be used in the classroom setting because it involves sensitive disclosures and really does not work unless each student has a chance to present.

Fifth, while some whole-group activities are very meaningful and lots of fun, they may or may not be feasible in the whole classroom format, depending upon the type and nature of the class. For example, the Me Too game from the Trust-Building and Communication Skills module and the Labeling game from the Ethnic Identity and Anti-Prejudice module involve a great deal of movement around the room. With a generally well-behaved and under-control class, these activities would be of great value, but if there are many disruptive children or the teacher does not feel that the class is generally controllable, chaos might ensue.

CHAPTER TWO

The SPARK Curriculum

The SPARK curriculum combines a group process model aimed at developing interpersonal skills and a psychoeducational model focused on building competence by development of specific skills needed by all youth, especially those at high risk. The goal of the first module of the curriculum, Trust-Building and Communication Skills, is to develop an atmosphere of increasing trust to set the stage for supportive interactions, meaningful self-disclosure, and respectful problem solving. In addition, throughout the curriculum, the group process orientation can be seen in the emphasis on discussing difficult interactions, developing a group identity, using the group-generated rules and consequences, and focusing on supportive, affirming responding.

The choice of the curriculum content after Module One is based on a psychoeducational model aimed at developing skills to alleviate common problems for high-risk youth. It begins with a module on Anger Management and Emotion Regulation Skills in order to build a framework and a set of skills for dealing with a variety of issues that are faced by today's youth, issues that are discussed in later modules. The anger management, problem-solving, and emotion regulation techniques advocated in this module are

brought up, emphasized, and reinforced throughout the rest of the curriculum to continue and expand skill building. The other modules were selected because they represent areas of significant concern for at-risk youth. Middle school and junior high years are crucial turning points for academic achievement, with many students beginning to fail, lose motivation, and earn poor grades in a downward spiral with deleterious consequences. Therefore, a module that focuses on educational aspirations, how to reach career goals, and the importance of developing study skills now seems essential. Similarly, peer relationships are crucial in this developmental stage. Peer pressure around a variety of areas, such as drugs, gangs, and sex, as well as forms of relational aggression such as bullying and gossip, represent serious challenges for at-risk youth and need to be addressed. For all students, and especially those living in multiethnic communities, exploration of ethnic identity, stereotypes, prejudice, and discrimination is necessary. Issues that arise in male–female relationships in adolescence including sex-role stereotypes are also addressed. In addition, application of problem-solving skills to complicated or disrupted family relationships is needed, as well as a focus on how parents can be a resource. Examination of community violence and posttraumatic stress reactions is part of the curriculum because this is a pervasive aspect of life for most inner-city children.

The SPARK curriculum consists of eight modules. Although the program is generally used in its entirety, it is possible to select specific modules that would be especially useful for a particular group of students. If only selected modules are used, we suggest that all concepts and core sessions in a particular module be presented. Modules can also be expanded to more sessions for specific issues that may require more time and care by having more discussions of the constructs involved and/or utilizing the optional sessions available for several modules. For example, in a school setting with a great deal of racial tension, the Ethnic Identity and Anti-Prejudice module might be expanded, with more opportunities for discussion and personalization to the particular school's situation. Similarly, for a group of especially aggressive students, the Anger Management and Emotion Regulation Skills module might be expanded from three to four sessions to allow for more practice of skills. If exposure to violence is not an issue in a particular community, the Exposure to Violence and Posttraumatic Stress Reactions module can be omitted, although the first session is useful in exploring students' scary experiences of all kinds.

Overview of Module Content

Module One: Trust-Building and Communication Skills

- Three or four sessions help students learn to trust each other, listen empathically, feel ownership of the group, and share their feelings.

Module Two: Anger Management and Emotion Regulation Skills

- Three sessions help students learn to recognize and manage angry feelings, develop emotion regulation strategies, and generate and practice alternatives to violence in dealing with anger and provocation.

Module Three: Ethnic Identity and Anti-Prejudice

- Two sessions help students develop positive feelings of ethnic pride, address and discuss prejudice, and understand and accept people from other ethnic groups.

Module Four: Educational Aspirations

- Three sessions, one of which is a field trip to a local university, help students set high but reasonable educational aspirations, address barriers to academic success, and identify specific steps they can take toward doing better in school.

Module Five: Peer Pressure, Bullying, and Gangs

- Two or three sessions help students generate and practice alternatives to giving in to peer pressure, examine relational aggression, and discuss alternatives to gang involvement.

Module Six: Male–Female Relationships

- Three sessions explore the impact of gender stereotypes and help students examine healthy versus unhealthy relationship characteristics and dating behaviors.

Module Seven:
Exposure to Violence
and Posttraumatic Stress Reactions

- One or two sessions help students discuss and understand their emotional reactions to witnessing or being the victims of violence and develop coping strategies for dealing with posttraumatic stress reactions.

Module Eight: Family Relationships

- One or two sessions help students understand and accept their families and the traits in themselves that are similar to those of family members—traits they like and those they wish were different.

Recruitment Criteria

Students appropriate for the SPARK program:

1. Currently experience academic, social, emotional, and/or family difficulties or have been exposed to high levels of violence.
2. Can work cooperatively in a group.
3. Attend school regularly.
4. Show interest in participating in the program.
5. Can miss one class period per week.
6. Do not display high levels of disruptive behavior.

See Chapter One for additional discussion of recruitment criteria.

Trust-Building and Communication Skills

Goal To help students learn to trust each other, listen empathically, feel owner-ship of the group, and share their feelings

Overview of Sessions

Session One
- ▪ *Purpose:* Develop process skills: cooperation, group cohesion, self-disclosure, universality of experience
- ▪ *Content:* (1) Discussion of confidentiality, (2) Me Too game, (3) selection of group name

Session Two
- ▪ *Purpose:* Develop process skills: group cohesion, group owner-ship, empathic responding, identifying and sharing feelings
- ▪ *Content:* (1) Selection of group rules, (2) Feelings Grab Bag

Session Three
- ▪ *Purpose:* Develop process skills: listening skills, I-statements, empathic responding
- ▪ *Content:* (1) Intent–impact model; (2) listening skills: Body Language game; role play; (3) speaking skills: you-statements and I-statements

Session Four (optional)
- ▪ *Purpose:* Develop process skills: self-disclosure, empathic responding, universality of experience
- ▪ *Content:* (1) Secret Pooling

Session One

Activities
- ✓ Trust ratings and introduction
- ✓ Discussion of confidentiality
- ✓ Discussion of member selection
- ✓ Me Too game
- ✓ Selection of group name
- ✓ Check-out

Materials
- ✓ Curriculum
- ✓ Trust ratings (one copy for each student—see Appendix B-la)
- ✓ Name tags
- ✓ Confidentiality Contracts (one copy for each student—see Appendix B-lb)
- ✓ Masking tape
- ✓ A pad of paper large enough to be seen by all students (or dry-erase board)
- ✓ Brightly colored pens for writing on the paper or board
- ✓ Three-ring binder for each student, with dividers labeled "Handouts," "Assignments," and "Points and Rewards." See Appendix A-8 for a sample title page.

Content

Pregroup Trust Ratings and Introduction

As students come in, ask them to fill out pregroup trust ratings. Say, **"Please fill out these sheets. We use these to check whether we need to do more to help build trust in the group. We will be asking you to complete these ratings again in a couple of weeks."**

1. Ask each student to write his or her name on a name tag.
2. Introduce leaders. Give name, background, and other information you feel would be useful.
3. Describe the group.
   a. Practical issues: dates and times (explain that the group will last through the semester).
   b. Overview of content: Say, **"We have different topics we will cover in the groups. For each topic, we will spend part of the time doing some fun activities and part of the time discussing your opinions and feelings about the topics."**
   c. Group goals: **"We want this to be a place where we can all feel safe to talk about things that are important to us."**

Confidentiality Contracts

It is important to discuss confidentiality in great detail because the success of the group depends on group members keeping confidentiality. Breaking of confidentiality can have severe consequences for individuals in the group.

1. Pass out the contracts and say, **"Don't sign these yet. Confidentiality is very important, and we want to make sure you think about this carefully before signing these contracts."**

2. Discuss the meaning of confidentiality: **"In a group like this, it is important to have complete confidentiality. Who can tell me what confidentiality means?"** Solicit responses. To reinforce responding, after each response make a motion or sound of approval, such as **"um-hm."** After hearing a nearly correct response, say, **"Right, so, in a nutshell, confidentiality means that nothing that is said in this room goes outside of the room."**

3. Discuss the importance of confidentiality: **"Can anyone tell me why this might be important?"** If no one can, prompt by asking, **"Imagine that you brought up something very important in the group. Then during the next week somebody in the group tells their friend what you said. Pretty soon, many people know what you said. How would you feel about talking in the group next week?"** Students will probably say that they would not feel like sharing.

4. Discuss the difficulty of confidentiality: **"Sometimes this can be really hard. One time when you might be tempted to break confidentiality is if you are talking to a person in this room when other people are around. Remember, you can't talk about what the person said in here. Or if you're talking to your best friend, you can't tell him or her what another person said here."**

5. Discuss the limits to confidentiality: **"I also will keep everything that you say in here confidential. That means I will not tell anyone what you say in here. Now there is one time when I will not be able to keep confidentiality. That is if I have reason to think that you or someone else is in danger—for example, if you tell us someone is hitting you or that you are thinking of hurting yourself or someone else. In that case, we will have to tell someone else what you said. This is because our first concern is your safety, and we need to make sure that you are safe. However, anything else you say in here will be kept confidential."** (If you are the person at your school who is the designated reporter for child abuse, you may want to modify the preceding statement to reflect that you will need to take the steps required to make sure the child is safe.)

6. Reading and signing of the contracts: **"Now let's read the contract carefully. Each student can read one sentence. Who wants to start?"** After the contract has been read completely, provide an opportunity for students to ask questions. Then say, **"Now think about this carefully. If you feel ready to sign a contract saying that you will keep everything said in the group confidential, please sign. If you are not sure, please think it over this week and sign the contract next week if you decide that you are willing to keep the group discussion confidential."**

7. A good way to reinforce confidentiality is to have group members teach other members what confidentiality means. For example, if a student arrives late for the group or misses the first week, you can have another group member explain to the newcomer what confidentiality means, and you can correct any misconceptions. Sometimes there are many students arriving late or missing the first week so that the students actually hear confidentiality explained four or five times by the end of the Trust-Building and Communication Skills module.

Why Students Were Selected for the Group

Explore participant reactions to being selected for the group. Begin to explore feelings about trusting other members in this setting. Many group members may fear that this will be a stigmatizing experience or that it means that they are bad.

1. As the program becomes established in the school and students hear that the groups are fun, this fear will be easier to overcome.

2. Explain that **"Almost all students will have various problems at different times. We chose you not because you were having problems, but because someone, either a teacher or a counselor, thought that you would be able to make the most of this type of experience. Some students can't work together in groups very well, but someone in the school thought you would be able to get along and work well with the other group members and gain something from the group."**

Trust-Building Activity: Me Too Game

This is a game similar to musical chairs. The goal of the game is for students to say something about themselves that they think other people will have in common with them. It encourages self-disclosure, creates a feeling of universality, and helps build group cohesion. This game provides a good opportunity for leaders to bond with the group. Try to laugh a lot and keep a light atmosphere. It is important to have a good time with the students and help them enjoy being part of the group.

1. Place chairs in the shape of a horseshoe, with one fewer chair than there are group members. Put a line of masking tape in the front of the horseshoe to mark the "it" zone, the line behind which everyone has to stand until the "it" person finds a seat.

2. Say, **"We're going to play a game called the Me Too game. One person stands in the empty space at the front of the horseshoe. The person says his or her name and something about himself or herself, such as shoe size, favorite color or movie, or feelings, like about homework or family. Then everyone else who has that thing in common with the person standing has to stand, come to the front of the horseshoe, wait for the 'it' person to sit, then scramble for the remaining chairs. Make sure you don't push anyone. The person left standing becomes 'it' and now has to say something about himself or herself. Let's try it. I'll be 'it' first."**

3. Say your name and something about yourself that you think others will have in common. Then ask, **"Is that true for anyone else? OK, everyone else who has that in common with me has to come up here, stand behind the tape, and wait until I find a seat."**

4. Sit down and remind students to find a seat once you are seated. Say, **"OK, looks like [student who is left standing] is 'it.' [Student], say your name and something about yourself."**

5. It helps to model increasingly personal disclosures as the game progresses, such as "I get mad at my mom sometimes" or "I wish I were a better student."

6. If there is a student who almost never stands up, specifically try to get that person to stand up when you are "it" by saying something you have in common with the student—for example, "I'm wearing black shoes," or "I have brown eyes."

Selection of Group Name (If Time Allows)

This activity builds group cohesion. The students decide on a name for their group that will be used throughout later sessions. Introduce this activity by saying, **"Now we'll need a name for our group. First let's try to come up with as many possible names as we can think of, then we'll vote on the one you all like best."**

1. Group members generate a list of names, which you write down on a large sheet of paper or a dry-erase board. Accept any name at this stage, no matter how strange or silly. Group names have included "The Trustworthy Club," "Yo Mama," the "UCLA Club," "The Hustlers," and even "Bruins [UCLA team name] and Buttheads." It is the members' group name, and it is up to them to decide on one they like. In some groups, the boys or the girls will take over this activity. Try to help both genders suggest names.

2. Vote on group name. Once students have generated a large list, say, **"OK, now we have a list of names. Everyone can have two votes, so look on the list and decide on the two names you like the best. Now, who votes for [first name on the list]?"** Tally responses. If there is a tie, have students vote between the two remaining names. **"We have a winner. Our group name is [Name of Group]."**

Check-Out

Check-out is a time for students to process their reactions to the group and for you to reinforce major points of each lesson. Introduce Check-out by saying, **"Our last activity for every group is called Check-out. This is a time for us to talk about our reactions to the group. What were your reactions to the group today? Was it the same or different from what you expected? What did you notice in the Me Too game? Were there parts of the group you liked or didn't like? Are there things that you would like to do more?"** Go around the circle and ask students to respond.

After everyone has had a chance to talk, hand out a three-ring binder to each student. Let students know that they can keep handouts and assignments in the binder. Describe the point and reward system you choose to use (see Chapter 1, pp. 4–5 for more information on setting up a reward system), and remind them that they can earn a point just for bringing their binder to the group each meeting.

Note: If the group is very difficult to manage, be prepared to develop group rules. See Session Two for directions.

Session Two

Activities	✓ Check-in
	✓ Introduce new members; discuss confidentiality
	✓ Group rules
	✓ Feelings Grab Bag
	✓ Group name (if not done in Session One)
	✓ Check-out
Materials	✓ Curriculum
	✓ Trust ratings (one copy for each student who was not present at Session One—see Appendix B-la)
	✓ Confidentiality Contracts (one copy for each student who did not sign during Session One—see Appendix B-lb)
	✓ A hat or bag for Feelings Grab Bag
	✓ Feelings for Feelings Grab Bag (one copy for each group—see Appendix B-lc; cut and fold each feeling)
	✓ A pad of paper large enough to be seen by all students (or dry-erase board)
	✓ Brightly colored pens for writing on the paper or board
	✓ Masking tape for putting up sheets of poster paper

Content

Check-In

This activity gives students an opportunity to bring up things that are happening in their lives that might need to be discussed in the group. Examples might be a death in the family, a loved one going to jail, or a fight in the school. It is also an opportunity to give out candy, stickers, or points for bringing the SPARK notebook to group (and later in the groups for bringing back completed assignments).

Introduce Check-in by saying, **"Each week we will start the group with an activity called Check-in. We would like to go around the circle and have each person say their name and tell the group how things are going for them. The reason we have this activity is to give you a chance to bring up things that you would like to talk about in the group. We have activities planned for each week, but sometimes things happen in people's lives, and we want to be able to have time to talk about those things, too. For example, in other groups we have done, students have had a birthday, have gotten in trouble at school, had a fun party, had family members who have died, gotten a good grade on a test, or have had parents divorce. These are things they have brought up in group. Who wants to start this week?"** Encourage participation from each member.

Introduce Any New Group Members

Use the same procedure as in Session One. Let other group members explain things like confidentiality, purpose of the group, and activities to help them feel ownership and to make sure they understand them. For example, the leader might ask, **"Who can tell James what confidentiality is?"**

1. Give new members Confidentiality Contracts to sign. Make sure all members have signed the contracts by the end of the session.

2. If students feel they cannot sign the Confidentiality Contract, they cannot continue in the group.

Group Rules

The goal is to help group members develop a feeling of group ownership. Group members are called on to generate, set consequences for, and enforce their own rules, rather than being required to follow rules that have been imposed on them. This shifts the role of disciplinarian from the leader to the group members (with the help of reminders from the leader). Setting up rules may need to be done in Session One, depending on the composition of the group. Middle school groups almost always need group rules by the end of Session Two; for high school groups, rules are instituted if and when needed.

GENERATING RULES

Say something like **"Now we're going to talk about group rules. We already have one rule, confidentiality. We also have some school rules that we need to keep. For example, we need to stay in the room during group rather than wandering around school. However, we don't have any other rules yet. We want this to be a place where you can feel comfortable talking about difficult subjects and can trust the other group members. We value and want to hear about everyone's opinions and feelings, and we want to make this a safe place to talk about them. Because this is your group, you can make the rules. Let's come up with possible rules. Then you can vote on which ones will help you best. Who has an idea for a rule that you think will make this the kind of place where you can talk about things that are important to you?"**

1. Generate a list of rules. Accept any suggestions at this point. Then say, **"OK, now we have a list of possible rules. Remember, the reason for the rules is to make this a place where you will feel safe and comfortable talking about things that are important to you. Let's talk about and vote on which rules will make the group feel safe."**

2. Allow for discussion of and a vote on each rule separately. If a rule is proposed that you perceive will be problematic and students do not first point out the difficulties, you can pose a question to get the group thinking about the possible

consequences of the rule—for example, "If we have a rule that people can throw things at other people, I wonder if the group will feel like a safe place."

GENERATING CONSEQUENCES

Say something like **"Now we have some group rules. What are going to be the consequences if a group member breaks a rule?"**

1. Generate a list; discuss the suggestions using a format similar to the one used for generating rules; then vote on the suggestions.

2. This part of the activity requires some careful responding by the group leader. The most useful consequences are something similar to one or two warnings, a time-out (remember to set a length, such as 3 or 5 minutes), then getting sent back to class for the day. Gently guide students toward such consequences.

   a. During the discussion, again ask questions to raise issues that might interfere with the success of the consequence—for example, "How long do you think it would take to write 'I will not bother other group members' 100 times?"

   b. If the group wants to set up other consequences that you think are reasonable, then these will be the consequences (e.g., do 10 push-ups, write a standard 10 times).

3. The goal of a time-out is time away from the attention of the group. When discussing time-outs, discourage attention-seeking time-outs such as "standing in the middle of the circle with a book on your head and your arms in the air."

   a. When in time-out, the student should sit in a chair in a corner of the room, facing away from the group. Do not lecture the student on the way to the chair because the added attention is often reinforcing, but quietly help the student to the time-out chair if necessary.

   b. If the student gets up or is disruptive, the time-out starts over again. Try to keep the group engaging for the other students while the time-out is taking place because you don't want the student in time-out to get attention (though he or she will probably try for attention).

   c. It is important to keep track of the time. When the time-out is over, invite the student to return to the group. Try to help make the student integral to the ongoing activity since the consequence is over and the student is not being punished.

ENFORCING RULES AND CONSEQUENCES

It is important to be consistent and careful in enforcing the rules and consequences. There is a temptation to overlook rule violations in early group sessions. Do not give in to this temptation, because then the group does not develop trust in the safety of the group environment. Even if you have to send a student back to class one week, the next week the student usually returns with increased respect for the rules and your ability to ensure the group's safety.

1. Group members are encouraged to be the ones who enforce the rules. If they do not call a rule violation that you see, you can say, **"Does anyone see a rule being broken?"** It is important for group cohesion and self-esteem to allow students to actively and effectively enforce the rules and consequences they have established.

2. After Session Two, use poster board or butcher paper to neatly write up the group rules and consequences. The heading should be the group's name to encourage group cohesion. This paper or board should be hung up in the room for each later session.

Trust-Building Activity: Feelings Grab Bag
(Adapted from Pedro-Carroll, 1985)

The goal of this activity is to increase awareness of one's own and others' emotions. It gives group members practice in identifying and reflecting feelings, the first building block toward developing empathic ways of responding. It is similar to charades, with the following steps: (1) a student draws a feeling out of the grab bag (a hat or bag); (2) the student acts out the feeling in front of the group, and members try to guess the feeling; (3) once the feeling is guessed, the student tells a time he or she has felt that feeling; (4) everyone else in the group gives an example of a time they felt the identified feeling.

1. Introduce this game by saying, **"Now we are going to play a game to help us learn how to help each other with problems. Have you ever had a friend tell you about a problem? Well, sometimes it's helpful just to let the person know that you understand how they feel by saying something like 'You must be mad' or That'd make me so sad.' Sometimes it can be hard to tell how someone else is feeling. So we're going to play this game to help us practice recognizing different feelings in our friends."**

2. **"This game is called Feelings Grab Bag. It's kind of like charades. Has anyone played charades? We have a number of feelings in this hat [or bag]. Each group member is going to get a chance to reach into the grab bag and draw a feeling. Then you'll come up to the front and act out the feeling for the other group members. Everyone tries to guess what the feeling is. Once someone guesses the feeling, the actor tells about a time when he or she felt that feeling. Then everyone else in the group tells about a time they felt like that. If you get a feeling that is really hard to act out, you can pick someone in the group to help you act out the feeling. OK, who wants to start?"**

3. If there's time after everyone has had a turn, discuss which feelings are the easiest and the hardest to express and why. Remind students that they can help people feel more comfortable talking about problems in the group just by recognizing and naming the other person's feeling.

Selection of Group Name

(If not done in Session One—see Session One for instructions.)

Check-Out

Generally, same as Session One. Ask, **"Why did we do Feelings Grab Bag? What did we learn that will help others when they are hurting?"**

Session Three

Activities
- ✓ Check-in
- ✓ Intent–Impact model
- ✓ Listening skills: Body Language game
- ✓ Listening skills: role play
- ✓ Speaking skills: you-statements and I-statements
- ✓ Check-out

Materials
- ✓ Curriculum
- ✓ Large pad of paper or dry-erase board and markers
- ✓ Papers with body language positions on them (see Appendix B-1d)
- ✓ Good Listening Skills handout (see Appendix B-1e)
- ✓ Secrets for Low-Trust Secret Pooling activity (see Appendix B-lf)— younger or older student version as appropriate
- ✓ Hat or bag in which to put body language papers and secrets
- ✓ Masking tape
- ✓ Rules and consequences. These should be put up in the room before each group session.

Content

Check-In

See Session Two.

Communication Skills: Listening and Speaking Effectively

These activities are meant to help group members communicate more effectively by learning to listen carefully, respond sensitively, and become aware of body language. It is hoped that developing these skills will help students more effectively utilize the rest of the SPARK curriculum as well as improve their interpersonal relationships outside of the group context.

Say, **"Last time we learned about how to recognize feelings and how to talk about a time when we experienced various feelings. Today we are going to look at positive ways to share our feelings as well as ways to really listen to others. Let's start by seeing how communication can sometimes go wrong."**

1. Explain the Intent–Impact model (Gottman et al., 1976). Draw two stick figures on the board, one with a big mouth (speaker) and one with big ears (listener), and note that what the speaker *intends* to say may not have the *impact* that was

intended (write the words *Intent* above the speaker and *Impact* above the listener; then draw a wiggly line between the two stick figures to indicate a disconnect). Give the following example or a similar one that is appropriate for your group. **"Your friend Jose made plans to hang out with you on Friday night. It's Friday morning and he says, 'I can't go with you tonight—I have to take care of some stuff.' What would be the message you hear?"** Elicit responses from group members. **"What did he really mean?"** Again elicit student response.

Discuss what was said versus what was meant versus what was heard by the other person. Ask students if they have ever felt misunderstood and elicit examples. Then ask students if they have ever misunderstood someone else and elicit examples.

2. **Listening skills.** The goal is to help students understand why it is important to listen to others and to learn skills to communicate that they are listening. Discuss why it is important to listen to others—mention that this relates to the *Impact* part of the communication drawing above. Try to elicit the following types of responses:

   a. People feel good when you make an effort to understand what they are thinking and feeling.

   b. You feel closer to people when you listen well to them and they to you.

   c. Listening carefully decreases misunderstandings.

   d. When people are upset, listening carefully helps calm things down.

Listening Skills: Body Language Game

This activity helps students understand how we communicate that we are listening or not listening. Put the papers with the body language positions listed below (from Appendix B-1d) in a bag or hat. Say, **"We're going to do an activity about what message our bodies give when people are talking. I'm going to walk around the room and talk to group members. As I come up to you, I'm going to ask you to draw a paper out of the bag. These papers mention ways our bodies can communicate whether or not we're listening to someone who is talking. Don't say what's on the paper, but follow the directions when I start talking."** If there is a co-leader of the group, first demonstrate with him or her looking out the window while the leader talks, and then proceed to other group members. After each demonstration, ask group members whether it seemed that the person was listening and then ask, **"What did their body do that showed they weren't really listening? What was the message their body was giving?"** Write the responses down on a large sheet of paper as they are discussed.

Body Language	*What Is Communicated*
■ Avoid eye contact	■ Shy, uninterested, nervous
■ Roll your eyes	■ Annoyed, mocking
■ Tap your foot fast	■ Impatient, nervous
■ Cross arms tight across chest	■ Not open, angry
■ Stand too close	■ Intimidating, scary

Give out the Good Listening Skills handout (see Appendix B-1e) and discuss the body language section. Ask someone to role play showing good listening skills through body language while the leader talks about something unrelated to the group (sports team, current news, etc.). Note the following body language positions that show good listening skills if the student displays these while the leader is talking: nodding head, good eye contact, leaning forward toward the speaker, and so forth.

Listening Skills: Role Play

Say: **"We've talked about ways our bodies show whether or not we're listening. Now let's talk about some ways that what we say shows that we're listening. What sorts of things do people say that let us know they're listening respectfully to us?"** Try to pull for the following points:

1. They *acknowledge what was said* by saying something like "uh huh" or "yeah," or even nodding their head.
2. They *summarize what was said* so we feel like what we said was heard and that they were listening carefully.
3. They *use reflective statements* that demonstrate they understand what we are feeling.
4. They *don't interrupt* but instead hear the person out.
5. They *ask open-ended questions* that encourage us to open up, tell more about what happened, or share feelings about it. Open-ended questions start with *what, why, how do, or tell me*. They can't be answered just *yes* or *no*.
6. They *share a similar experience they had* in a respectful manner.

Say, **"Let's try out our listening skills. We have some concerns here that people in other groups have shared. Let's divide into groups of three, then I'll give the concern to the person who is going to act it out and the other two people will demonstrate their good listening skills."** Get concerns from Secrets for "Secret Pooling"—Low-Trust Version (see Appendix B-1f). Divide students into groups of three that do not include best friends or more than one unruly member; each small group will then be performing in front of the entire group. Ask for a volunteer from each group to pretend it is their concern. Allow 5 minutes for problem sharing and good listening, then ask the concern sharer to talk about the particular listening skills used by his or her listeners and how they felt to the speaker. Focus on positive responses, but if negative ones arise (such as giving advice, putting the person down, laughing, or asking lots of irrelevant questions), ask how they made the concern sharer (and others in the group) feel. Elicit comments from other group members. Repeat the sequence with each group of three, using different concerns for each one. If there is not an even split, the leader(s) can participate in one of the groups or one group can have four members.

Speaking Skills: You-Statements and I-Statements

The goal of this activity is to help students learn to use I-statements rather than you-statements that are blaming and elicit defensiveness. This addresses the *Intent* part of the communication model presented at the beginning of this session. Say, **"Now we're going to talk about speaking skills, as we look at the *Intent* part of our communication model."** Start with a vignette that is relevant for your group. Examples might be:

1. **"You come home from school and you've been looking forward to eating some chips and watching your favorite program on TV. However, your older sister got to the TV first and is watching something you have no interest in, like reruns of *The Bachelor*, while eating the last of the Doritos. You're really mad. What might you say to her?"**

2. **"You see your friends gathered in a group on the lawn at school. You walk over to them and they are talking about the party they all went to on Saturday night and how much fun they had. You weren't invited to the party. You're really hurt. What might you say to them?"**

3. **"Your mom tells you to go clean the bathroom and the living room right now, going on and on about what a mess you made and how she has to do everything around the house. She says you're a lazy slob. You just got home from soccer practice and you're really tired and irritable. What might you say to her?"**

Use one of the above vignettes or make up your own. Write down on the large pad of paper or dry-erase board what students respond that they would say. After eliciting responses, ask whether they are statements that start with "I" or "you." Use a red marker to write "I" or "you" next to their responses. Point out that "you" statements usually are blaming and make the other person defensive and then not able to listen to you. Ask for some examples of the following "you" statements that they've said or had said to them and write them down as well. Say, **"What's an example of a blaming you-statement you've said or heard?"** Ask for one example of each of the following types of you-statements:

1. Blaming ("You can't do anything right")

2. Generalizing ("You always yell at me")

3. Name-calling ("You are such a jerk")

4. Accusing ("You are the one who doesn't care about anyone else but yourself")

5. Intimidating ("You clean up this stuff right now or I'll tell all your friends you still sleep with a stuffed animal")

INTRODUCE I-STATEMENTS

If one of the students' responses to the vignettes is an I-statement, highlight it and ask how the reaction to the I-statement differs from what they feel after hearing the you-statements. If no I-statements have been made, say **"Another** way of expressing yourself is to use I-statements. They are a much more effective way to share your feelings with others. The best thing about I-statements is that they're neutral and aren't threatening or blaming. They talk about our own feelings rather than about what the other person did. They take the form, 'I feel ___ when _____.' Or 'I would like _____.' Let's go back to the story we talked about earlier (i.e., the vignette), and come up with some I-statements for how we feel and what we would like." Elicit member responses and gently shape their responses into appropriate I-statements, first through eliciting help from other group members. If needed, the group leader can shape the I-statements.

Check-Out

"Today we talked about Intent–Impact in communicating. We learned about how to be a better listener and a more effective speaker. What are some things we can do to be a better listener? A better speaker?" Remind students to put their Good Listening Skills handout in their notebook.

Session Four (Optional)

Activities	✓ Trust ratings
	✓ Check-in
	✓ Secret Pooling
	✓ Check-out
Materials	✓ Curriculum
	✓ Trust ratings (one copy for each student—see Appendix B-la)
	✓ Secrets for Low-Trust Secret Pooling activity (see Appendix B-lf)—younger or older student version as appropriate
	✓ Paper and pencils for writing secrets in High-Trust version
	✓ Hat or bag in which to put secrets
	✓ Masking tape
	✓ Rules and consequences (if generated in previous session). These should be put up in the room before each group session.

Content

Check-In

See Session Two.

Trust Ratings

Have each group member fill out a trust rating slip. Collect them and put them aside. The level of trust in the group will be used to determine the version of the Secret Pooling activity you use in this session.

Trust-Building Activity: Secret Pooling
(Adapted from Goodman & Esterly, 1988)

This activity allows group members to practice and reinforce the skills in empathic responding taught in the first three sessions. It also reinforces self-disclosure skills when group members hear their secrets being read and hopefully met with empathy and understanding. In addition, hearing secrets that are similar to their own experiences reinforces feelings of universality for group members. This activity has the following steps: (1) a student draws a secret out of a hat or bag; (2) the student reads the secret as if it were his or her own secret; (3) the student says how he or she would feel if the secret were his or hers; (4) other students are encouraged to say how they think the person with that secret would be feeling; (5) group members are encouraged to discuss what they could say or do to help the person with the secret. There are High-Trust and Low-Trust versions of Secret Pooling. Prior to the group session, copy and cut out the prewritten secrets for the Low-Trust version (Appendix B-lf), fold them, and place them in a hat or bag, in case they are needed.

LOW-TRUST VERSION OF SECRET POOLING

The Low-Trust version is used if the trust ratings generated at the beginning of Session Four show an average trust rating of less than 3. Take out any secrets that were used in the Listening Skills role play in Session Three.

1. Say, "**Today we are going to use the listening skills that we learned last week when we play a game called Secret Pooling. Let's review those skills.**" Go over the Good Listening Skills handout from last week. "**We have a number of secrets written down and placed in this hat [or bag]. We'd like you to draw a secret out of the hat [or bag]. Then please read the secret to yourself and think about how you would feel if it were your secret.**"

2. "**Then when it's your turn, please read the secret out loud as if it were your own secret and say what feelings you'd be having. Other group members can help come up with feelings.**"

3. "**Finally, we'd like the other group members to think about what they could say that would help the person with this secret feel better. Ready? OK, who wants to begin?**"

HIGH-TRUST VERSION OF SECRET POOLING

The High-Trust version is used if the trust ratings generated at the beginning of Session Four show an average trust rating of 3 or higher. In this version, students are asked to generate their own secrets.

1. Say, "**Today we are going to use the listening skills that we learned last week when we play a game called Secret Pooling. Let's review those skills.**" Go over the Good Listening Skills handout from last week. "**Before we begin, we will ask each of you to write down a secret about yourself that you think no one in**"

the group will know. For example, people sometimes say something about their families (like if their parents are getting a divorce), about themselves (like if they've been arrested or used drugs), or about their relationships with others (like if they've had sex). Don't put your name on the paper. We don't want anyone to know that the secret is yours. Once we have your secrets, we're going to fold them in half, put them in the hat [or bag], and start the game." Pass out paper and pencils and ask the students to write down their secrets.

2. "We'd like you to draw a secret out of the hat [or bag]. If you get the secret that you wrote, put it back and draw another secret. Then please read the secret to yourself and think about how you would feel if that were your secret."

3. "Then when it's your turn, please read the secret out loud as if it were your own secret and say what feelings you'd be having. Other group members can help come up with feelings. Now the most important thing here is to talk about the feelings a person with this secret would have."

4. "We do not want you to try to guess whose secret it is or ask other group members if they wrote the secret. Also, do not reveal which secret is yours. And remember our Confidentiality Contract, and do not share anything with people outside the group."

5. "Finally, we'd like the other group members to think about what they could say that would help the person with this secret feel better. The two most helpful things are:

   a. Reflect the person's feeling, so they feel understood.

   b. Share a time when something similar happened to you and how you felt, so they don't feel so alone."

6. "Make sure to put empathy and helping the other person above curiosity. Ready? OK, who wants to begin?"

7. Leaders need to actively discourage members from trying to guess the author of the secret in the High-Trust version. A reminder about confidentiality can be helpful.

RESPONSES TO SECRET POOLING

In both versions, encourage group members to respond to the secret teller. The focus is on what will be helpful to the secret teller. Encourage reflection of feelings. If another student discloses a similar experience, the helpfulness of such self-disclosure to the person with the secret is emphasized.

1. Encouraged responses:

   a. *Reflections:* "That must be so hard for you," "You must feel sad all the time," and so on. If group members do not make feeling reflections, you can model them.

   b. *Self-disclosure:* "I think I know how you feel, because I also got picked up by the police (or had my dad leave without warning, etc.)."

2. Discouraged responses:

   a. *Advice-giving:* If students respond by giving advice, say **"I wonder how _____ feels. It will be more helpful for them to feel understood than be told what to do."**

   b. *Lots of specific questions about facts* (e.g., "What other drugs have you tried? Did the police pick you up other times too? How many guys have you had sex with?"): Say, **"I wonder how _____ feels. Let's see if we can help [him or her] feel understood."**

3. Especially when the secrets presented are highly personal (whether their own or given to them), there may be a tendency for students to react with nervous laughter or make jokes. It is important to quickly intervene and ask the group how they would feel if it were their own secret that they finally could share and people laughed or made fun of it.

4. After all the secrets are presented, hold a general discussion about what feels helpful when you are talking about something that is hard or scary to talk about and what makes you feel vulnerable.

Check-Out

Elicit general reactions to the session. Then ask, **"What did we learn from Secret Pooling? What things seemed to help the person with the secret feel understood? What felt helpful to you when you told the secret?"**

Anger Management and Emotion Regulation Skills

Goal To help students learn to understand their anger and develop emotion regulation strategies

Overview of Sessions

Session One
- *Purpose*: Understand internal and external anger triggers and body feelings associated with anger; learn emotion regulation strategies of muscle relaxation and deep breathing
- *Content*: (1) Anger Thermometer, (2) guess the body feeling game, (3) deep breathing, (4) muscle relaxation

Session Two
- *Purpose:* Examine typical responses to anger; introduce hot-headed and cool-headed responses; generate cool-headed coping thoughts and coping actions
- *Content*: (1) Generation of thoughts and actions when angry, (2) hot-headed and cool-headed thoughts and actions, (3) imagery exercise

Session Three
- *Purpose:* Further examine alternatives in dealing with anger, practicing cool-headed responses
- *Content*: (1) Hot-Head Cool-Head role play, (2) Hot-Head Cool-Head card game (optional)

Session One

Activities
- ✓ Check-in
- ✓ Anger management: Anger Thermometer
- ✓ Anger triggers
- ✓ Body feelings when angry
- ✓ Guess the body feeling game
- ✓ Deep breathing

✓ Muscle relaxation

✓ Check-out and handout

Materials ✓ Curriculum

✓ Anger Thermometer—two-sided (one copy for each student—see Appendix B-2a)

✓ Large Anger Thermometer drawn on poster paper or giant sticky note (should have hash marks 2/3 and almost all the way up the thermometer)

✓ Relaxation Log (one copy for each student—see Appendix B-2b)

✓ Red and black markers

✓ Large pad of paper or dry-erase board

✓ Masking tape

✓ Rules and consequences with the group name at the top of the rules and consequences pages. Put these up in the room before each session.

Content

Check-In

Anger Management Activity: Anger Thermometer

In this activity, students are encouraged to explore internal and external triggers for their anger and what they do when they are angry. In the next session, students will examine what kinds of coping thoughts and behaviors they might use to manage their emotional responses. In both sessions, the metaphor of a thermometer is used: the students examine what kinds of situations make their temperature rise; what body sensations and what thoughts help them know their temperature is rising and that they're getting angry; and what thoughts and actions they can use when angry that either escalate or de-escalate their angry feelings. It is important to leave about 15 minutes at the end of the first session to have time for the deep breathing and muscle relaxation exercises.

The leader introduces the Anger Thermometer by handing out the Anger Thermometer sheet from Appendix B-2a. The leader will have a large thermometer drawn on a piece of poster paper or giant sticky note. Say, **"We're going to use this thermometer to help us know what makes us angry and how our body tells us when our temperature is rising. As you can see, there are different degrees to which we can be mad. Here (point to near the bottom of the thermometer), we're not angry at all. Here (point to the mark about one-third way up the thermometer and fill it in with a red marker) we may be irritated or annoyed. When we get to here (point to mark about two-thirds up the thermometer and bring the red line up to that point), we're really mad, really pissed off. And when we get to here (almost at the top of the thermometer), we're enraged, so hot that we're about to explode. And here (pointing to the very top of the thermometer), we're in the danger zone and** what are we feeling?" Elicit responses from students. Summarize by saying, **"Yes, we're so mad it might even break the thermometer"**(draw the red line dramatically breaking through the top).

Anger Triggers

1. Give each group member the two-sided thermometer handout, with "Triggers" and "Body Feelings" on one side, and "Coping Thoughts" and "Coping Actions" on the other side.

2. Say **"Let's think of some things that make us mad, that *trigger* our anger, and see how mad they make us. We'd like you to write down at least one trigger or situation that makes you annoyed here** (point to one-third mark), **one that makes you really mad** (point to two-thirds mark), **one where you feel you'd be about to explode** (point to top mark), **and one where you're almost guaranteed to blow your top, if there is one"** (point to top of thermometer). Give students a few minutes to fill out their forms.

   a. Ask, **"What are some things that make you slightly irritated or annoyed?"** Write responses on the large sticky note or poster under "Triggers" at the one-third mark on the poster. If they put down something that seems like it would make people much madder, ask the group if this would make them slightly annoyed or if it belongs higher up on the thermometer.

   b. **"What makes us pretty mad, really pissed off?"** Record student responses as above, but this time near the two-thirds marker.

   c. **"What are some things that make us so mad, we feel like we'll explode?"** Point to the top mark and then record student responses at that level.

   d. **"Are there any situations where you're sure you'd lose control and blow your top?"** Point to the top of the thermometer and mark these at or above the top of the thermometer. In our studies, insulting one's mother seemed to be the thing that the male students especially felt they couldn't tolerate.

Body Feelings When Angry

1. Say, **"Over here (point to the right side of the page where the heading is 'Body Feelings'), let's think of some things that make us mad and see how we feel in our bodies then. Examples of body feelings are feeling hot, having your heart pound or veins stick out in your neck, or feeling your stomach tighten. We'd like you to write down at least one body feeling you have when you're annoyed** (point to one-third mark), **one body feeling that you experience when you're really mad** (point to two-thirds mark), **one that helps you know you're about to explode** (point to top mark), **and one body feeling you have when you're almost guaranteed to blow your top, if there is one"** (point to top of thermometer). Give students a few minutes to fill out their forms.

2. In the following discussion, try to elicit descriptions of physiological triggers such as racing heart, clenched fists or jaw, or hot face. Make a distinction between

those things we feel inside (racing heart, butterflies in stomach) and *those that show on the outside* (clenched fist, sweating, veins popping out on face).

3. **"How does our body feel when we are slightly annoyed?"** (point to one-third the way up the thermometer). Write down responses under "Body Feelings" on the large thermometer on the sticky note or poster.

4. **"What about when we're really pissed?"** Record student responses as above, but this time near the two-thirds marker.

5. **"How does our body feel when we're about to explode?"** Point to the top mark and then record student responses at that level.

6. **"And if our temperature rose so high we blew the top off?"** Mark these at or above the top of the thermometer.

Anger Management Activity: Guess the Body Feeling Game

1. Say, **"Now we're going to play a guessing game. Someone will show us how their body is when they are getting mad. We'll guess what they are experiencing in their body, and we'll vote on how mad we think the person is."**

2. Ask for volunteers to start. If no one volunteers, either give candy or points (if you are using these) to those who volunteer, or ask a student who has been active in other sessions to start. Encourage all students to participate but do not insist if someone prefers not to.

3. Have others guess what the body sensation is.

4. Ask students how mad the person was on the large thermometer in front of the group.

Emotion Regulation Activity: Deep Breathing

Say, **"One way to relax yourself quickly when you're mad without anyone knowing what you're doing is through deep breathing. It's a different kind of breathing and not how we usually breathe when we're mad. When we're mad, usually we breathe fast and shallow, like a dog panting** [exaggerate fast, shallow breathing with an angry face so it's funny]. **Deep breathing is slow and deep and it lowers our emotional temperature. It's often used by basketball players at the free-throw line or baseball players if they're being heckled."**

1. Turn off or dim the lights in the room if possible. **"Let's try it. We're going to breathe from our stomachs, so put your hand on your stomach. Take a very slow, deep breath, so deep that you can see your stomach rise with your breath. Now slowly let out your breath and watch your stomach fall. Watching your stomach is a good way to make sure you're taking deep breaths."**

2. **"A good way to make sure you're taking slow breaths is to count. Each breath in should take four counts and each breath out should take another four counts.**

Keep your hand on your stomach and let your breath follow my count: Breathe in, one, two, three, four. Breathe out, one, two, three, four. [Repeat this about 10 times.] Think about nothing but your breathing, let it flow in and out of your body."

3. Ask students how that felt and if they had any problems with the deep breathing. Suggest that they try using deep breathing this week at least twice when they feel their temperature rising.

Emotion Regulation Activity: Muscle Relaxation

Say, "Another way to relax when you're having lots of angry body feelings is through relaxing your muscles. Let's try this now. I'd like everyone to face toward the wall and get in a comfortable sitting or reclining position.

1. Loosen any tight clothing.

2. Now tense your toes and feet. Hold the tension, study the tension, then relax.

3. Now tense your lower legs, knees, and thighs. Hold the tension. Study the tension, then relax.

4. Tense your fingers and hands. Hold and study the tension, then relax.

5. Tense your lower arms, elbows, and upper arms. Hold it, study it, relax.

6. Tense your stomach, hold the tension, feel the tension, and relax.

7. Now tense your chest. Hold and study the tension. Relax. Take a deep breath and exhale slowly.

8. Tense the lower back. Hold and study the tension and relax.

9. Tense the upper back. Hold the tension, feel the tension, then relax.

10. Now tense the shoulders. Hold and study the tension. Then relax.

11. Now tense both the back and front of your neck. Hold the tension, study the tension, then relax.

12. Now tense your entire head. Make a grimace on your face so that you feel the tension in your facial muscles. Study the tension and then relax.

13. Now try to tense every muscle in your body. Hold it, study it, then relax.

14. Continue sitting or reclining for a few minutes, feeling the relaxation flowing through your body. Know the difference between muscles that are tense and muscles that are relaxed.

15. Now stretch, feeling renewed and refreshed."

Check-Out

Ask students what they learned about anger today. Collect their individual thermometer sheets and hold for use in Session Two. Remind them to use deep breathing at least twice before the next session and muscle relaxation at least once. Give each student a Relaxation Log so they can record these as well, and remind them to put it in their notebook. Let students know that they will receive a point or a candy when they return the sheet.

Session Two

Activities
- ✓ Check-in
- ✓ Review of Relaxation Logs
- ✓ Hot-headed and cool-headed thoughts and actions
- ✓ Guided imagery
- ✓ Development of own calming image
- ✓ Check-out

Materials
- ✓ Curriculum
- ✓ Thermometer sheets collected last session
- ✓ Large pad of paper or dry-erase board
- ✓ Colored markers (including red and blue markers)
- ✓ Blank paper, markers, and pencils
- ✓ Masking tape
- ✓ Cool-Head Thoughts and Actions handout (one copy for each student—see Appendix B-2c)
- ✓ My Anger Journal handout (one copy for each student—see Appendix B-2d)
- ✓ Rules and consequences with the group name at the top of the rules and consequences pages. Put these up in the room before each session.

Content

Check-In

Collect Relaxation Logs and discuss briefly when students used these coping strategies of deep breathing and muscle relaxation. Give each student who returned the Log a point or a piece of candy.

Anger Management Activity: Hot-Headed and Cool-Headed Thoughts and Actions

Use a poster or giant sticky note to write and list "Thoughts" in one column and "Actions" in another column.

1. Say, **"When we're mad, what kinds of thoughts do we think?"** Elicit students' thoughts when they're angry and write them down in the "Thoughts" column. Common thoughts are: I'd like to punch him; he's out to get me; what an %#@*%; maybe it was an accident that she bumped into me.

2. **"When we're mad, what kinds of actions do we do?"** Elicit students' actions when they're angry and write them down in the "Actions" column. Common actions are: I'd hit him; get my friends to go after him; say mean things back to her; walk away.

3. Introduce **hot-headed and cool-headed** thoughts and actions. Say, **"Most ways we deal with anger fall into two categories, and we're going to call those categories hot-headed and cool-headed responses. Hot-headed responses heat up the situation, while cool-headed responses bring down the temperature."** Point out that not expressing anger in some form may have negative consequences as well (e.g., exploding later on or taking out one's anger on an innocent victim). Make it clear that cool-headed responses *are* a response to anger and are not the same as not expressing anger.

   a. **"Let's look at the thoughts and actions we wrote down before. Which ones are hot-headed? Which ones are cool-headed?"**

      Have students categorize the thoughts. Put a big red *H* next to the hot-headed thoughts, and a big blue *C* next to the cool-headed thoughts. Repeat this process with the actions generated.

   b. Give out Cool-Head Thoughts and Actions handout. Go over the handout, with the focus first on **cool-headed coping thoughts.** Define these and have students generate examples.

   Types of Cool-Headed Coping Thoughts (Some adapted from Larson, 2005)

   ■ **Give the benefit of the doubt**—alternative explanations (e.g., "He probably didn't mean for it to come out the way it sounded"; "It was probably an accident").

   ■ **Calming self-talk**
      • "Let me stop and think" (reduces acting impulsively)
      • "Relax and breathe"—remind students about muscle relaxation and deep breathing from last time
      • "I can stay calm and bring the temperature down"

   ■ **Reframing the situation**
      • "This is an opportunity to really get to know him"
      • "If he hadn't shut my locker, I might have forgotten that I needed my history book from in there"

   c. Now focus on actions, discussing the types of **cool-headed coping actions** on the handout, and having students generate examples.

Types of Cool-Headed Actions

■ **Muscle relaxation and deep breathing** (remind them they experienced these both last session).

■ **Taking a time-out.** Say, "Some type of 'time-out' also is a good cool-headed response that lowers the emotional temperature. What are some ways you could take a time-out when your anger gets triggered?" Elicit responses from students. Try to guide them toward solutions such as walking away; ignoring the person; avoiding where they know the person they're angry at will be.

■ **Problem solving.** Say, "Another really good cool-headed coping action is to try to directly solve the problem. What would be some good cool-headed problem-solving strategies?" Elicit ideas from the students. If they come up with previously discussed ones like walking away under "taking a time-out," validate them and accept it. If students don't come up with some variation of trying to talk it out or negotiate or compromise and some variation of enlisting the help of someone like a teacher, principal, or parent, ask questions to try to elicit these responses.

■ **Seeking help from others** (e.g., trusted adults, counseling). Elicit from students when and how they might be able to get help from others when really angry and when they can't solve the problem themselves (e.g., someone is hurt or in danger).

■ **Imagery.** Say, "Another good way to help bring down your emotional temperature when you are really angry is to go to a calm relaxing place in your head. We'll do this in a few minutes, and later you'll develop your own calming image."

4. Distribute the students' anger thermometers that they started filling out last week. On the back side, have students spend a few minutes writing down cool-headed thoughts and actions they would be most likely to use.

Emotion Regulation Activity: Guided Imagery (Johnson, 2004)

The guided imagery exercise is preceded by a brief muscle relaxation. First ask students to turn their chairs toward the wall.

Say, "Close your eyes, as you scan your body for any tension. If you find tension, release it. Let it go and relax. Relax your head and your face. Relax your shoulders. Relax your arms and hands. Relax your chest and lungs. Relax your back. Relax your stomach. Relax your hips, legs, and feet. Experience a peaceful, pleasant, and comfortable feeling of being relaxed as you prepare to take an imaginary trip to a beautiful place. Take a deep breath, and breathe out slowly and easily. Take a second deep breath, and slowly breathe out. Allow your breathing to become smooth and rhythmic.

"Picture yourself on a mountaintop. It has just rained and a warm wind is carrying the clouds away. The sky is clear and blue, and the sun is shining down. Below you are beautiful green trees. You enjoy the fragrance of the forest after the rain. In the distance you can see a beautiful white, sandy beach. Beyond that, as far as you can see, is crystal clear, brilliant blue water. A fluffy cloud drifts in the gentle breeze until it is right over you. Slowly, this little cloud begins to sink down on you. You experience a very pleasant, delightful feeling. As the fluffy cloud moves down across your face, you feel the cool, moist touch of it on your face. As it moves down your body, all of the tension slips away, and you find yourself completely relaxed and happy.

"As the soft cloud moves across your body, it gently brings a feeling of total comfort and peace. As it sinks down around you it brings a feeling of deep relaxation. The little cloud sinks underneath you, and you are now floating on it. The cloud holds you up perfectly and safely. You feel secure. The little cloud begins to move slowly downward and from your secure position on it, you can see the beautiful forest leading down to the beach. There is a gentle rocking motion as you drift along. You feel no cares or concerns in the world, but are focused completely on the relaxed feeling you experience. The cloud can take you anyplace you want to go, and you choose to go to the beach. As you move to the beach, the cloud gently comes to the ground and stops. You get off the soft cloud onto the beach, and you are at peace. You take some time to look around at the white sandy beach, and the beautiful blue water. You can hear seagulls and the roar of the waves. As you feel the sun shining on you, you can smell the ocean air. It smells good. As you walk slowly on the beach, you enjoy the feeling of the warm clean sand on your feet. Just ahead on the beach is a soft blanket and pillow. You lie down and enjoy the feeling of the soft material on the back of your legs and arms. As you listen to the waves and the seagulls and feel the warmth of the sun through the cool breeze, you realize that you are comfortable, relaxed, and at peace. You feel especially happy because you realize that you can return to this special and beautiful place anytime you want to.

"Feeling very relaxed, you choose to go back to the place where you started, knowing that you will take these peaceful and relaxed feelings with you. There is a stairway close by that leads you back to the room where you started. As you climb the five steps, you will become more aware of your surroundings, but you will feel relaxed and refreshed. You are at the bottom of the stairs now, and begin climbing."

"Step 1 to Step 2: moving upward

Step 2 to Step 3: feeling relaxed and more aware

Step 3 to Step 4: you are aware of what is around you, and your body is relaxed

Step 4 to Step 5: your mind is alert and refreshed, open your eyes and stretch gently."

Emotion Regulation Activity: Developing One's Own Calming Image

Say, "**Now you can work on developing your own image.**" In introducing this as a coping action, it is important to have the students develop an image that they can use later. When someone is really angry, they will not be able to develop a calming image at that time.

"Begin by thinking of a place where you love to be, where you feel peaceful. Examples for different people might be a beach or a forest or a meadow or a park. Imagine yourself sitting or lying there and then really try to put yourself there by thinking about the sights, sounds, smells, temperature, and so forth. Now close your eyes and think about what place is peaceful and relaxing for you."

1. To help students develop and elaborate on their images, ask them to either **draw a picture** of their relaxing place **or write a paragraph** about it, with attention to smells, sounds, sights, and so on. Provide paper, markers, and pencils. Give students about 10 minutes to either draw or write about their relaxing place.

2. Ask students if some would be willing to share their drawing or writing. Allow all who want to share to have a turn telling about or showing their peaceful place. (If no student volunteers to share their image, leaders should be prepared to share an image they find very relaxing.)

Notes for Anger Management

1. At some point during this session, discuss justified anger. Ask, **"Are there any times when anger is justified, when the problem is really really big? What are some big problems where our solutions might not be enough?"** Elicit situations like child abuse, death of a loved one, or other major family problems.

2. If students simply cannot relate to cool-headed responses because they feel such responses would be too wimpy, you can raise the possibility of using "warm-headed" responses. Warm-headed responses involve giving back a verbal insult, making fun of the insult itself (e.g., "That line's so old you must have learned it from your great-grandmother"), or threatening to come back later. The possibility of warm-headed responses should be raised only after working to help students feel comfortable with cool-headed responses.

Check-Out

Elicit general reactions from the group. Give out My Anger Journal sheets and discuss the assignment. Remind them to put these sheets as well as the Cool-Head Thoughts and Actions sheet in their notebook. Let students know that they will earn points or candy for bringing in the completed sheet next week.

Session Three

Activities   ✓ Check-in

✓ Review of My Anger Journal homework

✓ Hot-Head Cool-Head role play

✓ Optional additional activity: Hot-Head Cool-Head card game

✓ Check-out

Materials   ✓ Curriculum

✓ (Optional) Hot-Head Cool-Head card game—see Appendix B-2e

✓ Rules and consequences with the group name at the top of the rules and consequences pages. Put these up in the room before each session.

Content

Check-In

Review of My Anger Journal Homework (If Not Already Discussed in Check-In)

Give each student who returned the Anger Journal a point or a piece of candy. Check on students' use of cool-headed responses during the last week. Have extra copies of the Cool-Head Thoughts and Actions handout. If a student chose a hot-headed response during the week, work with the group to generate a cool-headed response that the student would feel comfortable using in a similar situation.

Anger Management Activity: Hot-Head Cool-Head Role Play

The goal is to actively involve the students in evaluating cool-headed and hot-headed responses in simulated situations. Besides providing a review of problem-solving skills, the activity gives some understanding of how to resolve, or at least how not to exacerbate, conflicts between others. The activity has the following steps: (1) Group members are divided into two groups (with at least four members in each group), and each group does a role play. (2) In the role play, the "good guy" and "bad guy" get into an argument, then "freeze." (3) While they are frozen, the other two actors advise the good guy. The "hot-head" tries to get the good guy to respond violently. The "cool-head" tries to get the good guy to respond nonviolently. (4) The good guy chooses which response to use, and tells why that response was chosen. (5) Each group does their role play while the other group watches.

1. Introduce the activity by saying, **"Has anyone ever seen those cartoons where the character has an angel on one shoulder and a devil on the other, and they're trying to get him to do different things?"** Process reactions. **"Well, today's activity is kind of like that. We are going to break into two teams, and each team is going to put on a short play for the other team. OK, let's break into teams."** (You can assign teams or let group members choose.)

2. Say, **"Remember last time when we asked you about situations that make people angry? The play is going to be about those situations. Each team needs to pick one situation. Then each team picks who will play the characters. Each team's play should have a 'good guy,' a 'bad guy,' a 'cool-head,' and a 'hot-head.'"**

   a. **"The role of the cool-head is to serve as a kind of good 'conscience' and advise the good guy on ways to solve the problem without violence. The cool-head** character may suggest some of the 'cool-head coping thoughts and actions' we talked about last time."

   b. "The hot-head character may represent the good guy's automatic response or pressures to 'save face' and respond with violence. The hot-head character is to act like a 'bad conscience.'"

   c. "The purpose of the role play is for the good guy to examine the consequences of both the 'hot-head' and 'cool-head' responses. Then the good guy will tell us what he or she chooses and why."

3. "This is how it will work. The bad guy will start provoking and trying to get the good guy mad. When I say 'freeze,' the hot-head and the cool-head will each try to influence the good guy to follow them. After they finish, then the good guy will make the choice. Then you will do your play for the other group."

4. You should assist in the development of the role plays in order to ensure that the participants understand the purpose of the activity. Help assign characters in ways that will be productive. For example, it is best to avoid having a shy child play the cool-head role; if possible, the cool-head role should be performed by a student with high status in the group. It is helpful for you to facilitate the choice of a cool-headed response by asking questions about the consequences of a hot-headed response.

5. Once each group has planned the role play, they perform for the other group(s). Encourage good audience behavior from the group not performing (paying attention, not shouting out, etc.). The good guy and bad guy begin to argue; when it escalates, say "freeze" and the actors stop moving. Then the hot-head and cool-head try to convince the good guy of his or her next action.

6. If the role plays are not resolved in nonviolent ways, generate group discussion as to why. Sometimes students focus on the immediate consequence of winning or showing off and do not examine the longer-term consequences. Work with members to generate an alternative cool-headed response that they find acceptable.

Anger Management Activity: Hot-Head Cool-Head Card Game

(Use this activity if time permits.) This activity reinforces the concepts of identifying an anger-provoking situation, choosing cool-headed or hot-headed alternatives, and evaluating the consequences of the chosen alternative.

1. Set up the three stacks of cards, Problem, Alternative, and Consequence. Either use the preprinted problem cards from Appendix B-2e, or write out your own problem cards to fit the needs of the group.

2. The first player selects a Problem card and reads the problem aloud to the group.

3. The person to the left then selects an Alternative card, which will read either "hot" or "cool"; the player must provide an appropriate hot-headed or cool-headed response.

4. The next person to the left then draws a Consequence card (e.g., "Long-term for the other person") and must provide an appropriate consequence for the response just described.

5. Continue through as many problem cards as there is time for.

Check-Out

Elicit general reactions from the students. Then ask, **"What did we learn and practice today about dealing with situations that make us angry?"** If the students' responses do not mention cool-headed and hot-headed responses, looking at alternatives, and evaluating the consequences, reiterate these points.

MODULE THREE

Ethnic Identity and Anti-Prejudice

Goal To help students develop positive feelings of ethnic pride, to address and discuss prejudice, and to understand and accept people from other ethnic groups

Overview of Sessions

Session One
- *Purpose:* Increase awareness and understanding of prejudice and stereotypes
- *Content:* (1) Labeling game, (2) discussion of stereotypes and prejudice

Session Two
- *Purpose:* Continue discussion of prejudice, and to discuss and strengthen one's own ethnic identity
- *Content:* Ethnic identity posters

Session One

Activities
- ✓ Check-in
- ✓ Labeling game
- ✓ Discussion of stereotypes and prejudice
- ✓ Check-out

Materials
- ✓ Curriculum
- ✓ Name tags or mailing labels with adjectives written on them for labeling exercise (see Appendix B-3)
- ✓ Masking tape
- ✓ Rules and consequences with the group name at the top of the rules and consequences pages. Put these up in the room before each session.

Content

Check-In

Anti-Prejudice Activity: Labeling Game

The goal is to increase awareness and understanding of prejudice and stereotypes. This game has the following steps: (1) Place a label on each group member's forehead; (2) group members mingle, treating each other as if the labels were true; (3) group members try to guess their label based on the way they were treated.

1. Before the group meets, prepare adhesive labels (mailing labels or name tag stickers) with adjectives or descriptions written on them. Some should be positive (e.g., Friendly, Helpful, Sexy, Good Athlete, Good Student) and others should be slightly negative (e.g., Snobby, Teacher's Pet, Bossy, Lazy, Shy). Suggested adjectives are given in Appendix B-3. Use the ones most appropriate for your group or those that will be most helpful to your group.

2. Introduce the activity by saying, **"Now we are going to play a game called Labeling. I am going to place a label on each person's forehead so that no one can see his or her own label. Then we will mingle and chat with each other, and you should treat each person as if his or her label is true. For example, if my label said Leader, you might want to ask my advice or follow my lead. The object of the game is to try to guess your label based on how others treat you. There are only three rules:**

   a. **You can't look at your own label.**

   b. **You can't tell anyone what his or her label says.**

   c. **You can't ask other people to tell you what your label says.**

   OK. Let's start."

3. Place the labels on students' foreheads. Model the interactions by treating group members stereotypically as if their label were true. Make sure to interact with any students who may not be actively participating.

4. After 5 or 10 minutes of interacting, ask group members to guess what their labels say. Then have them take off their labels and see what they say.

   a. Encourage students to explain how they guessed their labels from clues from other students by asking, **"How could you tell?"**

   b. Probe how it felt to be treated as if the label were true by asking: **"How did it feel to be treated as if you were _____?"**

Discussion of Prejudice and Stereotypes

Say, **"We all wear labels, and people treat us as if the labels were true. Many people look at us and make assumptions. Race or ethnicity is one characteristic that often leads people to make assumptions about others."**

DEFINING RACE AND CULTURE

"**Who knows what 'race' means?**" Elicit and discuss responses from group members. "**Who knows what 'culture' means? How is it different from 'race'?**" Elicit and discuss responses from group members. "**Sometimes people don't like to talk about race because it makes them feel uncomfortable and makes us seem different from each other. People** *are* **different, and there's nothing wrong with that. In fact, differences make life interesting. Our race and cultural background are real and important parts of us, and there is nothing wrong with talking about them. It can help us understand ourselves and others better.**"

DEFINING AND DISCUSSING PREJUDICE

"**Who can tell me what 'prejudice' means?**" (Support all answers, working toward correct definition): Prejudice—to prejudge; a feeling, opinion, or attitude about members of a certain group.

1. Ask, "**What's the name for prejudice against:**
   a. **people from other racial groups?**" Racism.
   b. **women?**" Sexism.
   c. **people with little money or poor people?**" Classism.
2. It helps group members open up to group leaders of different ethnic backgrounds if you say something like "**I really hope that you will feel comfortable talking about prejudice with me. I will not feel any differently about you or be mad at you if you say something negative about [leader's ethnicity] people. What's most important to me is to hear your true reactions and feelings about things.**"

DEFINING AND DISCUSSING STEREOTYPES

"**Prejudice is often based on stereotypes. Who can tell me what 'stereotype' means?**" Stereotypes—exaggerated beliefs about characteristics of members of certain groups (e.g., Asians are good in math and very quiet; African Americans are violent and good at basketball).

1. Ask, "**What are some examples of stereotypes you've heard, either about your own group or others?**"
2. Elicit examples of people who do not fit these stereotypes.

ORIGINS OF PREJUDICE AND PERSONAL EXPERIENCES WITH PREJUDICE

Say, "**It is probably impossible to grow up without any prejudice because it is such a problem in our society and is very common.**"

1. Examine origins of our racial attitudes. **"Where do these attitudes come from? Where did you learn some of the stereotypes you have?"** Common sources are parents, media, and school.

2. The following are suggested questions for discussion.

   a. **Describe the earliest memory you have of an experience with people of a cultural or ethnic group different from yours.**

   b. **Who or what has had the most influence on how you feel about people of different cultural or racial groups, and in what ways?**

   c. **Describe an experience where you feel you were discriminated against for any reason, not necessarily race or culture.** (Point out that all people experience some kind of prejudice, maybe because of race, gender, class, religion, or style of dress, but acknowledge that some groups experience more prejudice than others.)

3. If members have trouble talking about experiences of prejudice, share a personal experience of prejudice, including feelings and coping style.

WHAT CAN WE DO ABOUT DISCRIMINATION AND PREJUDICE?

If appropriate, say, **"It sounds like many of you have had experiences with racism and that prejudice seems unfair and hurtful. Several of you raised the question 'What can we do about this?'"** (If no one raised that question, say, **"Let's talk about what we can do to stop prejudice."**)

1. Explore students' own stereotypes. **"One of the biggest ways we can make a difference is by changing our own behaviors. Because of the way our society is, most people hold stereotypes and have acted in a way that was prejudiced. Who can tell us about a stereotype they've held or something they've done or said that you think might have been kind of prejudiced?"**

   a. Reinforce being brave enough to speak up. Encourage others to share their attitudes and experiences.

   b. In schools with much racial tension, this may be a difficult and emotionally charged activity. Acknowledge that by saying, **"We know that discrimination and prejudice occur right here in our school, so it's kind of a touchy subject. But it's important to own up to what's happening so that we can do something about it. Who can give some examples of discrimination or prejudice going on at our school?"**

2. Generate ideas about things group members can do to lessen racism. Say, **"Who has ideas about what *we* can do to eliminate racism?"** If students are unable to come up with ideas, suggest some of the following (or your own ideas): not laughing at racist jokes, asking friends and relatives not to tell racist jokes or make prejudiced statements, talking in a friendly manner with and getting to know members of other ethnic groups.

Check-Out

Elicit general reactions to the session. Ask, **"What did we learn from the Labeling game? What did we learn about prejudice and racism? What positive steps can we take to end prejudice and discrimination?"** Begin planning for the field trip now. See Module Four, Session Two for details on how to plan for the field trip.

Session Two

Activities
- ✓ Check-in
- ✓ Finish "What can we do about discrimination and prejudice?" if not completed last session
- ✓ Ethnic Identity posters
- ✓ Check-out

Materials
- ✓ Curriculum
- ✓ Poster boards (at least enough for each ethnic group represented)
- ✓ Colored markers (lots)
- ✓ Permission slips for field trip to local university or college
- ✓ Masking tape
- ✓ Rules and consequences with the group name at the top of the rules and the consequences pages. Put these up in the room before each session.

Content

Check-In

What Can We Do about Discrimination and Prejudice?

If the discussion from Session One feels unfinished, say, **"Last week, we started talking about people's experiences with racism and some of the anger and fear that people feel when they are discriminated against. We also started talking about things we can do to help end prejudice and discrimination. I'm wondering if you have thought any more about this during the week."** Process responses according to the guidelines in Session One.

Ethnic Pride Activity: Ethnic Identity Posters

(Requires at least a half hour.) The goal is to develop and share a sense of ethnic identity and to celebrate differences and diversity. This activity has the following steps: (1) Members break up into small groups of the same ethnicity; (2) groups share ideas and feelings about what it means to be a member of that ethnic group; (3) group members draw symbols representing these ideas and feelings on posters;

(4) the groups come together and present their posters to each other; (5) students identify differences and similarities among posters.

1. Students break into groups by ethnicity. If, for example, all students are Latino, then the groups are broken down by country of origin (e.g., Mexico, Puerto Rico, El Salvador).

    a. Say, **"One way that we can feel better when other people treat us in a prejudiced way is to remember the things we like about our own ethnic groups. Today we are going to think about what we especially like about our ethnic groups by making Ethnic Identity posters. We'll make one poster for each ethnic group here. Let's make this area the African American poster, this one the Latino poster, and this one . . . "**

    b. **"First discuss your ideas about what it means to be a member of your group and what symbols or concepts or feelings represent your cultural or racial identity. After you have come to an agreement, draw those things on your poster."**

    c. If students have trouble thinking about symbols or ideas, suggest foods, music, dress, history, and so on as possible things to think about. Circulate and assist any groups that may be having difficulty.

2. Come together again after 15 to 20 minutes. Discuss feelings about the activity. Ask questions such as the following to stimulate discussion:

    a. **"How did it feel to separate into small groups of the same race or ethnicity?"** (Uncomfortable, similar to how it usually is at school, more comfortable talking about your racial identity with people from your ethnic group?)

    b. **"How did it feel to come back into one group?"**

    c. **"How did the size (relative largeness or smallness) of your group make you feel? Did size affect your discussion or your poster? How might the size of a group affect ethnic identity?"**

3. Present the posters. Each group presents its poster, explaining the meanings of the symbols and objects. Possible discussion questions are

    a. **"What were the similarities among posters? What were the differences?"**

    b. **"Were there differences and/or disagreements within your group about what ethnicity meant to people? How did it feel to have a different idea about your culture than others in your group?"** Add, **"There are many differences among individuals within racial groups, and there are many commonalities among ethnic groups."**

    c. **"What experiences have led to the development of positive feelings about your cultural heritage and background?"**

    d. **"What experiences have led to the development of negative feelings, if any, about your cultural heritage and background?"**

Check-Out

Elicit general reactions to the group. Ask, **"What did we learn about ethnic identity? How does ethnic identity relate to prejudice?"** Pass out permission slips for the field trip to the local college or university to be held in a few weeks, specifying where the students should return the permission slips.

MODULE FOUR

 # Educational Aspirations

Goal To help students set high educational aspirations, to address barriers to academic success, and to identify specific steps students can take to do better in school

Overview of Sessions

Session One
- ■ *Purpose:* Think about educational and career aspirations, discuss steps required to reach goals, and examine barriers to reaching these goals
- ■ *Content:* (1) Peer introduction of career goals, (2) Education and Career Ladder, (3) barriers to education

Session Two
- ■ *Purpose:* Give students the experience of being on a college campus and expose students to positive role models
- ■ *Content:* Field trip to local college or university

Session Three
- ■ *Purpose:* Associate positive feelings with being a good student and help students define behaviors and skills necessary to do well in school
- ■ *Content:* (1) *Rudy* movie clips, (2) goal setting

Session One

Activities
- ✓ Check-in
- ✓ Peer introduction of career goals
- ✓ Education and Career Ladder
- ✓ Barriers to education
- ✓ Goal setting
- ✓ Check-out

Materials   ✓ Curriculum

✓ Education and Career Ladder (one for each student—see Appendix B-4a)

✓ My Goals sheets (two-sided, one for each student—see Appendix B-4b)

✓ A pad of paper large enough to be seen by all students (with questions sheet and blank Education Ladder completed *prior* to session—see below)

✓ Real or pretend microphone (optional)

✓ Brightly colored pens

✓ Masking tape

✓ Rules and consequences with the group name at the top of the rules and consequence pages. Put these up in the room before each session.

Content

Check-In

Peer Introduction of Career Goals

The goal is to help students think about what type of career or work they want for themselves in the future. Students are asked to interview their partner in front of the group.

1. Say, "**Today we will be talking about what you want to do when you have finished high school, and how you can reach that goal. You are going to be reporters and interview each other about your future goals. Then we'll come back together, and you will use our reporter's microphone to interview your partner so that the whole group knows about their goals. Each person in the pair will take a turn being the reporter and being the person interviewed.**"

2. Have students divide into pairs. Assign pairs, or have students pick partners.

3. Say, "**Ask your partner the following questions**" [questions should be written on the large pad of paper so students can refer to them]:

   a. "**What is your name? (if you don't already know)**"

   b. "**What do you want to do when you grow up?**"

   c. "**What is your backup career plan?**"

   d. "**What education or training do you need to become what you want to be? What do you need for your backup plan?**"

4. Allow 5 to 10 minutes for students to interview each other and find out the answers to the above questions. After about 5 minutes, suggest that students switch roles once they have answered the questions, so that the reporter becomes the interviewee and vice versa.

a. Circulate and help students who may need assistance in coming up with their career plan and their backup career plan, as well as those who may be shy and have difficulty sharing.

b. If there is an odd number of students, pair yourself with one student; the student should interview you, and you should interview the student.

5. After the interviews, gather the students in a circle again and say (using real or imaginary microphone), **"We will now present interviews of group members about what they want to do for a job or career, their backup plans, and how they will get there. Who will be the first reporter?"** (Give real or imaginary microphone to the reporter.) Each student presents their partner's career goals and the steps needed to reach the goal. If an answer is left out, ask the reporter, for example, **"So what kind of education or training will Bryan need to be a fireman [lawyer, NBA player, etc.]?"**

6. Accept all career goals. However, if the goal is something illegal (e.g., pimp), gently question whether this is a reasonable goal.

Educational Aspirations Activity: Education and Career Ladder

The goal is to provide students with a picture of the educational or training steps that they need to take in order to reach their career objectives. Before the beginning of the session, use the Education and Career Ladder handout as a guide and write the steps on one of the large sheets of paper or on the dry-erase board. Make a straight line on the left for age and years in school. Make sure to include spaces for preschool, elementary school, middle school, high school, college/university/ vocational school, and graduate/professional school. The ladder (with no steps filled in) should be made before the start of the session. Give each student an Educational and Career Ladder handout.

1. Ask, **"What educational steps have you already taken?"**

a. Start with preschool and elementary school so that students feel they have already accomplished some of the steps.

b. As students mention different steps, fill them in on the Education and Career Ladder. Make sure to go in order up the Education and Career Ladder.

2. After high school is on the board, ask students what comes next, making clear that the next steps will differ depending on their career goals.

a. Using each student's previously given career goal, ask him or her, **"What kind of education or training after high school do you need to become a _____?"**

b. If the student does not know, ask other group members. If that still does not elicit the appropriate answer, supply the answer. If you do not know, brainstorm with the group about how the student might find out what is needed to reach the particular career goal.

1. Examples of resources are the school's career guidance counselor, profes-sional organizations (e.g., the Plumber's Association), and the Internet.

2. You can volunteer to find out for the student if it feels as if the task would be overwhelming.

3. Be sure to discuss educational or training steps needed for the backup career goal as well as the main career goal.

c. Remind students that each step prepares them for the next one, and that they need to try their best at each level because reaching the next level depends on how they do on the previous level. It will not work to begin trying after they finish high school.

d. If students are interested, share information about your own education.

3. Ask students to write on their Education and Career Ladder handout the specific steps past high school necessary to reach their particular goal. Say, **"On your own handout, please write down your career goal and the education or training steps we just talked about that you need to reach your goal."**

Barriers to Education

Say, **"Many of you have goals that would require you to go to college. What are some things that might stop you from going to college?"** Elicit their concerns and worries, and discuss them. Speakers at the field trip will also address some of these issues. The following concerns are common (possible student and leader responses are in parentheses):

1. *Financial.* (Scholarships are available; community/junior colleges.)

2. *Social.* ("People in college will be different from me, I'd feel scared to be away from my friends"—but there are usually people from all backgrounds in college; ethnic studies or other organizations exist to help students feel more supported.)

3. *Deserting my community.* (Many low-income students may feel that they are sell-ing out or be afraid it will look like they think they are better than others from their communities. Some students may have been told this by peers or family. It is important to acknowledge this, but to point out ways that education can be used to help one's community. Education does not have to change you in ways you don't want to be changed.)

4. *Deserting my family.* (In some cultures, there may be a lot of pressure to stay in the neighborhood or live at home. Parents very often have not attended college. They may be ambivalent about having the student go to college; while they are excited for the student, they may also have concerns that their children will leave them or become different from them. It is important to be sensitive to what the child wants and to his or her culture. If the student wants to go away to college, discuss concerns about the family and the student's own need for autonomy. If the student feels more comfortable staying near family, explore nearby colleges where the student could visit often or live at home).

Goal Setting

The goal is to help students translate their long-term career goals into short-term goals that will help them do better in school now. Say, **"I'm passing out a goal sheet (My Goals sheet from Appendix B-4b) to all of you. In order to reach the top of your Education and Career Ladder, you need to do well in school. Please take this sheet home, fill out the front side, which asks you to list your goals for the year, and bring it back when we meet after the field trip. You can earn a point or candy for bringing back your filled-out goals sheet. You don't need to complete the back side yet, as we will do that together when we meet next time."**

1. Elicit one or two students' goals and what is needed to achieve them to make sure students understand the assignment.

2. Examples of useful goals are to get better grades, not fail any classes, and not get suspended or sent to the principal's office.

Check-Out

Elicit general reactions. Ask, **"Why is it important to think about how you might reach your career goals now?"** Remind students to put their Education and Career Ladder and their My Goals sheet in their notebook. Additionally, remind them to return their signed parent permission slips for the field trip and to bring a lunch or money to buy lunch next week for the field trip.

Session Two: Field Trip to Local College or University

(NOTE: While this session takes some planning and organization, it is definitely worth it because of the powerful inspiration it can provide to the students. If it is not possible to organize as outlined below, it is also possible, though less desirable, to simply call and arrange a campus tour at a local college.)

Activities
  ✓ Travel on bus
  ✓ Academic demonstration
  ✓ Inspirational speakers and snack
  ✓ Visit dorms, gyms, and student union
  ✓ Lunch
  ✓ Meet athletes (both genders) or enjoy entertainment (often provided by ethnic studies centers)
  ✓ Group discussion and Check-out
  ✓ Return to school on bus

Materials
  ✓ Curriculum
  ✓ Parent permission slips

✓ Snack foods and drinks

✓ Extra My Goals sheets (see Appendix B-4b)

✓ College search and scholarship websites handout (see Appendix B-4c)

✓ Money to loan students for lunch (optional)

✓ Camera and film to take pictures of the students at various locations (optional)

Notes about the Field Trip

1. The goals of the field trip are to expose students to college and make it real for them; to give them the experience of feeling comfortable and welcome on a college campus; and to provide students with role models with whom they can identify.

2. Planning for the field trip must begin at least a month prior to the selected date; sometimes arranging for a bus must be done even earlier.

3. In choosing a site, we suggest picking a public college or university that has high status in the community. However, if such a site is not convenient or available, utilize the college or university that is available.

4. If several groups are running at a school or several schools in a district are participating in the program, all groups can arrange to go on the field trip the same day. If necessary, modules can be switched around so that the Educational Aspirations module comes at the time of the field trip. However, the field trip should not occur until after the Trust-Building and Communication Skills module has been completed.

5. The order of activities and the specific activities are suggestions only; details will depend on the availability of resources at the particular college or university. If you cannot arrange all the suggested activities, do your best. It may take a great deal of effort to set up the field trip the first time, but once it has been arranged, coming back for future field trips is relatively simple.

Content

Travel to College or University on Bus

PARENT PERMISSION SLIPS

1. These should be passed out at least 2 weeks prior to the field trip so that you have at least one session to remind students to get the permission slips signed and returned.

2. Permission slips should be turned in to the group leader or the counseling office several days before the trip so that students without permission slips can be tracked down.

DISCUSSION ON BUS

1. Share the day's schedule with students.

2. Emphasize when the bus must leave to return to school.

3. Set guidelines for the visit to the college campus:

    a. Stay with the group at all times.

    b. The group rules apply on the field trip.

    c. Listen to and be polite to speakers and guides.

    d. Set up a lunch meeting place and time in case anyone gets lost.

4. Elicit and answer student questions.

Academic Demonstration

1. Most colleges and universities have interesting and absorbing demonstrations for prospective students that can be accessed through the admissions office, the ethnic studies centers, or the public information office. It is worth making several phone calls to access such a demonstration because the instructors are used to making presentations to secondary-school students and almost always put on an interesting show.

2. Examples are physics or chemistry demonstrations or a planetarium.

3. If no demonstration is available, arrangements can be made for students to sit in on the class of an interesting and entertaining professor. Do not expect to drop in on a class at random; doing so may be boring and counterproductive, and professors often are not open to having a group of potentially disruptive visitors unless previous arrangements have been made.

Inspirational Speakers and Snack

1. Can be done inside or outside.

2. Snack

    a. If resources are available, it is helpful to provide a mid-morning snack (generally chips or cookies and soda or juice). If resources are not available, ask students to bring a snack from home.

    b. Having the snack also helps students pay attention to the inspirational speakers.

3. Aim for two inspirational speakers, one of each of the following types:

    a. Minority or low-income students who have overcome adversity to attend college and are doing well.

        1. These speakers can usually be found through ethnic studies centers or the admissions outreach office.

        2. They tell their own inspirational stories.

b. Financial aid officers.

    1. They discuss ways in which students from families with few or no financial resources can receive funding that allows them to attend the college or university.

    2. They often have pads or pencils or even T-shirts that they may give to students as souvenirs—be sure to ask if they have any material or souvenirs to share with the students when you arrange for them to speak.

4. Suggest that each speak for 10 to 15 minutes.

5. Introduce the speakers. Say, **"We have arranged for two people to speak to you about how college can be a reality for each of you. One is a student who comes from a neighborhood like yours, and the other is the person who helps students who think they cannot afford to go to college get the money to be able to study here. Please listen carefully, and then you can ask any questions you have."**

Visit Dorms, Gyms, and Student Union

1. After listening to the speakers, this is a good time for students to tour the fun places of college. If you are familiar with the campus, you can lead an informal tour. If not, or if you would prefer not to lead the tour, college students who give tours for prospective students can give the tour (requires prearrangement, usually through the admissions office).

2. *Dorms.* It is helpful and interesting for students to tour the dorms, see what a student room looks like, explore the recreational facilities, and see where college students eat.

3. *Gyms or other recreational areas* (e.g., swimming pool, fitness center). If the campus has a sports stadium that students might have seen on TV, they enjoy visiting it. The fitness center is also often a big draw. Be sure to ask as you enter whether it is OK for students to use equipment such as treadmills or weights, and let the students know before they begin exploring.

4. *Student union.* This should be the last stop before lunch. Allow students to wander around the student store, check out various eating facilities, and so on. Many student unions have arcades, which are a huge draw for middle school and high school students. If you allow students to play in the arcade, set a clear time limit, and make sure they put their lunch money in a safe and separate place before playing.

Lunch

There are three options for lunch: (1) Students bring their lunches; (2) students buy their lunches at campus eateries; (3) lunch is provided for students. Sometimes, a campus group will be willing to donate lunch (e.g., pizzas or sandwiches and soda). This is worth inquiring about when setting up the trip. If lunch is not provided, encourage students to bring a sack lunch. However, if they wish, they can bring money to buy food on campus. If the last stop on the campus tour is the student union, they can buy lunch there. Prearrange where students will eat lunch, depending on what or who the entertainment or speakers will be. Usually the speakers or entertainment will suggest a particular location—either indoors or outdoors.

Athlete Speakers and/or Entertainment

1. *Athlete speakers.* If available, athletes whose names or feats are known to the group members are highly valued. Arrangements can be made through the athletic department or sometimes through the admissions outreach office. The sports figures who choose to speak to students generally speak of their own struggles to go to college and talk about the importance of studying and getting good grades in order to be able to play sports in college. They often bring photos they have signed or that they will personally autograph, providing a very special souvenir. The ideal situation is to have both a male and a female athlete.

2. *Entertainment.* This can usually be arranged through the ethnic studies centers and can take the form of a step or salsa dance demonstration, singers, and so on.

3. If you have to choose between athlete speakers and entertainment, athletes who are known are usually more highly valued by group members. However, whatever can be arranged, either athlete speakers, entertainment, or both, is fine.

Group Discussion and Check-Out

1. After lunch and the speakers or entertainment, find a quiet place where the group can sit in a circle (on the lawn if it's nice out or at a round table in the student union).

2. Ask, **"So what are some of your impressions from our visit today?"** Guide the discussion with such questions as:

   a. **"Do you think you would like to go to a college like this? Why?"**

   b. **"What are some things you especially liked today?"** Students are often impressed that there are no bells and that you do not *have* to go to class. They also may be very taken with the sports figures, the tour guides, "the cute guys," or "the sexy girls."

   c. **"Were there any scary parts or things that made you uncomfortable?"** Sometimes students worry about the size of the campus, getting lost, not knowing anyone, or being away from home. If they say they think they could never go to college, then find out what they see as obstacles, and make sure to include the obstacles in the discussion during the next session.

   d. **"Are there other questions you have?"** Tell students that if they think of questions in the future, they should be sure to ask their teachers or school guidance counselor, or remark that lots of useful information is available online. Distribute the handout about college search websites and scholarship opportunities (see Appendix B-4c).

3. Say, **"Remember to bring in your goal sheets next week, and we'll talk about what you need to do to reach your goal for this year and for your future."**

Board Buses for Return to School

Session Three

Activities   ✓ Check-in

✓ Athlete analogy/clips from the movie *Rudy*

✓ Discussion of being a good student

✓ Discussion of goals

✓ Check-out

Materials   ✓ Curriculum

✓ Extra My Goals sheets (see Appendix B-4b)

✓ DVD of the movie *Rudy*

✓ Student Strategies for Success handout (see Appendix B-4d)

✓ Large pad of paper or dry-erase board

✓ Markers

✓ Masking tape

✓ Rules and consequences with the group name at the top of the rules and consequences pages. Put these up in the room before each session.

Content

Check-In

Educational Aspirations Activity:
Analogy of the Athlete on the Road to Success

1. Say, **"We've been talking a lot about our goals in life and the importance of education to achieve those goals. We will be doing that again today, but first let's watch a few minutes of the movie *Rudy*.** The movie is about a young man who dreamed about playing football at Notre Dame since the time he was a kid, but before he could play football at Notre Dame, he first had to be a student at Notre Dame."

2. Show scenes from the movie *Rudy*. If possible, use the DVD and view chapters 16 and 18, which depict Rudy's hard work at a junior college and his eventual acceptance to Notre Dame. Then show chapter 20 and the beginning part of chapter 21, which depict Rudy's tryouts for the Notre Dame football team.

3. After showing the movie, ask, **"How do you think Rudy felt when he fulfilled his dream of becoming a Notre Dame football player?"** Help students identify the positive emotions associated with success.

4. Say, **"Just like each of you has goals and dreams for your life, Rudy had a dream. But to achieve this dream, he had to put in a lot of hard work. What are some**

of the things he did to achieve this dream?" Elicit some of the following examples: studying hard; many, many hours of practice and training; running, lifting weights, and sweating; enduring pain and injuries; ignoring all of those, including his family, who said that it could never be done; and enduring all the ridicule of teammates.

Discussion of Being a Good Student

ADVANTAGES OF BEING A GOOD STUDENT

Say, **"Even though Rudy's goal was to be a football player, he had to learn to be a good student in order to achieve his dream. There are many advantages to being a good student. What are some of the reasons to be a good student?"** Pull for the following points:

1. Being a good student gives you more options for future careers that you would enjoy.
2. Being a good student and getting more schooling usually means you will make more money.
3. Being a good student allows you to participate in sports and other fun activities.
4. Being a good student makes your family happy.
5. Being a good student stops teachers from yelling at you.

DISADVANTAGES OF BEING A GOOD STUDENT

Ask, **"Are there some negative things about being a good student?"** Pull for the following points:

1. Being a good student may make you feel different than your friends.
2. You may be teased by your friends or brothers and sisters.
3. If you study, you may miss out on some time hanging out with friends.

Discussion of Goals

Discuss goal sheets passed out in Session One of Educational Aspirations.

1. Ask, **"Who brought back their My Goals sheets?"**
   a. Give the promised candy, sticker, or point to those who brought back completed sheets.
   b. Pass out goal sheets to anyone who forgot, and allow time for students to fill out the sheets.
2. Ask, **"What are your goals for this school year?"** Have students share their goals with one another.

3. Say, **"While it is very important to have goals, it is just as important to identify the specific steps that one needs to take to achieve those goals."**

   a. Distribute the Student Strategies for Success handout to each group member. As a group, review each item on the handout.

   b. Ask students about obstacles that might interfere with "strategies for success" (e.g., peer pressure to joke around in class, responsibilities at home that take time from doing homework), as well as ways in which they might reward themselves for following through (e.g., calling a friend, watching TV, taking a bubble bath, having a fun snack).

   c. Tell students to use the back side of their goal sheets to write down their own strategies for success. Emphasize the importance of including rewards for a job well done.

4. Let students know you will be checking with them next week on how they are doing with their goals and strategies for success.

5. If time permits, show the final two chapters of *Rudy* (chapters 27 and 28), which depict the highly emotional finale to Rudy's football career at Notre Dame. Tell students, **"Now we'll watch the end of the movie. Though Rudy made the walk-on team, he did not play in an actual game until the last play of the last game of his senior year. Let's watch."**

Check-Out

Elicit general reactions to the group. Ask, **"How does it feel to commit to being a better student? Do you feel you will be able to or willing to carry out your commitment? What might get in your way?"** Remind students to put their My Goals and Student Strategies for Success handouts in their notebook.

MODULE FIVE

Peer Pressure, Bullying, and Gangs

Goal To help students generate and practice alternatives to giving in to peer pressure, examine relational aggression, and discuss alternatives to gang involvement.

Overview of Sessions

Session One:
- *Purpose:* Help students develop strategies and skills for resisting peer pressure
- *Content:* (1) Situations and Strategies posters, (2) Tag-Team Peer Pressure game, (3) costs and benefits of resisting peer pressure

Session Two:
- *Purpose:* Explore a type of bullying called "relational aggression" (e.g., gossip and spreading rumors) and its consequences
- *Content:* (1) Introduction/Feather in the Wind, (2) aggressor role/"Is it OK?" survey, (3) victim role/Bruised Banana or Wrinkled Heart analogy, (4) Aggressor, Victim, Bystander activity

Session Three (optional)
- *Purpose:* Prevent or decrease gang membership
- *Content:* (1) Positive and negative aspects of gang involvement, (2) alternate options to obtain the advantages that gangs provide

Session One

Activities
- ✓ Check-in
- ✓ Follow-up on good student behaviors
- ✓ Situations and Strategies posters
- ✓ Tag-Team Peer Pressure game
- ✓ Costs and benefits of resisting peer pressure
- ✓ Check-out

Materials   ✓ Curriculum

✓ A large pad of paper or poster board

✓ Brightly colored pens

✓ Candy as reward for the game (optional)

✓ Resisting Peer Pressure handout (see Appendix B-5a)

✓ Masking tape

✓ Rules and consequences with the group name at the top of the rules and consequences pages. Put these up in the room before each session.

Content

Check-In

Follow-Up on Strategies for Success in School

Check how students did with the strategies for success to which they committed last week. Ask, **"Who was able to use at least one of the strategies for success they committed to last week? How did it feel to accomplish that goal?"** Make sure to give lots of praise to those who were successful in using these strategies. For those who were not successful, discuss obstacles that may have come up and generate solutions for overcoming the obstacles. Ensure that each student makes a commitment to an original or modified strategy for success for the next week as well.

Generate Peer Pressure Situations and Strategies Posters

The goal is to help students become aware of situations in which they may give in to peer pressure and to generate acceptable alternative strategies to "going along with the crowd."

SITUATIONS POSTER

Group members are asked to generate situations in which they might encounter peer pressure. Say, **"Today we are going to talk about peer pressure. What is peer pressure? What are some situations in which people encounter peer pressure? When do people try to talk you into doing something that you don't know if you should do? I'll write the situations down on this poster."**

1. Write the situations on a poster labeled "Peer Pressure Situations."
2. The following are situations commonly listed by middle school and high school students (in no particular order). If members fail to mention one that you feel is important, ask, **"What about _____? Has anyone ever been pressured to _____?"**

   a. Ditching class.

   b. Fighting.

c. Drugs.

d. Stealing or shoplifting.

e. Gangs.

f. Cheating.

g. Picking on other kids.

h. Sex.

STRATEGIES POSTER

Group members are asked to generate strategies to resist peer pressure. Say, **"Now that we have some peer pressure situations, let's try to think of ways to resist peer pressure."**

1. Write the strategies on a poster labeled "Strategies to Resist Peer Pressure."

2. Common strategies generated are listed below. As with the situations, ask questions to elicit the following strategies if they are not brought up by group members.

   a. Saying no.

   b. Changing the subject.

   c. Walking away or ignoring the person.

   d. Avoiding situations where they might encounter pressure.

   e. Hanging around with people who set good examples and who don't exert peer pressure on them.

   f. Identifying a person to whom they can talk when they feel pressured.

Peer Pressure Activity: Tag-Team Peer Pressure Game

The goal of this game is to allow students behavioral practice in using strategies to resist peer pressure. This activity is a verbal version of tag-team wrestling (in which two people wrestle and are relieved by partners who tag in when things get tough). The activity involves the following steps: (1) group members are divided into two teams, and each team chooses a captain; (2) you assign the role of "pressurer" (the person doing the pressuring) to one captain, and the role of "pressuree" (the person getting pressured) to the other captain (or the captains can choose their roles); (3) the pressurer picks a peer pressure situation from the Situations poster and tries to pressure the pressuree; (4) the pressuree selects resistance strategies from the Strategies poster and tries to resist the pressurer; (5) the pressurer's team gets a point if the pressurer successfully pressures the pressuree into doing the activity, while the pressuree's team gets a point if he or she successfully resists; (6) the other team members can tag in for the pressurer or the pressuree if they're having difficulties pressuring or resisting.

1. Say, "For this game, we need to divide into two teams and have each team pick a captain. Let's do that now so we can start the game." After teams and captains are picked, say, "This game is called the Tag-Team Peer Pressure game. Can anyone tell me what 'tag-team' means?" Discuss their responses in relation to the activity. "In this game, one person from each team comes into the ring."

    a. "One person is the pressurer. This person tries to pressure the other person to do one of the things on our list of situations. If the pressurer succeeds in getting the other person to do it, the pressurer's team gets the point."

    b. "The other person is the pressuree. This person tries to resist the pressurer by using the strategies we listed or any other strategy—whatever is needed to resist. If the pressuree successfully resists, that team gets the point."

2. *Tagging in.* "The tag-team part comes in if one person is having a hard time. For example, if it looks like the pressuree is about to give in, a teammate can tag in for the pressuree and take over. On the other hand, if the pressurer is not having much success pressuring, a teammate can tag in and take over. OK, any questions? Ready to begin? Let's have the captain from each team begin. Which one wants to be the pressurer and which the pressuree?" If you feel it would work better, you can assign the roles of pressurer and pressuree. For example, it is sometimes hard for a shy or passive student to start out as the pressuree because he or she may give in too quickly.

3. *Picking a situation.* Say, "OK, [pressurer's name], you're the pressurer. What situation are you going to use to try to pressure [pressuree's name]? Look on the list and see which one you want to use. OK, now go ahead and try to pressure him or her. [Pressuree's name], remember, you can use any of the strategies on our resistance strategy list, or any other strategy as well. Team members, don't forget to tag in if your teammate needs help or if you have a good idea. Good luck." If there is a disagreement about who should get a particular point, you should be the referee and decide who gets it, explaining specifically which behaviors led to the decision, or declare a tie.

4. *Rewards* (optional). If rewards are used, generally each member of the winning team gets two pieces of candy, and each member of the losing team gets one piece.

Evaluating Costs and Benefits of Resisting Peer Pressure

The goal of this discussion is to consider whether students can use some of these strategies themselves and to examine potential obstacles to using resistance strategies.

1. Say, "Great job. Seems that it was pretty hard to resist some of those things. What are some reasons that it's sometimes hard to resist peer pressure in real life?" (Uncool, afraid of rejection, etc.) "Which of these strategies do you think might work in real life? Which ones have you tried, and how did they work?"

2. Hand out Resisting Peer Pressure sheets (see Appendix B-5a). Say, **"We'd like you to notice one situation over the next week where your friends pressure you to do something. See if you can resist the pressure, and next week we'll talk about what strategies you used to resist and how they worked."**

Check-Out

Elicit general responses to the session. Ask, **"What did you learn that might be useful to you in resisting peer pressure?"** Remind students to notice a situation where they are pressured and to reflect on how they responded. Also, remind them to put their Resisting Peer Pressure handout in their notebook.

Session Two

Activities   ✓ Check-in

✓ Follow-up on resisting peer pressure

✓ Introduction/Feather in the Wind story

✓ Discussion of aggressor role/"Is it OK?" survey

✓ Discussion of victim role/Bruised Banana or Wrinkled Heart analogy

✓ Aggressor, Victim, Bystander activity

✓ Check-out

Materials   ✓ Curriculum

✓ "Is it Ok?" survey (one copy for each participant; see Appendix B-5b)

✓ Either one banana *or* a piece of paper with a heart drawn on it

✓ A large pad of paper or dry-erase board

✓ Brightly colored markers

✓ Aggressor, Victim, Bystander handout (one copy for each participant; see Appendix B-5c)

✓ Three sets of footprints (see Appendix B-5d)

✓ Masking tape

Content

Check-In

Follow-Up on Resisting Peer Pressure

Give a point or piece of candy to all students who brought back their Resisting Peer Pressure handout.

PRESSURE SITUATIONS

Say, "Remember from last week that you were going to notice when friends pressured you about something? Who can share an example of when that happened to them? Who else has examples?"

RESISTANCE STRATEGIES

Ask, "Who tried to resist the pressure? How did you do it?" Ask members for examples of how they tried to resist. Also ask if members decided not to resist the pressure, and what made them give in to it.

EVALUATING THE OUTCOME

Ask, "How did you feel about resisting the pressure (or giving in to the pressure)?" Be accepting of their answers, discussing again the costs and benefits of resisting peer pressure.

Introduction to Concept of Relational Aggression/Feather in the Wind

Say, "Today we're going to be talking about a form of bullying called 'relational aggression.' Typically, when we think of bullying, we think of one person physically hurting—or threatening to hurt—another person. The type of bullying called 'relational aggression' is a little different. Listen closely to this story": (If all group members are boys, you may want to change the gender of bully and victim in the story to males and change the specific rumor).

Once there was a girl named Maria who seemed to run the whole school. She was very popular, but mostly she was popular because other kids were scared of her. Sometimes she teased them, other times she threatened them, and sometimes she just ignored them. Maria decided to make Ashley her next victim, so she spread lots of rumors about Ashley. She told everyone that Ashley had hooked up with four boys the previous weekend, including the boyfriend of Ashley's best friend.

When Ashley finally told a teacher what was going on, both girls were asked to report to the principal's office. Ashley had tears in her eyes when she explained what was going on, and for the first time Maria realized the seriousness of what she had been doing. She told Ashley that she was sorry and wanted to make it up to her. The principal said, "If that is true, here is what you need to do: go home, take a feather pillow from your house, cut it up, and let the feathers scatter to the wind. Then, both of you come back to my office tomorrow."

Maria thought the principal's punishment sounded kind of odd, but she did it anyway. The next day, both girls returned to the principal's office. Maria wondered if she had been forgiven, so she asked Ashley and the principal, "Is everything cool now?" The principal replied, "Everything will be cool after you go and gather up all the feathers." "But I can't," replied Maria. "The wind has scattered them." "That's exactly the point," said the principal. "Once you have spread rumors about someone, it is impossible to undo the damage—your words are out there in the school halls, spreading hate, even as we speak."

After reading the story, note that this type of bullying involves hurting someone emotionally instead of physically.

The Aggressor Role/"Is it OK?" Survey (Randall & Bowen, 2007)

Say, **"In the story, Maria was the aggressor, the bully. Ashley was the victim. Almost all of us have been the bully at times and the victim at other times. Let's first think about times we may have bullied others."**

1. Have students take the "Is it OK?" survey (see Appendix B-5b). Tell students that their responses are confidential and that they do not need to turn in their surveys or show them to other group members.

2. After they take the survey, remind students that, at one time or another, we all have been bullies (including the group leaders). If the group leaders feel comfortable, they might give an example from their own lives. Then, discuss the various kinds of bullying/relational aggression listed in the survey. Encourage students to describe times that they have bullied others or times that they have seen someone be bullied.

3. Note to students that the various types of bullying/relational aggression have one thing in common: they make one person feel powerful by making the other person feel bad about him- or herself. Also, note that this type of bullying is more common among girls, but that boys do it as well.

The Victim Role/Bruised Banana or Wrinkled Heart Analogy*

Say, **"Now we're going to talk a little more about what it is like to be the victim of gossip, teasing, or other forms of relational aggression."** [Depending on the maturity level of the group, use either the bruised banana analogy or the wrinkled heart analogy.]

BRUISED BANANA ANALOGY FOR (MORE MATURE GROUPS):

Say, **"We're going to pass this banana around the circle. Each group member needs to press hard (one time) on the banana."** After passing the banana around the circle, say, **"Now we will peel the banana. Look at all the bruises on the inside. Over time, that's what gossip, rumors, teasing, taunting, or ignoring someone will do—these types of bullying may not leave a visible bruise on the outside, but, they leave lots of 'bruises' and hurts on the inside"**

---

* Reprinted with permission of Youth Light, Inc.

WRINKLED HEART ANALOGY (FOR LESS MATURE GROUPS):

Say, **"We're going to pass around this piece of paper with the heart drawn on it. Each group member needs to fold the paper in half and then pass it to the next person to fold in half."** After all group members have had a chance to fold the paper, the group leader opens the paper and says, **"Look at all of the wrinkles on this heart. Over time, that's what gossip, rumors, teasing, taunting, or ignoring someone will do—these types of bullying leave a permanent mark on the victim's heart. Once the wrinkle or hurt is there, it can never be ironed out—it's permanent."**

AFTER EITHER ACTIVITY:

1. *Consequences to the victim.* Have students generate a list of consequences to the victim. Write the suggestions on the pad of paper or dry-erase board. Consequences may include the following: being depressed; feeling lonely; feeling bad about oneself; feeling weak; difficulty trusting others; being angry; being scared or worried; getting bad grades; ditching school or dropping out; or turning to alcohol or drugs to cope.

2. *Consequences to the school culture.* Next, ask students to consider consequences of relational aggression on the broader school culture. Ask what it would be like to attend school at a place where relational aggression is widespread versus attending a school where relational aggression is not tolerated.

Relational Aggression Activity: Aggressor, Victim, Bystander

Say, **"So far, we have talked about the different types of relational aggression that a bully might use, as well as the consequences to the victim. Of course, most of the time, there are bystanders too—these are the people who see what is happening, but do nothing to stop it. Usually, bystanders don't do anything because they are scared of drawing attention to themselves—they don't want to become a victim too. But, I think we all can agree that this kind of bullying is very harmful and needs to stop. There are things that the bully can do to stop his or her behavior, and there are things the victim and bystander can do too. This handout gives some examples of what we can do."** [Distribute Aggressor, Victim, Bystander handout (Senn, 2007) (see Appendix B-5c) and place three sets of footprints on the floor—one set marked "Aggressor," the second set marked "Victim," and the third set marked "Bystander" (see Appendix B-5d)].

1. Tell students, **"This handout is divided into three parts: Aggressor; Target/Victim; and Bystander."** Then group leaders read aloud the various suggestions listed on the handout for each of the three roles.

2. Next say, **"Let's take turns imagining what it would be like to walk in the shoes of an aggressor, a victim, and a bystander. I'm going to read aloud some situations that involve bullying or relational aggression. After I read the first situation, some of you will stand in the footprints marked 'Aggressor.' Each student in that**

group will need to say one feeling that the bully or aggressor may be experiencing, and then give one suggestion from the handout of how to stop the bullying. Another group of students will stand in the footprints marked 'Victim.' Each student in this group needs to state one feeling that the victim may be experiencing and give one suggestion from the handout in terms of how to stop being a victim. Finally, the rest of you will stand in the footprints of the 'Bystander' and each person needs to state one feeling and action that could be taken. Each of you will have a chance to stand in all three sets of footprints."

3. Separate students into three groups: those that will stand in the Aggressor footprints; those that will stand in the Victim footprints; and those that will stand in the Bystander footprints. Read the following scenario (adapted from Taylor, 2005): "You don't have any plans for the weekend and you overhear some of your friends talking about having a sleepover. You ask if you can go too. Your friends say 'Sure, as long as you promise not to talk. PSYCH!' They roll their eyes at you and walk away." Encourage students in each of the three groups to express one emotion that the person in their role might be feeling and to read one possible solution from the handout.

4. Have students rotate to a new set of footprints (e.g., those in the Aggressor group should move to the Victim group, those in the Victim group should move to the Bystander group, and those in the Bystander group should move to the Aggressor group). Read the following scenario (adapted from Taylor, 2005): "It's the first day of school and you're wearing a new outfit, hoping to make a good impression. Some of the kids look at you and start laughing. They say, 'Wow—where did you get that outfit? I wouldn't be caught dead wearing that.' For the rest of the day, every time they see you, they point at your clothes and start to laugh." Again, encourage students in each of the three groups to express how the person in their role might be feeling and to read one possible solution from the handout.

5. Have students rotate to the final set of footprints (e.g., those in the Aggressor group should move to the Victim group, those in the Victim group should move to the Bystander group, and those in the Bystander group should move to the Aggressor group). Read the following scenario: "You've been looking forward to the school dance for weeks. You leave the dance for a few minutes to make a call and use the restroom. When you return, some of the kids are spreading a rumor that you left the dance to make out with someone that they think is a dork. They're making fun of you and trying to ruin your reputation." Again, encourage students in each of the three groups to express how the person in their role might be feeling and to read one possible solution from the handout.

Check-Out

Elicit general reactions to the session. Ask, "What are some ways in which you think you can use what we learned today to reduce bullying?" Remind students to put the "Is It OK?" survey and the Aggressor, Victim, Bystander handout in their notebook.

Session Three

(If gangs are not a threat in a particular school, this session may be omitted.)

Activities
- ✓ Check-in
- ✓ Discussion of group members' gang involvement and knowledge
- ✓ Advantages and disadvantages of joining gangs
- ✓ Different ways than gangs to get the same advantages
- ✓ Check-out

Materials
- ✓ Curriculum
- ✓ A large pad of paper or dry-erase board
- ✓ Brightly colored pens
- ✓ Masking tape
- ✓ Rules and consequences with the group name at the top of the rules and consequences pages. Put these up in the room before each session.

Content

Check-In

Discussion of Group Members' Gang Involvement and Knowledge

Say, **"This week we are going to talk about gangs."** If appropriate, say, **"This topic has come up before, and several of you have mentioned knowing people in gangs or being in a gang yourself. We know this topic can be hard to talk about, but we want you to know that we will not judge you if you are in a gang or know people who are. Also, remember that everyone must keep everything said in the group confidential. We know that there are a lot of reasons that people join gangs, and we want to talk about some of the advantages and disadvantages of being in gangs. We'd like to start by talking about experiences you may have had, both positive and negative, with gangs. Is anyone in a gang or has anyone had an experience with gangs?"** In facilitating this discussion, it is important to be neutral and nonevaluative about gang involvement.

Advantages and Disadvantages of Joining Gangs

ADVANTAGES

Say, **"Now we're going to talk about the reasons people join gangs. What are some advantages of being in gangs? What can people get out of being in a gang?"**

1. Often respect, admiration, love, support, and safety and security are mentioned.

2. Write the reasons on a large piece of paper or dry-erase board labeled "Advantages of Gangs."

DISADVANTAGES

Say, **"What are some reasons not to join gangs? What are some disadvantages of belonging to gangs?"**

1. Getting killed and killing are often included on this list.

2. Write the reasons on another large piece of paper labeled "Disadvantages of Gangs."

Brainstorming Different Ways to Obtain Advantages That Gangs Provide

Say, **"There seem to be some important advantages and disadvantages to joining gangs. It seems like the cost can be very high if you join a gang. What if you decide not to join a gang? It still seems like you would want some of the advantages we talked about before. [Point to "Advantages" poster.] What are some other ways of getting these important things besides being in a gang?"**

1. Sports (respect, admiration).

2. Family and extended family (love, support).

3. After-school clubs, church groups (love, support).

4. A trusted adult, big brother, school security guard, and so on (security, support).

Check-Out

Elicit general reactions to the session. Ask, **"What are some other ways besides being in a gang that you personally can get some of the same advantages?"**

Male–Female Relationships

Goal To explore media and personal gender stereotypes and to help students learn appropriate romantic relationship behaviors

Overview of Sessions

Session One
- ▪ *Purpose:* Explore gender stereotypes in the media and discuss their personal impact
- ▪ *Content:* Creation of collages of actual and ideal gender depictions

Session Two
- ▪ *Purpose:* Identify healthy versus unhealthy relationship characteristics and dating behaviors
- ▪ *Content:* (1) Relationship Rights game, (2) dating role plays, (3) distribution and discussion of Dating Dos and Don'ts

Session Three
- ▪ *Purpose:* Explore "Crossing the Line" from flirting to sexual harassment and from consensual sexual activity to date rape
- ▪ *Content:* (1) Generation of list of written, verbal, visual, and physical forms of sexual harassment, (2) myths and facts about date rape, (3) assertiveness role plays

Session One

Activities
- ✓ Check-in
- ✓ Collage making of actual and ideal gender depictions
- ✓ Discussion of personal impact of gender stereotypes
- ✓ Check-out

Materials
- ✓ Curriculum
- ✓ Magazines to use in collage making (e.g., *Cosmo Girl*, *Seventeen*, *Sports Illustrated*, various videogame magazines)

✓ Four poster boards
✓ Markers
✓ Scissors
✓ Glue sticks

Content

Check-In

Gender Stereotypes Activity:
Collage Making of Actual and Ideal Gender Depictions

Say, "**For the next three sessions, we will be exploring gender relationships, including ways in which the media shows males and females, as well as things that make for good and bad romantic relationships. Today, we will be making collages from these magazines showing how we think about men and women. First, let's break into groups of boys and girls. Each group will be making two collages. The first collage will show how our society stereotypes boys and girls, men and women.**"

1. Have students break into a group of boys and a group of girls. Give each group one poster board, scissors, glue, markers, and a stack of magazines (some general, like *Time* or *Newsweek*, and some gender specific, like *Cosmo Girl* or *Sports Illustrated*). Allow 10–15 minutes for this activity.

2. Have each group present their collage.

3. Invite group members to share how gender stereotypes have affected them or someone they know.

4. Have students again break into a group of boys and a group of girls. Say, "**Next, we will be making collages of how we would like males and females to be shown.**" Using the same supplies, allow 10–15 minutes for developing this collage.

5. Have each group present their second collage and note differences between the two.

Check-Out

Elicit general reactions to the session. Then ask, "**How do you think differently about the opposite gender after making and seeing these collages?**"

Session Two

Activities   ✓ Check-in
✓ Relationship Rights game
✓ Dating role plays
✓ Check-out

Materials ✓ Curriculum

✓ Two sets of Relationship Rights cards (see Appendix B-6a)

✓ Cell phones to use in role plays

✓ Signs saying "Scene 1" and "Scene 2"

✓ A large pad of paper or dry-erase board

✓ Brightly colored markers

✓ Masking tape

✓ Dating Dos and Don'ts handout (see Appendix B-6b)

Content

Check-In

Male–Female Relationships Activity: Relationship Rights Game

Say, "Today we're going to be talking about dating and romantic relationships (depending upon the culture of the school and community, use alternative wording for "dating" if appropriate). First, we're going to play a card-sorting game. Each card has a word that can describe a relationship. We will be sorting the cards into two piles: one pile of cards for good or healthy relationships and the other for bad or unhealthy relationships. Like last week, let's break into a group of boys and a group of girls."

1. Have students break into groups. Hand out complete sets of cards, with healthy and unhealthy characteristics shuffled together randomly (see Appendix B-6a).

2. After students are done sorting, the group leader will read each characteristic aloud and have both groups state whether it was rated as good/healthy or bad/unhealthy.

3. Group leader then asks each group to identify the three most important good/healthy characteristics, and the entire group discusses the responses.

Male–Female Relationships Activity: Dating Role Plays

"We are going to do an activity that deals with some of the problems that get in the way of having a healthy relationship. We will put on two mini-plays and hopefully you will all have a chance to be in one of them. Who would like to be an actor or actress for the first one? We need one girl and at least two boys."

1. Leader takes the actors aside to tell them about the content of the role play.

   a. Say to the girl: "You are to pretend that you like one of the boys. In Scene 1, you are at home and you are calling him all the time (give girl cell phone). He doesn't answer or return your calls. In Scene 2, you are at school, and you go up to the boy you like and his friend(s) and begin flirting with another boy to make him jealous so that he'll want to be with you."

b. Leader randomly picks one of the boys to be the object of affection. Say to that boy: **"We will pretend that she likes you but you're not sure if you like her. Your phone rings and you notice that it is her calling and so you ignore the call. This happens several times. In Scene 2, you are at school hanging out with your friend(s) and she starts flirting with your friend(s) right in front of you. You ignore her."**

c. Leader randomly picks another boy to be the object of flirtation. Say to him: **"You will only be in Scene 2. She will start flirting with you in order to make your friend jealous. Your job is to flirt back as much as you want."**

2. Let actors rehearse and then the group presents their mini-play.

3. Ask the audience to identify dating "don'ts" that they noticed in the role play. Write them down on big pad of paper. Ask students what the girl could do instead when she likes someone. Discuss if anything would be different if the situation were reversed and it was a boy who really liked a girl.

The leader then introduces the second mini-play and tries to include the other group members. At least one boy and one girl must be available as actors.

1. Leader takes the actors aside to tell them about the content of the role play.

a. Leader picks one boy to be the main character. Say to this boy: **"In Scene 1, you want to break up with your girlfriend of 3 weeks but you know she'll be mad and cry and carry on. So you send her a text message at 11 p.m. indicating that the relationship is over. You turn off your cell phone and go to sleep. In Scene 2, it is the next day at school. You hope that if you ignore her, the whole thing will go away."**

b. Leader picks one girl as the heartbroken rejectee. Say to the girl: **"In Scene 1, you are about to go to bed when you notice a text message on your phone. Your boyfriend has broken up with you in the message. You immediately call him but he doesn't answer or return any of your messages. You forward the message to his friend and several of your closest girlfriends and ask for their opinions. In Scene 2, you are at school the next day. Your ex is ignoring you, so you ask your friends to ask him what is going on. Before you know it, the whole school is talking about the breakup."**

c. Leader tells remaining students to gossip about the breakup in Scene 2.

2. Let actors rehearse and then present their mini-play.

3. Ask the audience to identify dating "don'ts" that they noticed in the role play. Write them down on big pad of paper. Ask students for other, healthier ways of breaking up with someone, and how the gossiping that happened might be avoided.

Leader passes out the Dating Dos and Don'ts handout (see Appendix B-6b). Ask each group member to read one, and allow for group discussion.

Check-Out

Elicit general reactions to the session. **"What are some qualities you would look for in a boyfriend or girlfriend? What are the most important Dating Don'ts to avoid?"**

Session Three

Activities   ✓ Check-in

✓ What is harassment?

✓ Discussion of responses to Survey of Relationship Attitudes

✓ Assertiveness role play

✓ Check-out

Materials   ✓ Curriculum

✓ Survey of Relationship Attitudes for each student (see Appendix B-6c)

✓ A large pad of paper or dry-erase board

✓ Brightly colored marker

✓ Masking tape

Content

Prior to Check-In, as students arrive for group, hand each member a copy of the Survey of Relationship Attitudes (some items adapted from Roden and Abarbanel, 1993) and ask them to fill it out. Have students fill it out anonymously, reminding them to indicate their own gender in the space indicated. Collect them in a non-identifying way.

Check-In

What Is Harassment?

Say, **"Today we are going to talk about crossing the line: how flirting can cross the line and be harassment (Wiseman, 2002), and how dating can cross the line and be date rape. Then we'll talk about how to prevent this."**

1. Say, **"Flirting is a time-honored ritual—it's a chance to develop our romantic skills, and it's fun. But it also can cause communication problems and lead to hurt feelings."** Ask, **"When does flirting cross the line into harassment?"**

2. Elicit group ideas and discussion.

3. Give definition: **"Flirting makes both people feel good, but sexual harassment makes one person feel small, uncomfortable, powerless, and intimidated."**

4. On a large pad of paper or dry-erase board, write the following headings: Verbal/Written; Visual; Physical (Wiseman, 2002). The leader then asks students to give examples of these different types of harassment. Some examples are listed below.* If students do not immediately give examples, the leader can give an example of each type for clarification.

Verbal/written	*Visual*	*Physical*
■ Sexually explicit notes	■ Hand gestures	■ Pinching
■ Cat calls	■ Licking lips	■ Grabbing
■ Showing lewd pictures	■ Staring at body parts	■ Unwanted hugging/kissing
■ Calling someone bitch or ho	■ Flashing	■ Rubbing
■ "Can I get some of that?"	■ Grabbing crotch	■ Grinding (e.g., while dancing)

Discussion of Responses to Survey of Relationship Attitudes

Prior to this discussion, group leaders should sort the survey responses into separate piles for boys' and girls' responses. Then say, **"Just as flirting can cross the line into harassment, our dating attitudes and behaviors can also cross a line. Let's talk about the survey that each of you completed at the start of today's group."**

1. Ask, **"What were your reactions to the survey?"**

2. If student discussion doesn't cover most of the issues in the survey, go over the questions one at a time.

3. Ask if students think boys and girls answered the questions differently. Quickly look over responses and give the results for boys and girls for each question. Use responses for further discussion.

Dating Relationships Activity: Assertiveness Role Play

Say, **"We've talked about harassment and looked at attitudes about sex-role stereotypes. Now let's set up a scene and see how we can deal with potential harassment and unwanted sexual advances."**

1. Ask for a boy and a girl volunteer.

2. Say to the boy: **"You have been dating the same girl for 2 months and believe it is time to have sex. Your parents are going out on Saturday night to a party in another town, and you ask your girlfriend to come over to watch a movie. You start watching the movie. You ask if she wants to have sex. She says no, but you think she's playing hard to get, and so you keep trying to convince her."**

3. Say to the girl: **"In the mini-play, you're excited about going over to your boyfriend's house. You want to look really nice, so you dress up for him. When he**

---

* Reprinted with permission of Rosalind Wiseman.

asks you to have sex, you start to feel really uncomfortable but you don't want to disappoint him, or even possibly lose him. You tell him, 'No, I'm not ready,' but he's persistent. It gets harder and harder to say no."

4. Tell both actors to end the mini-play without sexual contact. Make it clear that a rape does not occur.

5. After the mini-play, the group leader asks each actor how they might feel in that situation.

6. Note that several things that happened in the role play relate to the assumptions discussed in survey items.

   a. Elicit suggestions from the other group members about ways in which the girl could have been more assertive, as well as ways in which the boy could have responded more appropriately.

   b. Discuss obstacles to being assertive. Try to elicit the following ideas, along with any others they may have.

      1. A girl might be afraid that her boyfriend will break up with her if she says no.

      2. Sometimes it feels frightening or isolating to be assertive.

      3. Alcohol or drugs can impair decision making

   c. Make sure to get or give examples of clearly communicated, assertive statements the girl could give.

Say, **"The message from these sessions is:**

1. "You have a right not to be harassed or forced into unwanted sex.

2. "You can clearly and assertively communicate your thoughts to your partner and feel empowered to say 'no.'

3. "If someone forces you into something you are uncomfortable with, get help from a trusted adult (e.g., parent, older sibling, teacher, pastor/priest, or counselor)."

Check-Out

Elicit general reactions to the session. Acknowledge that this was a serious session with the difficult topics of harassment, unwanted sex, and date rape. Be vigilant about students who appear uncomfortable and follow up with them individually. Also, if students make disclosures of sexual abuse or date rape, follow required reporting procedures; make sure to have ongoing follow-up with the student and provide appropriate treatment referrals.

Exposure to Violence and Posttraumatic Stress Reactions

Goal To help students share their experiences as victims or witnesses of violence; to normalize and understand posttraumatic stress; to discuss coping strategies for posttraumatic stress reactions; to encourage students to seek help if they have significant symptoms of posttraumatic stress disorder (PTSD)

Overview of Sessions

Session One
- *Purpose:* Facilitate discussion of exposure to violence and related feelings
- *Content:* (1) Scary Art Gallery, (2) reintroduction of emotion regulation strategies

Session Two (if needed to continue processing drawings and feelings; necessary for groups with high violence exposure)
- *Purpose:* Introduce concept of posttraumatic stress
- *Content:* (1) Continuation of Scary Art Gallery (if needed), (2) posttraumatic stress discussion and game, (3) coping strategies for posttraumatic stress reactions

Session One

Activities
- ✓ Check-in
- ✓ Preparation for termination
- ✓ Scary Art Gallery
- ✓ Calming activity
- ✓ Check-out

Materials   ✓ Curriculum

✓ One piece of blank drawing paper for each student, plus some extras

✓ Lots of brightly colored pens/markers

✓ Masking tape

✓ Rules and consequences with the group name at the top of the rules and consequences pages. Put these up in the room before each session.

Content

Check-In

Preparation for Termination

It is important to discuss the ending of the group early so that students can have a chance to reflect on and express any feelings they may be having. These may include feelings of regret about having to go back to class, missing group leaders or other students, or being happy that summer is coming. Goals are (1) to help students feel some control over the process of ending the group by accepting and validating all feelings about termination; (2) to help members reflect on the gains they have made by pointing out changes they have noticed; (3) to provide an opportunity for group members to bring up any topics they wished had been covered and would like to address in the last weeks of the group.

Say, **"We only have about three more groups left after today, and I am wondering what feelings you have about the group ending."** Elicit responses. If it is hard for group members to respond, you can share your own feelings about the ending of the groups (e.g., feeling attached to them or knowing you will miss them; being pleased with the changes you've seen and with their hard work; having enjoyed the group). **"OK. We'll talk more about our feelings about ending in the next few weeks, and we'll also plan our party. It's something we like to talk about now so that the end of the group doesn't sneak up and surprise us."**

Exposure to Violence Activity: Scary Art Gallery

The goal is to allow students to graphically display traumatic experiences in their lives. This activity includes the following steps: (1) Students draw something really scary that has happened to them; (2) drawings are posted in the "art gallery"; (3) students describe the event to the other group members; (4) students process feelings, fantasies, and prevention strategies. Representative student drawings are shown on pages 96–100.

1. Give each group member a piece of paper and different-colored markers.

2. Introduce the activity by saying, **"Today we're going to do an activity called Scary Art Gallery. Think of something really scary that has happened to you.**

These should be things that have really happened to you, not things that you are scared of like Chuckie from a movie. A lot of scary things happen every day. For example, people are killed, fires happen, people are beat up." [If appropriate, add, "Several of you have already talked about times that you have seen or been the victims of violent events."] You can draw the situation with stick figures if you'd like. The important thing is not how nice your drawing looks, but that you are able to draw about something important to you. It should be something serious—this isn't a funny subject."

3. Give students time to draw their pictures.

4. Tape students' drawings on the wall to exhibit them in the gallery. When all are completed, students should sit facing the gallery.

5. Ask members to describe the event in their drawing. Say, "Looks like you all drew about some pretty scary and important things. Now we'd like each of you to tell the group about what is in your drawing and how you felt when it happened." For each presentation, make sure to deal with the following issues:

   a. *Feelings.* "How did you feel when that happened?" (If the student is unable to share his or her feelings, the leader can reflect the feelings—e.g., "That must have been really upsetting or scary; you must have felt so helpless.")

   b. *Fantasies.* "That's a scary situation. Sometimes people imagine ways they would have liked to act that wouldn't be possible in real life because they're too dangerous. Is there anything that you would have liked to do in that situation to make it better if you had super powers?"

   c. *Empowerment strategies.* "There's no way to totally prevent what happened, but is there any way you can think of to help keep yourself safe if this happens again (or reduce the likelihood of it happening again)?" If the student cannot think of any safety strategies, ask for input from other group members: "Can anyone think of something [student's name] could do to prevent this from happening again or to keep safe if it does happen?"

   d. *Shared experience.* "Has anyone else been in a situation like this or had something like this happen to them?" Encourage commonalities among the students' experience to help them feel less isolated.

6. Sometimes the intensity of some disclosures causes anxiety in the group. If this is expressed by inattention or laughter or silliness, it is important to comment that when scary stuff is being discussed, sometimes it makes people nervous and they have trouble listening respectfully.

7. This activity, with the full discussion, may take more than one session. If so, finish up during the next session. Especially in groups with high levels of community and/or family violence exposure, it is important for students to be given the opportunity to discuss their experiences fully if they wish and are able.

Calming Activity

1. Because the Scary Art Gallery activity may cause significant anxiety and even fear, it is helpful to end this session with one of the emotion regulation strategies discussed in the Anger Management and Emotion Regulation Skills module. Choose the one that seemed to resonate best with the group (e.g., muscle relaxation, imagery, deep breathing).

2. Say, **"Often thinking about something really scary that happened to you can make you feel frightened, anxious, or upset all over again. So let's end today by using one of the coping strategies we learned earlier that you guys seemed to really like."**

3. Take the script from the anger management module and readminister the technique that seemed most effective. If doing imagery, do the following section to relax the students: Say, **"Close your eyes, as you scan your body for any tension. If you find tension, release it. Let it go and relax. Relax your head and your face. Relax your shoulders. Relax your arms and hands. Relax your chest and lungs. Relax your back. Relax your stomach. Relax your hips, legs, and feet. Experience a peaceful, pleasant, and comfortable feeling of being relaxed as you prepare to make an imaginary trip to a beautiful place. Take a deep breath, and breathe out slowly and easily. Take a second deep breath, and slowly breathe out. Allow your breathing to become smooth and rhythmic."** Once students are relaxed, ask them to go to the special place they developed as a calming image for themselves and to fully experience it.

Check-Out

Elicit general feelings about the session. If it has elicited a great deal of emotion or very difficult disclosures have occurred, reflect the feelings of the group: **"Several students shared very difficult experiences and feelings today; sometimes it was hard, but I think we all appreciate their openness and willingness to share."** If any students seem very upset or extremely emotionally aroused, ask them to stay after the group, and try to bring them back to the mundane moment by asking them what class they have next, where they will be going after school, and so on.

Students' Scary Art Gallery drawings
(re-creations of actual drawings)

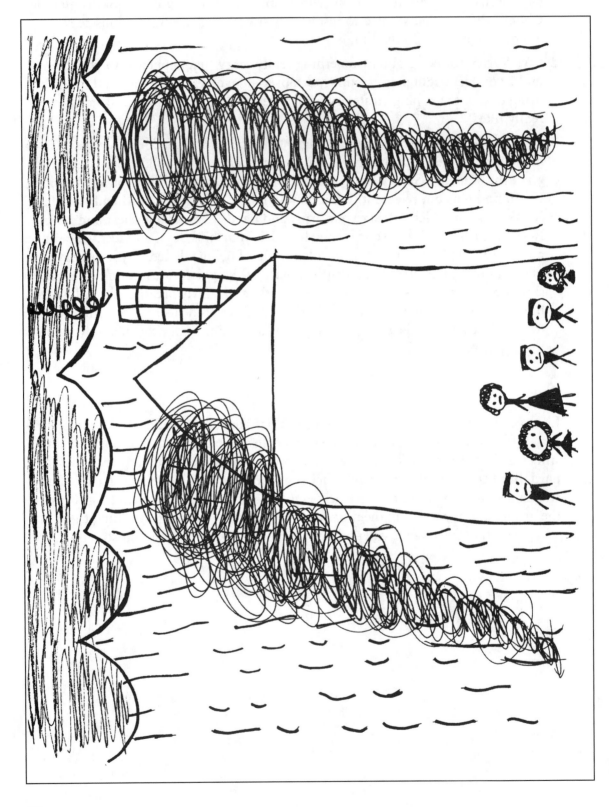

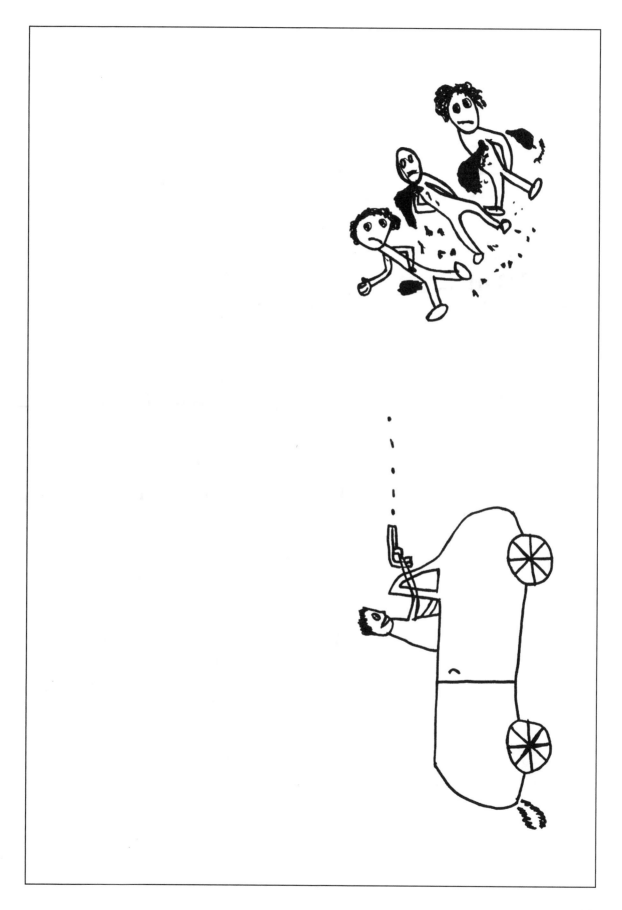

Session Two

(Optional for groups without high violence exposure; necessary for groups with high violence exposure. For groups with high exposure where the Scary Art Gallery discussion continues in Session Two, it may be necessary to add a third session to this module.)

Activities

✓ Check-in

✓ Finish Scary Art Gallery (if not completed last session)

✓ Posttraumatic Stress Reactions handout and discussion

✓ PTSD disk game

✓ Ways to cope with posttraumatic stress

✓ Muscle relaxation

✓ Check-out

Materials

✓ Curriculum

✓ Scary Art Gallery drawings from Session One (post these on the wall)

✓ Posttraumatic Stress Reactions handout—two-sided (one copy for each student—see Appendix B-7a)

✓ Disks for posttraumatic stress reactions activity (50 copies of each of the three types of disks with each type a different color—see Appendix B-7b)

✓ Candy to exchange for disks at the end of the session (optional)

✓ Masking tape

✓ Rules and consequences with the group name at the top of the rules and consequences pages. Put these up in the room before each session.

Content

Check-In

Scary Art Gallery (Continued from Last Week)

If some group members need to finish presenting or discussing their drawings, continue with the Scary Art Gallery exhibit until completed. Follow the instructions in Session One.

Exposure to Violence Activity:
Posttraumatic Stress Reactions Handout, Discussion, and Game

The goal is to help students learn about common reactions to trauma that they may have had, to help them understand why these reactions occur, and to develop strategies to deal with the reactions. An additional goal is for students to identify a safe person to whom they can talk about their traumatic experiences.

INTRODUCING THE CONCEPT OF POSTTRAUMATIC STRESS

Say (if appropriate), **"We saw from people's drawings in Scary Art Gallery that many frightening and traumatic things have happened to group members—like hearing shots, seeing someone stabbed or beaten, or having it happen to you. We now know that when such horrible things happen to people, they tend to react in certain ways to try to cope. These are totally normal reactions to abnormal events. They are called posttraumatic stress reactions. Has anyone ever heard of that? We're going to give you a handout with the different types of reactions that people have after something traumatic happens, then play a game to see which of these reactions you may have had. Then we'll talk about some ways to cope with these reactions."** Give out Posttraumatic Stress Reactions handout (Appendix B-7a).

POSTTRAUMATIC STRESS REACTION CLUSTERS

Say, **"There are three basic categories of reactions. Some people who have been exposed to a trauma will have only one type, while some will have reactions of all types. Many of you may have been exposed to lots of violence and trauma, which makes these reactions more likely."**

1. **"The first category is *reexperiencing the trauma*. We're going to talk about each way people may reexperience the trauma. If that has happened to you, tell us your experience, and you will get a reexperiencing token."**

   a. **"Having memories or thoughts of the bad thing that happened suddenly pop into your mind."** Ask students if this has ever happened to them. Ask for specific examples, and give a green reexperiencing token to each person who gives a personal example.

   b. **"Dreaming about what happened over and over."** Ask students if this has ever happened to them. Ask for specific examples, and give a green reexperiencing token to each person who gives a personal example.

   c. **"Having the feeling that the traumatic event is happening again, like flashbacks."** Ask students if this has ever happened to them. Ask for specific examples, and give a green reexperiencing token to each person who gives a personal example.

   d. **"Getting really nervous or uncomfortable if you get near the place where the bad thing happened."** Ask students if this has ever happened to them. Ask for specific examples, and give a green reexperiencing token to each person who gives a personal example.

2. **"The second category is *avoiding* stuff about the traumatic thing, or *feeling numb*. We'll talk about the different ways people cope by avoiding anything that reminds them of the bad thing or avoiding feelings. If that has happened to you, tell us your experience, and you will get an avoiding token."**

a. **"Avoiding people, places, or activities that remind you of the bad thing that happened."** Ask students if this has ever happened to them. Ask for specific examples, and give an orange avoiding token to each person who gives a personal example.

b. **"Feeling detached or cut off from other people or numb."** Ask students if this has ever happened to them. Ask for specific examples, and give an orange avoiding token to each person who gives a personal example.

c. **"Being less interested and involved in things you liked to do before the bad thing happened."** Ask students if this has ever happened to them. Ask for specific examples, and give an orange avoiding token to each person who gives a personal example.

d. **"Thinking you won't have a career or a family or that you will die young."** Ask students if this has ever happened to them. Ask for specific examples, and give an orange avoiding token to each person who gives a personal example.

3. **"The third category is *feeling more on edge* than you did before the bad things happened. We'll talk about the different ways people might feel more on edge. If that has happened to you, tell us your experience, and you will get an edge token."**

a. **"Trouble falling asleep or staying asleep."** Ask students if this has ever happened to them. Ask for specific examples, and give a purple edge token to each person who gives a personal example.

b. **"Being irritable or getting angry easily."** Ask students if this has ever happened to them. Ask for specific examples, and give a purple edge token to each person who gives a personal example.

c. **"Getting distracted and having trouble paying attention."** Ask students if this has ever happened to them. Ask for specific examples, and give a purple edge token to each person who gives a personal example.

d. **"Being super-aware of where danger might be, or startling easily."** Ask students if this has ever happened to them. Ask for specific examples, and give a purple edge token to each person who gives a personal example.

IDENTIFYING TYPICAL PATTERNS OF REACTING

Say, **"We can see that these posttraumatic stress reactions happen to everybody and are part of coping with bad things that happen to us or that we see happen. You can tell from the colors of your tokens which types of reactions you yourself have. What color tokens did you have the most of?"**

Have students tell their ratios of tokens. The goal is for them to recognize their typical patterns of reaction. For example, **"So Juan, you have more purple tokens than green and orange combined. So what are the ways you have learned to react to traumatic things?"** Wait for his answer. Or elicit an answer from other group members if he does not know, then restate: **"That's right, you tend to get on edge— you can't sleep well and get angry easily."**

Ways to Cope with Posttraumatic Stress

Say, **"Why do you think it might be important to know how each of us reacts when faced with bad and traumatic things?"** Elicit their reactions and shape them to make the following points:

1. It helps us understand otherwise puzzling reactions and see them as normal reactions to abnormal events.

2. If we know why we feel these ways, it gives us choices to act differently than we usually do. For example, if I know I feel nothing because I'm avoiding feelings about my brother getting shot, I need to allow myself to feel the feelings of grief about his death that I'm avoiding. Or if I get angry at every little thing, I probably need to recognize that I'm still in a rage about what happened to my cousin, and not take it out on everyone around me who had nothing to do with what happened to my cousin.

COPING STRATEGIES

Some good strategies that are particularly helpful for reexperiencing and being on edge are (adapted from Jaycox, CBITS program, 2004):

1. **Thought stopping.** Ask students to think about the trauma they drew in Scary Art Gallery, what it felt like, and what smells, sounds, and sights are associated with it. After a minute or two, say "STOP!" loudly to distract the group. Ask group members what they are thinking now. Most will say that they're thinking about the group leader, other members, or nothing at all. Explain that this is **thought stopping.** Encourage them to talk about ways they can use this technique when upsetting thoughts are bothering them.

2. **Distraction.** Ask group members how they distract themselves when they feel upset. Possible distractors are reading a book, watching TV, playing a game, exercising, or talking to friends.

3. **Imagery.** Remind students about the relaxing image that they developed in the anger management module. Ask students to state again a few details of their image. Note that they can use this relaxing and positive image to counteract the negative images associated with the trauma.

4. **Relaxation techniques.** Remind group members about the deep breathing and muscle relaxation skills learned in the anger management module. Let them know that you will end the session today with a brief muscle relaxation exercise.

HELPING STUDENTS WHO HAVE MANY POSTTRAUMATIC REACTIONS

In groups where there has been a great deal of traumatic stress, some students may be having many and intense posttraumatic reactions that are interfering with their functioning or well-being. These children may be suffering from developmental trauma disorder or posttraumatic stress disorder (PTSD). To address the needs of these children, two additional concepts are helpful, both relating to safety.

1. **Who can you talk to about your traumatic feelings and what happened to you?** Ask students who would be a safe adult to talk to about what happened to them and the feelings and reactions they are continuing to have that interfere with their lives. Discuss what would make it safe to talk to that person, shaping to try to elicit the following points: (1) Someone who cares a lot about them and has their safety and best interests in mind; (2) someone who is a good listener and who the student feels understands them; (3) someone who can be discreet and not spread the disclosure all over the school. Again stress that posttraumatic reactions are *normal* reactions to abnormal events. If no one mentions a counselor, make sure to say that there are specially trained counselors and therapists who can help people to overcome their posttraumatic reactions.

2. **What can you do to keep yourself safe?** Ask students what they themselves can actively do to keep themselves safe and minimize getting even more traumatized. Examples might be not hanging around gang members, knowing where to go in school if you feel unsafe, avoiding parties where there is a good chance of violence occurring, telling one of the trusted people discussed above if you are being hurt at home, and so forth.

Muscle Relaxation

End the session by doing a muscle relaxation exercise. Either take this from the anger management module or use another muscle relaxation exercise if you prefer. Say, **"We talked a lot about trauma today, so let's end by using one of the strategies we discussed for coping. Let's use the muscle relaxation technique."**

Check-Out

Elicit general reactions to the group. Ask how they feel they might use what they learned about their reactions to trauma. Encourage them to talk to their safe person if their posttraumatic reactions are interfering with their lives, and again mention that there are specially trained counselors available to help children with these reactions. Give members one or two small pieces of candy in exchange for their tokens. Remind students to put the Posttraumatic Stress Reactions handout in their notebook.

MODULE EIGHT

 Family
Relationships

Goal To understand and accept one's family

Overview of Session

Session One ■ *Purpose:* Sharing feelings about one's family; working toward acceptance of families

■ *Content:* (1) Family Me Too game; (2) Personality Family Album game; (3) Ideal Family Movie

Session One

(May be expanded to two sessions.)

Activities ✓ Check-in

✓ Planning for termination

✓ Family Me Too game

✓ Personality Family Album game

✓ Ideal Family Movie

✓ Assessing family support

✓ Check-out

Materials ✓ Curriculum

✓ Masking tape

✓ Rules and consequences with the group name at the top of the rules and consequences pages. Put these up in the room before each session.

Content

Check-In

Planning for Termination

DISCUSSION OF TERMINATION

Given that this is the next to last session, it is important to again bring up feelings about the ending of the group. The goals are to help students share their feelings about the ending and to point out positive changes they (or you) have noticed about individual members or about the group as a whole (e.g., more trusting, more able to talk about difficult topics). Remember that it is fine to share your own feelings if that feels comfortable. Refer back to Module Seven, Session One, for other ideas about discussing termination.

PLANNING THE PARTY

Say, **"It's clear that people have lots of feelings about the group ending. In our last session, we'd like to celebrate our group with a party. Who has ideas about what we should bring to eat and drink?"**

1. Solicit ideas about food and drink. In very poor schools, the leaders generally supply the refreshments. If there are budgetary constraints, it is fine to set guidelines, such as **"Do you guys prefer cookies, cupcakes, or chips and dip?"** In other schools or groups, group members want to volunteer to bring food for the party; if so, it is useful to give each student a card with what they chose to bring on it to help them remember to bring it next week.

2. Students sometimes suggest bringing decorations or having music, and these generally add to the party atmosphere. However, there is an important termination activity, so it is not a good idea to plan to watch a movie or play games, since the time is generally limited to one school period. The party parameters should be set to meet the needs and resources of the particular group, leader, and school.

Family Relationship Activity: Family Me Too Game

The goal of all the activities in this module is to help group members speak about family issues, some of which may have been discussed in previous modules and some of which will be new. The idea is to illustrate that everyone has feelings about and problems related to family and that it may help to share these feelings.

1. Say, **"Today we're going to talk about our families. Our first activity is going to help us look at the things we like and things we wish were different about our families. Does anyone remember the game we played on our first day of the group?"** Wait for response. **"That's right, we played the Me Too game. Today we're going to play the same game, only instead of saying things about ourselves, we're going to say things about our families that we like and that we wish were**

different. Remember that you want to say things that you think other people will have in common with you." (See Module One, Session One to review the Me Too game.)

2. **"Let's start with things we like about our family."** Examples are: "My mom is a really good cook," "My brother helps me with hard homework," or "My mom almost always listens when I have a problem." Leaders may need to model responses to begin the activity.

3. After 5 or 10 minutes, say, **"Now let's switch to things we wish were different about our family."** Examples are: "My dad never has time for me," "My sister always takes my things without asking," or "My mom yells at me all the time." Spend another 5 to 10 minutes on this.

Family Relationship Activity: Personality Family Album

The goal of this activity is to help students connect with personality characteristics they share in common with family members. Say, **"Next, let's talk about ways our families have influenced us. Family members have a strong influence on our personalities and the way we act. We hardly ever stop and think about the ways our families shape our personalities and make us the way we are. So now we're going to play a game called Personality Family Album. We're going to go around the circle and ask each of you to describe two qualities that you have in common with someone else in your family (e.g., just like your mother, father, sister . . .). We'd like one of these qualities to be one that you like and one that you don't like. Also describe how it makes you feel to have those qualities. I'll start to show you how it's played (e.g., I get my sense of humor from my dad, and I like that. I get my temper from my mom, and I don't like that. My sister is a brat, and sometimes I am too)."** Go around the circle so that each student takes a turn. When appropriate, ask the other group members whether they have similar feelings about and reactions to their own families.

Family Relationship Activity: Ideal Family Movie

The final family relationship activity is meant to help students think about how they would like their families to be. Say, **"We can choose our friends, but we don't get to pick our families. Our next activity is called Ideal Family Movie. If you were going to make a movie about your family, and you were the writer and the director so you could make it the way you really wanted your family to be, what would you change about your family for the movie?"**

1. If students suggest changes that are reasonable (e.g., "My mom would spend more time with me; my sister and I wouldn't fight all the time"), wonder out loud

   a. what might happen if the student asked for the changes.

   b. whether there is something the student might do to help this change take place.

2. If they suggest changes that are not realistic (e.g., "My dad wasn't in jail; my

mom would stop taking drugs; my parents would get back together again"),
reflect the student's feelings with an empathic comment (e.g., "You miss your dad
and it's really upsetting that he's in jail; it's been 6 years, and you still wish that
your parents would get together again").

Assessing Family Support

Ask students who they can go to in their families for help when they have a problem
or when they are upset. How do they ask for help? Have group members give suggestions to any students who don't know who to go to for help or support or how
to ask for help. If a student feels that no one in the family could understand or help,
try to identify another adult they trust and to whom they could go for help.

Check-Out

Elicit general reactions about the session. Ask, **"Did you notice any patterns about
families from our activities?"** Remind students that next session will be the last
group.

Termination Session: The Party

Activities
- ✓ Trust ratings
- ✓ Check-in
- ✓ Party—eat treats and talk socially
- ✓ Group memories
- ✓ What I like about you
- ✓ Certificates
- ✓ Check-out

Materials
- ✓ Curriculum
- ✓ Trust ratings (one for each student—see Appendix B-la)
- ✓ Treats (see last session for hints about this)
- ✓ What I Like about You sheets (one for each student—see Appendix B-8a)
- ✓ Certificates (one for each student—see Appendix B-8b for a sample)
- ✓ Colored markers
- ✓ Masking tape
- ✓ Rules and consequences with the group name at the top of the rules and consequences pages. Put these up in the room before each session.

Content

Trust Ratings

As students come in, ask them to fill out another trust rating.

Check-In

This is usually informal over treats.

Party

Eat treats and enjoy group members.

Process Group Memories

Discuss group members' experience of the group. Say, **"We've done a lot of things together over the time of the group. We're wondering what kinds of things you liked or found difficult. What special things do you think you'll remember from the group?"** Process reactions. Group leaders can share their experiences as well (i.e., unique things they have learned from the group or group members, effect the group has had on them, reasons they will not forget the group members).

Termination Activity: What I Like about You

The goal of this final activity is to focus on positive connections between group members and to leave the members with a written reminder of their own special qualities. Say, **"Our last activity is to make a souvenir for each of you. It's so easy to give put-downs, but we rarely take the time to give put-ups. So today we're going to concentrate on put-ups. I have a sheet for each of you. We'll go around the circle, and each person will say one nice thing that they like about you. I will write these on your sheet, and you can take it home at the end of the group. Who wants to begin?"** Wait for a volunteer. **"Great! What color do you want your name written in? OK, we'll start with [name of student to left of volunteer]. What's one nice thing you like about [name of volunteer]?"** Write each statement on the sheet, then give it to the student.

1. You also participate in giving put-ups, but you do not usually have sheets written about you. If students really want to do put-up sheets for you, then it should be allowed.
2. Sometimes, students will say mean things. Refocus them on something nice that they like about the student. Ask, **"Is that a put-up? Think of something positive that you like about _____."**
3. Sometimes, students will say things that may be taken as mean or nice. If this happens, ask the target student if he or she thinks it's nice and wants it written down. "Loudmouthed" is an example of this ambiguous category. If it does not feel like a put-up to the target student, ask the person giving feedback to pick something else that they like about the person.

Distribute Certificates

Check-Out

Elicit general reactions to the group. Help students say good-bye. Sometimes groups will want to have a reunion in a few months. This can serve as a booster session to reinforce major concepts discussed in the groups (e.g., hot-headed versus cool-headed responses, problem-solving strategies, talking about feelings and responding empathically, dealing with traumatic events). Be sure to say your own good-byes to students. Some members want to hug you—this is fine if you are comfortable with it.

Congratulate yourself for completing the SPARK program!

CHAPTER THREE

Effectiveness of SPARK Groups

In this section, we first describe the characteristics of the hundreds of adolescents who have already participated in the SPARK groups, based on individual pregroup interviews. We then discuss the demonstrated effectiveness of the SPARK group curriculum, comparing time 1 (pregroup) and time 2 (postgroup) interview responses. Finally, we present pilot data involving our major revisions for the second edition—our new module, Male–Female Relationships, and our completely revised module, Anger Management and Emotion Regulation Skills.

Characteristics of Participating Group Members

All of the students who participated in SPARK were from urban schools in the Los Angeles area, including six public middle schools and two public high schools. Among group members, there were more middle school than high school participants and more boys than girls. Students were primarily African American and Latino.

Family Structure and Distress

Participants in the SPARK program typically did not come from intact families.

Although 37% lived with both parents, 51% lived with just one parent, and 12% lived with neither parent (most frequently living with other relatives or less frequently in a foster home). Participating youth also reported high rates of family distress. For example, in our sample, 37% reported having a family member in jail or prison; 27% reported that a family member had a drug and/or alcohol problem; 10% had parents who divorced in the previous year; 26% were bothered by their parents' arguing with one another; and 39% were bothered by arguments with their parents.

Characteristic	Percentage
Grade level	
6th	30%
7th	25%
8th	30%
9th	14%
10th or higher	2%
Gender	
Male	60%
Female	40%
Ethnicity	
African American	49%
Latino/Latina	39%
Mixed/other	12%

Exposure to Community Violence

In addition to family distress, participants in the SPARK program reported alarmingly high rates of exposure to community violence. For example, 42% had seen someone being killed, and 9% had been shot or shot at with a gun. Percentages of those exposed to violence are given in the chart below.

We have found that exposure to community violence is associated with numerous emotional, cognitive, and behavioral consequences. For example, among youth in the SPARK groups, exposure to community violence is significantly linked with increased psychological distress, including depression, anxiety, and posttraumatic stress. Adolescents with more exposure to violence also have significantly lower levels of self-esteem. Finally, exposure to community violence is significantly linked with increased physical aggression (i.e., hitting, kicking, and slapping others) and gang involvement (i.e., having friends in a gang, believing it is necessary to be in a gang). These findings are consistent with other samples of inner-city youth around the country.

Violent event	Percentage
Chased by gangs	22%
Beaten up or mugged	14%
Attacked or stabbed with a knife	6%
Shot or shot at with a gun	9%
House broken into when at home	11%
Saw someone carrying a gun or knife	55%
Heard a gun fired while at home	62%
Saw someone being killed	42%

Outcomes of the SPARK Groups

To examine the effectiveness of the SPARK groups, information collected from 241 students before the groups began (time 1) was compared with information from their interviews after the groups ended (time 2). In addition, information from these 241 students was compared to information from 78 students who were initially placed in a wait-list control group. Of course, students in the wait-list control group were subsequently placed in SPARK groups, and they were interviewed again after they had completed the groups. Hence, students in the control group were interviewed on three occasions: twice before the groups began and once after the groups ended.

Time 1 and Time 2 Differences for Those in the Treatment Group

Those in the treatment group reported significant gains in a number of areas. After participating in the SPARK groups, the adolescents had significantly higher educational aspirations, and although their math grades did not change significantly, they did achieve significantly higher English grades (see Figure 1). Additionally, those in the treatment group reported significant gains in self-esteem and in psychological adjustment, including decreased anxiety, depression, and posttraumatic stress. Finally, those in the treatment group felt significantly more attached and connected to their peers following participation in the SPARK groups.

After completing the groups, SPARK participants were also asked to complete

FIGURE 1. English grades.

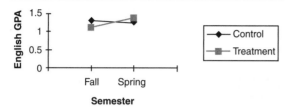

a brief satisfaction survey. In general, the participants agreed that they "got a lot out of counseling," and that counseling helped them feel better about themselves and do better in school. Additionally, group leaders were asked to complete a brief evaluation for each student who participated. As part of the evaluation, group leaders were asked the question "Overall, how much did this student benefit from the group?" Responses were given on a 5-point scale (1 = not at all; 2 = mild; 3 = moderate; 4 = much; 5 = very much). Altogether, group leaders indicated that 75% of students who completed the SPARK groups benefited "moderately," "much," or "very much."

Time 1 and Time 2 Differences for Those in the Control Group

Adolescents in the wait-list control group were interviewed at the same time as those in the treatment group. In general, from time 1 to time 2 (both before they participated in SPARK), those in the control group did not report the same gains as those in the treatment group. In fact, in comparing their time 1 and time 2 interviews, those in the control group reported a significant increase in gang involvement (i.e., number of friends in a gang). However, those in the control group did report a significant decrease in depression and alienation from peers.

Comparisons between the Treatment and Control Groups

Although we tried to randomly assign students to treatment and control groups, students in major distress were immediately placed in the treatment group. As a result, at time 1, adolescents in the treatment group were significantly more distressed in a number of areas when compared to those in the control group. In particular, adolescents in the treatment group had significantly lower levels of self-esteem, ethnic identity, peer attachment, and educational aspirations than those in the control group at time 1. At time 2, however, none of these differences were significant. Furthermore, when each student's time 1 score was taken into account, comparisons between time 2 scores indicated that those in the treatment group were significantly less likely to believe that it is necessary to be in a gang than those in the control group (see Figure 2).

In addition to these gains, a doctoral student involved in the SPARK program found that the groups were effective in the area of perceived control. In particular, compared to those in the control group, students in the treatment group reported a decrease in their perceptions of external control (i.e., that their fate was in the hands of others). In addition, changes in perceived control were associated with increased educational aspirations and decreased aggressive behavior (Watt, 1998).

FIGURE 2. Necessity of being in a gang.

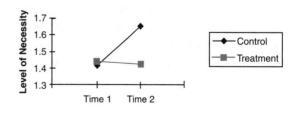

Pilot Evaluations of New and Revised Modules in This Edition

In order to begin assessing the effectiveness of the new module for the second edition, Male–Female Relationships, a small sample of ninth graders was given the Survey of Relationship Attitudes (see Appendix B-6c) prior to the module and again after the completion of the module. This survey looks at sex-role stereotypes about males and females, mostly involving dating relationships. Data showed that students had significantly less stereotyped attitudes in group posttesting on 6 of the 10 items, indicating that the module was successful on changing students' attitudes on items such as "Guys only want one thing from girls," and "If a guy takes a girl out on an expensive date, he can expect the girl to show him some affection in return."

To assess the impact of the major revisions to the Anger Management and Emotion Regulation Skills module, we gave a different small sample of students the subscales of the Multidimensional School Anger Inventory (Smith & Furlong, 2008) to be used in the pregroup and postgroup interview in Appendix A-5 before and after administering the module. After the intervention, students showed significantly lower scores on the Anger Experience subscale, indicating they would feel less angry than before the module about things such as being sent to the principal's office when other students were acting worse, having someone start a mean rumor that spreads all over the school, and so forth. In terms of coping skills, students scored marginally significantly higher on the Positive Coping subscale after intervention, but there was no change in the Destructive Expression subscale. This may be due to the focus in the module on development of emotion regulation and prosocial coping strategies.

Summary and Conclusions

The SPARK group counseling curriculum has been implemented in a number of secondary schools in the Los Angeles area. In our groups, more males than females, more middle school than high school students, and primarily African American and Latino or Latina adolescents have participated. In general, participants did not come from intact families, and they reported alarmingly high rates of family distress and exposure to community violence. In turn, exposure to community violence was linked with numerous deleterious consequences, including psychological distress, lowered self-esteem, increased physical aggression, and gang involvement.

The SPARK curriculum appears to be effective in a number of domains, including academic goals and achievement, psychological adjustment, self-esteem, and gang involvement. With respect to academics, group members report an increase in educational aspirations and also achieve significantly higher English grades following participation in the groups. With respect to psychological adjustment, following participation in the SPARK groups, members report significant decreases in anxiety, depression, and posttraumatic stress, as well as a significant increase in self-esteem. Participants also report increased attachment and connectedness to peers following the groups. Finally, compared to those in the control group, adolescents who participate in the groups are less likely to view gang involvement as necessary.

Although participants in the SPARK groups reported significant gains in a number of areas, the gains tended to be relatively modest. For example, although the students achieved significantly higher English grades following participation in the program, their grades were still quite poor. One possible explanation for the modest findings is that adolescents in our groups are particularly at risk; they all live in the inner city, contending with such chronic stressors as poverty, community violence, and family distress. A second possible explanation involves treatment studies in general. Typically, treatment studies that are relatively brief and circumscribed yield modest results, especially those involving at-risk adolescents (see Kazdin, 1993). As in other treatment studies, we did not expect dramatic improvements, as such gains would most likely require a very intensive, multicomponent, long-term, and costly intervention. Our hope is that students will continue to make gains in the months and years following participation as they practice skills acquired through the program.

Contrary to our expectations, students who participated in the groups did not report a significant decrease in physical aggression despite an emphasis on anger management in the curriculum and despite group leader reports of students' increased use of cool-headed responses in a variety of situations. This may have been due to the questionable validity of our measure of physical aggression (i.e., "How many times have you hit, kicked, or slapped someone in the last month?"). This one question is an inadequate measure of physical aggression; it was developed for this project, has statistical prob-

lems, and does not discriminate between sibling squabbles and serious interpersonal aggression. Given that significant gains were made in other areas (e.g., self-esteem, psychological adjustment) that were assessed with established and widely used measures, it is possible that we would have found significant results in the area of physical aggression had we used a more reliable and valid measure. We have tried to address the possible inadequacies in the anger management module by completely revising it for the second edition, and to deal with the possible problems with measurement of anger and aggression by using the Multidimensional School Anger Inventory (Smith & Furlong, 2008), a standardized measure of these constructs.

Overall, the groups yield benefits in a variety of areas, including academic achievement, psychological adjustment, self-esteem, peer connectedness and attachment, and alternatives to gang involvement. The SPARK group counseling curriculum is applicable to a wide variety of adolescents, including the general population as well as adolescents at high risk for developing severe behavioral, emotional, and/or academic problems.

Information Regarding Data Analyses

For more detailed information regarding the data analyses, please contact the authors through Jill Waterman, PhD, Department of Psychology, UCLA, 405 Hilgard Avenue, Los Angeles, CA 90095-1563.

APPENDIX A

Sample Materials for Beginning SPARK Groups

SPARK Counseling Groups Referral Form

SPARK counseling groups are for students who are currently experiencing academic, social, emotional, and/or family difficulties or have been exposed to high levels of violence. The groups will meet for one class period per week for 15 to 20 weeks. Topics covered in the groups include: anger management, educational aspirations, family relationships, and peer pressure/gangs. If you know of a student who could benefit from such an experience and who can work cooperatively in a group, please refer him/her in the space below.

Student's Name: _____

Gender: _____

Grade: _____

Ethnicity: _____

Reason for Referral (please place an "X" next to all relevant concerns):

____ Family problems

____ Disruptive or disobedient

____ Inattentive

____ Anxious or nervous

____ Sad or withdrawn

____ Academic problems

____ Exposure to violence

____ Other (please specify) _____

Teacher's/Counselor's Name and Date: _____

Thank you for referring this student to the SPARK program. We will be contacting him/her in the next few days.

Sample Script for Presenting SPARK Groups to Potential Group Members

1. Introduce yourself.

2. Explain the purpose of SPARK groups: "I'm here to talk to you about SPARK groups here at school. The groups are a place where kids come to talk about things that are going on in their lives—like things that happen at school or at home. We'll also be talking about certain things that are important to people your age. For example, we'll be talking about your future plans, ways to control anger, racism, and family relationships. Everything talked about in the group is confidential, unless we are concerned that you or someone else might get hurt. This means that what happens in the group—what gets talked about—won't be shared with your parents, teacher, or friends."

3. Outline the structure of SPARK groups: "The SPARK groups meet for one class period every week for 15 to 20 weeks. Every time we meet, you'll have a chance to talk about what is going on in your life. In addition, we will have a fun activity that is related to the topic for that day. Later, we'll be taking an all-day field trip to a local university where you can learn more about college life. Before the group starts and after it ends, we will need to ask everyone who participates some questions. Responses to these questions will be kept private."

4. Explain why the child was referred to participate in the group: "The reason you've been invited here today is because someone, either a teacher or a school counselor, identified you as a person who works well with other students, who might like to be in this group, and who could benefit from the topics that are discussed. We've done a lot of these groups before and students seem to like them."

5. Answer any questions students might have.

6. Give Parent Consent Forms to all students who are interested in participating.

SPARK Parent Consent Form

What Are SPARK Groups?

SPARK counseling groups are for students who have been identified by a school counselor or teacher as a student who could work cooperatively in a group and who may benefit from this type of experience. For SPARK groups, students will miss one class period per week for a total of 15 to 20 weeks. In the group sessions, the following topics will be covered: trust building, anger management, coping strategies, the importance of education for the future, ethnic pride, dealing with discrimination, avoiding peer pressure and gangs, male–female relationships, family relationships, and dealing with community violence. Specific activities will be presented in each session and students will be encouraged to share their own feelings and experiences.

Students will be interviewed before and after participation in the groups. The interview contains questions about the student's feelings, attitudes and beliefs, experiences, level of stress, and problem behaviors.

Confidentiality

Students' responses to the interview questions and his/her participation in the SPARK groups will be kept confidential, except as required by law. The privilege of confidentiality does not extend to information about sexual, emotional, or physical abuse of a child, or to neglect of a child. If the SPARK leader has reasonable suspicion of abuse or is given such information, the leader is required to report to the authorities. Also, if the SPARK leader believes that a student is at significant risk of harming him/herself, the leader will need to ensure the student's safety by telling the child's parent or guardian and the school counselor.

Participation and Withdrawal

Participation in the interview and in the SPARK groups is voluntary. If a student does not participate, there will be no negative effects on the relationship with the school or treatment in the classroom. The SPARK leader can be reached at the number below if any questions or concerns about the interview or the groups arise.

I give permission for my child to participate in SPARK groups, as described above. In signing this form, I acknowledge that I have received a copy of the consent form.

_____   _____
Parent's Signature and Date   **Student's Name**

_____   _____
SPARK Leader   **SPARK Leader's Phone Number**

SPARK Student Assent Form

I am being invited to participate in SPARK counseling groups. This means that I will miss a class period once a week for a total of 15 to 20 weeks. In the group sessions, topics covered include: trust building, anger management, coping strategies, the importance of education for the future, ethnic pride, dealing with discrimination, avoiding peer pressure and gangs, male–female relationships, family relationships, and dealing with community violence. Specific activities are presented in each session and students are also encouraged to share their own feelings and experiences.

I will be asked to complete a brief interview now and another one after the groups have ended. During the interview, I will be asked to talk about things in my life. I can skip whatever question I do not wish to answer and I can stop the interview at any time. If I am feeling upset at the end of the interview, the interviewer will give me the phone number of a counselor with whom I can talk about problems I may be having.

What I say during the interview and in the SPARK groups will be kept confidential. This means that what I say will not be shared with my parents, teachers, or friends. The SPARK leader will not tell anyone what I say without my permission unless there is something that could be dangerous to me or to someone else. If I indicate that someone is or has been hurting me, the leader will have to tell the people who are responsible for protecting children, so they can make sure that I am safe. If I indicate I am thinking about hurting myself, the leader will have to tell my parents and school counselor in order to keep me safe.

My parents or I can always call the SPARK leader if we have any questions about the groups or the interview. I have read this form and I understand it.

_____   _____
Student's Signature   **Date**

_____   _____
SPARK Leader   **SPARK Leader's Phone Number**

Pregroup and Postgroup Interview

Student's Name: _____ **Ethnicity:** _____ **Gender:** _____

Administered by: _____ **Date:** _____

Circle One: **Pregroup**   **Postgroup**

Section I: Background Information

Demographics

I'm going to start by asking you some general questions.

1. What grade are you in? _____

2. What is your birthdate? _____   So, you're _____ years old?

3. Who do you live with? (list) _____

   Does anyone else live in your home with you? (list) _____

   List siblings: Brother/sister   Age   Lives with you?

   _____   _____   Y/N

   _____   _____   Y/N

   _____   _____   Y/N

4. So you don't live with (mom, dad, mom or dad)? Why is that? (circle M for mom, D for dad)

Divorce	M	D	Parent in jail	M	D
Separated	M	D	Other (specify) _____		
Death	M	D	Don't know		
Never married	M	D			

Family Stressors

I'm going to read you a list of things that sometimes happen to people your age. For each event, tell me if it has happened to you during the last year. Then, if it has happened during the last year, tell me how stressful it was for you when it occurred. (*Show response scale 1.*)

No		Yes		
1	2	3	4	
no trouble	bothersome	stressful	very stressful	

During the last year . . .

1. Did one of your parents start or stop working?	N	1	2	3	4
2. Did your parents separate or get a divorce?	N	1	2	3	4
3. Did you argue more with your parents?	N	1	2	3	4
4. Did your parents argue much more with each other?	N	1	2	3	4
5. Did someone in your family have a problem with drug or alcohol use?	N	1	2	3	4
6. Did someone important to you go to jail or prison?	N	1	2	3	4

Community Violence Exposure[†]

How often have any of the following happened to you either at home, in your neighborhood, or in school? *(Show response scale 2.)*

0	1	2	3
Never	Sometimes	Often	Very often

1. *You* being told by someone that they were going to hurt you	0	1	2	3
2. Seeing *someone else* being told they were going to get hurt	0	1	2	3
3. *You* being slapped, punched, or hit	0	1	2	3
4. *Seeing* someone else being slapped, punched, or hit	0	1	2	3
5. *You* being beaten up	0	1	2	3
6. Seeing *someone else* being beaten up	0	1	2	3
7. *You* being attacked or stabbed with a knife	0	1	2	3
8. Seeing *someone else* being attacked or stabbed with a knife	0	1	2	3
9. *You* being shot at or shot with a **real** gun	0	1	2	3
10. Seeing *someone else* being shot at or shot with a **real** gun	0	1	2	3

[†]Adapted with permission from Singer (1997).

Section II: Other Information Relevant to SPARK Groups

Educational Aspirations

Next, I will be asking you some questions about school. *(Show response scale 3.)*

1	2	3	4	5
Much less than other kids	Less than other kids	About the same as other kids	More than other kids	Much more than other kids

APPENDIX A-5. From Waterman and Walker (2009). Copyright by The Guilford Press.

1. Compared to other kids in your school, how likely is it that you will finish high school?_____

2. Compared to other kids in your school, how likely is it that you will go to college?   _____

3. Compared to other kids in your school, how important is it to you that you do well   _____
in your schoolwork?

Adjustment

I'm going to read you a list of things that some kids your age experience. Please tell me how often each of these things happens to you. (*Show response scale 2.*)

0	1	2	3
Never	Sometimes	Often	Very often

	0	1	2	3
1. Feeling lonely.	0	1	2	3
2. Remembering things you don't want to remember.	0	1	2	3
3. Trouble concentrating on things at home or at school.	0	1	2	3
4. Wanting to break things.	0	1	2	3
5. Wanting to hurt yourself.*	0	1	2	3
6. Feeling afraid.	0	1	2	3
7. Feeling sad or unhappy.	0	1	2	3
8. Can't stop thinking about something bad that happened to you.	0	1	2	3
9. Trouble falling asleep or staying asleep.	0	1	2	3
10. Wanting to yell at people.	0	1	2	3
11. Wanting to kill yourself.*	0	1	2	3
12. Trying not to feel anything (bad feelings).	0	1	2	3
13. Worrying about things.	0	1	2	3
14. Feeling unlike anybody else.	0	1	2	3

*Mark items 5 and 11 for follow up at end of interview.

Anger Experience and Expression[†]

Multidimensional School Anger Inventory—Revised (MSAI-R) (Smith & Furlong, 2008)

Anger Experience Subscale (*Show response scale 4.*)

1	2	3	4
I wouldn't be mad at all	I'd be a little angry	I'd be pretty angry	I would be furious

	1	2	3	4
1. You didn't notice that someone put gum on your seat and you sit on it.	1	2	3	4
2. At school, two bigger students take something of yours and play "keep away" from you.	1	2	3	4

APPENDIX A-5. From Waterman and Walker (2009). Copyright by The Guilford Press.

3. You tell the teacher you are not feeling well but she/he does not believe you. 1 2 3 4

4. Someone in your class acts up, so the whole class has to stay after school. 1 2 3 4

5. You ask to go to the bathroom and the teacher says "no." 1 2 3 4

6. You go to your desk in the morning and find out someone has stolen some of your school supplies. 1 2 3 4

7. Someone in your class tells the teacher on you for doing something. 1 2 3 4

8. You get sent to the principal's office when other students are acting worse than you are. 1 2 3 4

9. The teacher's pet gets to do all of the special errands in class. 1 2 3 4

10. Somebody cuts in front of you in the lunch line. 1 2 3 4

11. You are trying to do your work in school and someone bumps your desk on purpose and you mess up. 1 2 3 4

12. You study really hard for a test and still get a low grade. 1 2 3 4

13. Somebody calls you a bad name. 1 2 3 4

Anger Expression Subscale (*Show response scale 2.*)

0	1	2	3
Never	Sometimes	Often	Very often

When you get mad, what do you do?

1. When I'm angry, I'll take it out on whoever is around. 0 1 2 3

2. I talk it over with another person when I'm upset. 0 1 2 3

3. When I get angry, I think about something else. 0 1 2 3

4. When I'm mad, I hate the world. 0 1 2 3

5. When I get mad at school, I share my feelings. 0 1 2 3

6. When I'm mad, I break things. 0 1 2 3

7. Before I explode, I try to understand why this happened to me. 0 1 2 3

8. When I'm upset, I calm myself down by reading, writing, painting, or some similar activity. 0 1 2 3

9. I get so mad that I want to hurt myself 0 1 2 3

10. If something makes me mad, I try to find something funny about it. 0 1 2 3

11. When I'm mad, I let my feelings out by some type of physical activity like running, playing, etc. 0 1 2 3

12. If I get mad, I'll throw a tantrum. 0 1 2 3

13. When I'm angry, I cover it up by smiling or pretending I'm not mad.   0 1 2 3

14. I punch something when I'm angry.   0 1 2 3

15. When I get a bad grade, I figure out ways to get back at the teacher.   0 1 2 3

16. When I'm mad at a teacher, I make jokes in class to get my friends laughing.   0 1 2 3

17. When I get a bad grade on a test, I rip the test paper into little pieces.   0 1 2 3

†Reprinted with permission of the authors.

Self-Esteem

I'm going to read you some statements and I'd like you to tell me how much you agree or disagree with each statement. (*Show response scale 5.*)

1	2	3	4
Strongly agree	Agree	Disagree	Strongly disagree

1. I feel that I am a person of worth, at least on an equal basis with others.   _____

2. I feel that I have a number of good qualities.   _____

3. All in all, I am inclined to feel that I am a failure.   _____

4. I am able to do things as well as most other people.   _____

5. I feel I do not have much to be proud of.   _____

6. I take a positive attitude toward myself.   _____

7. On the whole, I am satisfied with myself.   _____

8. I wish I could have more respect for myself.   _____

9. I certainly feel useless at times.   _____

10. At times I think I am no good at all.   _____

Ethnic Pride

In a minute I'm going to read you some different statements but first I'd like to ask you a question.
What word would you use to describe your ethnic or racial group? _____
(*If the child has trouble, say: " Martin Luther King might say he is Black or African American; Cesar Chavez might say that he is Hispanic or Latino . . . "*)

OK, so for these questions, whenever I say "ethnic group" I mean _____.
I'd like you to tell me how much you agree or disagree with each statement.
(*Keep response scale 5.*)

1	2	3	4
Strongly agree	Agree	Disagree	Strongly disagree

1. I am happy that I am (*ethnic group from above*).   _____

2. I feel little sense of belonging to my own ethnic group.   _____

APPENDIX A-5. From Waterman and Walker (2009). Copyright by The Guilford Press.

3. I have a lot of pride in my ethnic group and its accomplishments.   _____

4. I feel little attachment towards my own ethnic group.   _____

5. I feel good about my cultural or ethnic background.   _____

Peer Attachment

These questions ask about your relationships with important people in your life—your close friends. Please tell me how true each statement is for you now. (*Show response scale 2.*)

0	1	2	3
Never	Sometimes	Often	Very often

1. When we discuss things, my friends care about my point of view.   _____

2. I feel my friends are good friends.   _____

3. I feel angry with my friends.   _____

4. I trust my friends.   _____

5. My friends help me to talk about my difficulties.   _____

6. It seems as if my friends are irritated with me for no reason.   _____

It is necessary to belong to a gang.	YES	NO
Has anyone ever tried to jump you in a gang?	YES	NO

The interview part is completed. Process any distress responses to items 5 and 11 of the Adjustment Scale.

If this is a pregroup interview, say "OK, we're done. Thanks for answering all of these questions. Do you have any questions about any of the things we talked about today? The groups will be starting soon and they should be a lot of fun."

For older groups of students, it may be helpful to readminister the Survey of Relationship Attitudes (Appendix B-6c) at the postgroup interview. Please see below for scoring instructions.

If this is a postgroup interview, say "OK, we're done with this part of the interview. I just have one more thing for you to do. I'm going to give you a paper with some questions about the SPARK groups. You don't have to write your name on the paper, so be as honest as possible. When you're done, put your answers in this envelope and seal it so that your answers will be anonymous." (*Give the student an envelope and the last page of the interview.*)

SPARK Group Evaluation

1	2	3	4	5
Not at all	Just a little	Somewhat	Pretty much	Very much

1. Using the numbers on the response scale above, how much did the SPARK groups help you to

   a) Use cool-headed responses when angry? _____

   b) Feel better about yourself? _____

   c) Express your feelings? _____

   d) Resist peer pressure? _____

   e) Cope with bullying? _____

   f) Feel more accepting of people who are different from you? _____

   g) Understand your reactions to bad things happening to you? _____

   h) Want to do better at school? _____

2. How much did you like the SPARK groups? _____

3. How helpful were the group leaders? _____

4. Overall, how helpful were the SPARK groups? _____

5. What suggestions do you have for improving the SPARK groups?

   _____

   _____

   _____

Thanks for being a member of SPARK!!

Response Scale 1 for the Interview

NO		YES		
	No trouble	Bothersome	Stressful	Very stressful
N	1	2	3	4

APPENDIX A-6. From Waterman and Walker (2009). Copyright by The Guilford Press.

Response Scale 2 for the Interview

0	1	2	3
Never	Sometimes	Often	Very often

APPENDIX A-6. From Waterman and Walker (2009). Copyright by The Guilford Press.

Response Scale 3 for the Interview

1	2	3	4	5
Much Less Than Other Kids	*Less Than Other Kids*	*About the Same as Other Kids*	*More Than Other Kids*	*Much More Than Other Kids*

APPENDIX A-6. From Waterman and Walker (2009). Copyright by The Guilford Press.

Response Scale 4 for the Interview

1	2	3	4
I wouldn't be mad at all	I'd be a little angry	I'd be pretty angry	I would be furious

Response Scale 5 for the Interview

1	2	3	4
Strongly agree	Agree	Disagree	Strongly disagree

APPENDIX A-6. From Waterman and Walker (2009). Copyright by The Guilford Press.

Scoring Instructions and Additional Information about the Interview

Some of the measures in the interview were developed specifically for the SPARK program. Whenever possible, however, we used measures that were already in existence and well documented. In some cases, we adapted those measures for the purposes of the SPARK program. Below is a description of the various measures. References for the measures can be found in the References section at the end of the manual.

Section I: Background Information

Demographics: The items in this section involve basic information, including grade level, family structure, and living situation.

Family Stressors: This scale includes items drawn from the Junior High Life Experiences Survey (Swearingen & Cohen, 1985) that pertain specifically to stress and distress within the immediate family. *Scoring:* "No" responses are scored as "0"; sum the responses to the 6 items and divide by 6 to get the mean Family Stressors score.

Violence Exposure: This scale is an adaptation of the Exposure to Violence Scales: Grades 3–12 (Singer, 1997; Singer, Anglin, Song, & Lunghofer, 1995): Sum the responses to the 10 items and then divide by 10 to get the mean Violence Exposure Score.

Section II: Other Information Relevant to SPARK Groups

Educational Aspirations: These items were developed specifically for the SPARK program. *Scoring:* Sum the responses to the 3 items and divide by 3 to get the mean Educational Aspirations score.

Adjustment: Most of the items from this scale were drawn from the Trauma Symptom Checklist for Children (TSCC; Briere, 1996). The TSCC has several subscales, including: Depression, Anxiety, Anger, and Post-Traumatic Stress Disorder (PTSD). Several additional items were also developed specifically for the SPARK program in order to assess the 3 symptom clusters of PTSD: Re-experiencing the traumatic event, Avoidant behaviors, and Hyperarousal. In this shortened version, we included the 2 items from the Depression, Anxiety, and Anger subscales that had the highest item-scale correlation in our sample. We also included 6 PTSD items—the 2 items from each of the 3 symptom clusters (i.e., Re-experiencing, Avoidance, and Hyperarousal) that had the highest item-scale correlation in our sample. Finally, we included 2 items that assess for suicidality (i.e., Wanting to hurt yourself; Wanting to kill yourself); these 2 items can be included in the Depression subscale. *Scoring:* sum the responses to items 1, 5, 7, and 11, and then divide by 4 to get the mean Depression score; sum the responses to items 6 and 13, and then divide by 2 to get the mean Anxiety score; sum the responses to items 4 and 10, and then divide by 2 to get the mean Anger score;

sum the responses to items 2 and 8, and then divide by 2 to get the mean PTSD—Re-experiencing score; sum the responses to items 12 and 14, and then divide by 2 to get the mean PTSD—Avoidance score; sum the responses to items 3 and 9, and then divide by 2 to get the mean PTSD—Hyperarousal score; sum the responses to items 2, 3, 8, 9, 12, and 14, and then divide by 6 to get the mean PTSD score; sum the responses to all 14 items and divide by 14 to get the mean Adjustment score.

Anger Management: This scale includes the Anger Experience and Anger Expression subscales of the Multidimensional School Anger Inventory—Revised (Smith & Furlong, 2008). To score the Inventory visit the website *www.education.ucsb.edu/csbyd*, scroll down to the Multidimensional School Anger Inventory, and click on the link. For the Anger Experience subscale, sum the responses on items 1 through 13 and divide by 13 to get the mean Anger Experience score. The Anger Expression scale is divided into Destructive Expression (DE) and Positive Coping (PC) subscales (see website above for which items make up these scales). Sum the responses for the Destructive Expression items and divide by 9 to get the mean Destructive Expression score, and sum the responses for the Positive Coping items and divide by 8 to get the mean Positive Coping score.

Self-Esteem: This scale is an unmodified version of the Rosenberg Self-Esteem Scale (Rosenberg, 1979). *Scoring:* Reverse score items 3, 5, 8, 9, and 10 (e.g., a score of "4" would be a "1", a score of "3" would be a "2", etc.); sum the responses to the 10 items and then divide by 10 to get the mean Self-Esteem score.

Ethnic Pride: These items were adapted from the Affirmation and Belonging subscale of the Multigroup Ethnic Identity Measure (Phinney, 1992). *Scoring:* Reverse score items 2 and 4 (e.g., a score of "4" would be a "1", a score of "3" would be a "2", etc.); sum the responses to the 5 items and divide by 5 to get the mean Ethnic Pride score.

Peer Attachment: These items were drawn from the Peer scale of the Inventory of Parent and Peer Attachment (Armsden & Greenberg, 1987). The Peer scale includes 3 subscales: Trust, Communication, and (Lack of) Alienation. In our shortened version of the Peer scale, we included the 2 items from each subscale that had the highest item-scale correlation in our sample. *Scoring:* Reverse score items 3 and 6 (e.g., a score of 5 would be a 1, a score of 4 would be a 2, etc.); total the responses to items 2 and 4, and divide by 2 to get the mean Trust score; total the responses to items 1 and 5, and divide by 2 to get the mean Communication score; total the responses to items 3 and 6, and divide by 2 to get the mean (Lack of) Alienation score; total all 6 items, and divide by 6 to get the mean peer attachment score.

Survey of Relationship Attitudes: For this survey (Appendix B-6c), given as part of the Male–Female Relationships module, we adapted items from a questionnaire given by the Rape Treatment Center at Santa Monica-UCLA Medical Center (Roden & Abarbanel, 1993) and added several new items. We recommend that students take the survey again as part of postgroup testing. *Scoring:* Reverse score items 6 and 8 (e.g., a score of 4 would be a 1, a score of 3 would be a 2, etc.); total responses to the 10 items and divide by 10 to get the mean Relationship Attitudes score.

Title Page for Student Notebooks

SPARK Groups

Topics to be covered:

1. Trust-Building and Communication Skills
2. Anger Management and Coping with Difficult Emotions
3. Ethnic Identity and Coping with Prejudice and Racism
4. Educational Goals and Academic Success
5. Peer Pressure, Bullying, and Gangs
6. Male–Female Relationships
7. Exposure to Violence and Posttraumatic Stress
8. Family Relationships

Your Name: _____

Group Name: _____

Attendance/Good Behavior/Homework Tracking Log (for Group Leaders)

Attendance (place an X in the relevant box if student attended the session)*

Student Name	Session Number																			
	1	2	3	4	5	6	7	8	9	10	11	12	13	14	15	16	17	18	19	20
1.																				
2.																				
3.																				
4.																				
5.																				
6.																				
7.																				
8.																				
9.																				
10.																				

Good Behavior (place an X in the relevant box if student had no more than 1 warning)*

Student Name	Session Number																			
	1	2	3	4	5	6	7	8	9	10	11	12	13	14	15	16	17	18	19	20
1.																				
2.																				
3.																				
4.																				
5.																				
6.																				
7.																				
8.																				
9.																				
10.																				

Homework (place an X in the relevant box if student completed homework)*

Student Name	Homework Assignment					
	Anger Thermometer	Relaxation Log	My Anger Journal	Permission Slip	My Goals	Resisting Peer Pressure
1.						
2.						
3.						
4.						
5.						
6.						
7.						
8.						
9.						
10.						

*If desired, students may choose candy instead of accumulating points to later be traded in for small prizes at the end of the group.
If a student chooses candy instead of points, circle the X to show the point has been used.

APPENDIX B

Curriculum Materials and Handouts

Module Five: Peer Pressure, Bullying, and Gangs

Module Six: Male–Female Relationships

Module Seven: Exposure to Violence and Posttraumatic Stress Reactions

Termination Session: The Party

Module One: Trust-Building and Communication Skills

Session One

1. *Trust Ratings* (Appendix B-1a)
   a. Make enough copies for each student to complete one rating slip.
   b. Cut slips along dotted line.
   c. Ask students to complete these forms at the beginning of the first session.
   d. You may need to bring some trust ratings to Session Two for new members.
   e. Trust ratings for each student are also needed in Session Four of this module, and at the Termination Session of the SPARK program.
2. *Confidentiality Contract (Appendix B-1b)*
   a. Make enough copies for each student to complete one contract.
   b. You may need to bring some Confidentiality Contracts to Session Two for students who did not attend Session One, or who wanted to think about whether they were willing to sign.

Session Two

1. *Feelings for "Feelings Grab Bag"* (Appendix B-1c)
   a. Cut paper to separate individual feelings and fold in half.
   b. Add other feelings if they seem important for your particular group.
   c. Place the folded "feelings" in a hat or bag.

Session Three

1. *Body Language Positions* (Appendix B-1d)
   a. Cut paper to separate individual body positions and fold in half.
   b. Add other body positions if they seem important for your particular group.
   c. Place the folded "body positions" in a hat or bag.
2. *Good Listening Skills* (Appendix B-1e)
   a. Make a copy for each student.
3. *Secrets for "Secret Pooling"*—Low-Trust Version) (Younger Students)
   Secrets for "Secret Pooling"—Low-Trust Version) (Older Students) (Appendix B-1f)
   a. Cut up secrets for the appropriate age group.

Session Four (Optional)

1. *Trust Ratings* (see Session One)
2. *Secrets for "Secret Pooling"*—(Low-Trust Version) (see Session Three)
   a. Use prepared secrets if the average of the trust ratings at the beginning of the session is less than "3."
   b. Select "younger" or "older" version of Secrets as appropriate for the group.
   c. Bring one copy for each group you are running.
   d. Cut paper to separate individual Secrets and fold in half.
   e. Place in hat or bag.
   f. If the average trust rating is 3 or more (high trust), have students write down their own secret on the blank forms.

Trust Ratings

Name: _____   Date: _____

How much do you trust the other members of the group?

1	2	3	4	5
Not at All	Just a Little	Somewhat	Pretty Much	Very Much

- -

Name: _____   Date: _____

How much do you trust the other members of the group?

1	2	3	4	5
Not at All	Just a Little	Somewhat	Pretty Much	Very Much

- -

Name: _____   Date: _____

How much do you trust the other members of the group?

1	2	3	4	5
Not at All	Just a Little	Somewhat	Pretty Much	Very Much

- -

Name: _____   Date: _____

How much do you trust the other members of the group?

1	2	3	4	5
Not at All	Just a Little	Somewhat	Pretty Much	Very Much

- -

Name: _____   Date: _____

How much do you trust the other members of the group?

1	2	3	4	5
Not at All	Just a Little	Somewhat	Pretty Much	Very Much

- -

Name: _____   Date: _____

How much do you trust the other members of the group?

1	2	3	4	5
Not at All	Just a Little	Somewhat	Pretty Much	Very Much

- -

Name: _____   Date: _____

How much do you trust the other members of the group?

1	2	3	4	5
Not at All	Just a Little	Somewhat	Pretty Much	Very Much

- -

Confidentiality Contract

I understand that anything I say or do during the group will not be revealed by the group leaders to anyone outside the group, including my parents, friends, and teachers. I understand that the only exception is if I reveal information about myself or someone else being in danger; then, the group leaders will have to tell someone in order to keep me or someone else safe.

I also understand that I cannot talk to anyone else about what other people say or do in the group. This includes talking to my parents, brothers and sisters, and friends. I understand that the other members of this group will be trusting me with their secrets, and that to talk about what they say would be breaking their trust. I understand that for the group to be as helpful as possible, I must honor this confidentiality contract.

By signing this contract, I agree not to talk to anyone outside of the group about what others say or do in the group.

_____   _____

Group Member's Signature   **Date**

Feelings for "Feelings Grab Bag"

Scared	Proud
Shy	Disappointed
Brave	Confused
Sad	Happy
Surprised	Embarrassed
Frustrated	Excited
Relaxed	Stressed
Ashamed	Confident

Body Language Positions

Avoid eye contact
Roll your eyes
Tap your foot over and over
Cross arms tight over chest
Stand too close

 # Good Listening Skills

Body Language

1. Look at the other person when they are talking.

2. Turn your body toward rather than away from the other person.

3. Keep a respectful distance between you and the other person.

4. Keep your body open and arms relaxed.

5. Keep your face friendly or neutral.

6. Avoid nervous fiddling with clothes, hair, etc.

Verbal

1. Acknowledge what was said by saying "uh huh," "yeah," etc., or nodding.

2. Summarize what you heard so the other person knows you were listening carefully.

3. Use reflective statements that show you understand what the other person is feeling.

4. Don't interrupt but instead hear the person out.

5. Ask open-ended questions—they start with "what," " why," "how do," or "tell me," and cannot be answered just "yes" or "no."

6. Share a similar experience you had in a respectful way.

APPENDIX B-1e. From Waterman and Walker (2009). Copyright by The Guilford Press.

Secrets for "Secret Pooling"— Low-Trust Version (Younger Students)

(Includes blanks to fill in other secrets as appropriate for a particular group.)

Secret

I have been jumped into a gang.

Instructions:
1. Read this secret out loud as if it were your own secret.
2. Say how you would feel if this were your own secret.

Secret

I have smoked marijuana.

Instructions:
1. Read this secret out loud as if it were your own secret.
2. Say how you would feel if this were your own secret.

Secret

I have shoplifted.

Instructions:
1. Read this secret out loud as if it were your own secret.
2. Say how you would feel if this were your own secret.

Secret

I have been held back a grade.

Instructions:
1. Read this secret out loud as if it were your own secret.
2. Say how you would feel if this were your own secret.

Secret

I have been picked up by the police.

Instructions:
1. Read this secret out loud as if it were your own secret.
2. Say how you would feel if this were your own secret.

Secret

My parents are getting a divorce.

Instructions:
1. Read this secret out loud as if it were your own secret.
2. Say how you would feel if this were your own secret.

Secret

I cheat on tests.

Instructions:
1. Read this secret out loud as if it were your own secret.
2. Say how you would feel if this were your own secret.

Secret

My dad is in jail.

Instructions:
1. Read this secret out loud as if it were your own secret.
2. Say how you would feel if this were your own secret.

Secret

I have gotten drunk.

Instructions:
1. Read this secret out loud as if it were your own secret.
2. Say how you would feel if this were your own secret.

Secret

I sometimes feel like killing myself.

Instructions:
1. Read this secret out loud as if it were your own secret.
2. Say how you would feel if this were your own secret.

Secret

_____

Instructions:
1. Read this secret out loud as if it were your own secret.
2. Say how you would feel if this were your own secret.

Secret

_____

Instructions:
1. Read this secret out loud as if it were your own secret.
2. Say how you would feel if this were your own secret.

- -

Secret

_____

Instructions:
1. Read this secret out loud as if it were your own secret.
2. Say how you would feel if this were your own secret.

- -

Secret

_____

Instructions:
1. Read this secret out loud as if it were your own secret.
2. Say how you would feel if this were your own secret.

- -

Secret

_____

Instructions:
1. Read this secret out loud as if it were your own secret.
2. Say how you would feel if this were your own secret.

- -

Secret

_____

Instructions:
1. Read this secret out loud as if it were your own secret.
2. Say how you would feel if this were your own secret.

- -

Secret

_____

Instructions:
1. Read this secret out loud as if it were your own secret.
2. Say how you would feel if this were your own secret.

- -

Secrets for "Secret Pooling"—Low-Trust Version (Older Students)

(Includes blanks to fill in other secrets as appropriate for a particular group.)

Secret

I have been jumped into a gang.

Instructions:
1. Read this secret out loud as if it were your own secret.
2. Say how you would feel if this were your own secret.

- -

Secret

I have smoked marijuana.

Instructions:
1. Read this secret out loud as if it were your own secret.
2. Say how you would feel if this were your own secret.

- -

Secret

I have shoplifted.

Instructions:
1. Read this secret out loud as if it were your own secret.
2. Say how you would feel if this were your own secret.

- -

Secret

Girls: I got pregnant and had an abortion.
OR
Guys: I got my girlfriend pregnant and she had an abortion.

Instructions:
1. Read this secret out loud as if it were your own secret.
2. Say how you would feel if this were your own secret.

- -

Secret

I have been picked up by the police.

Instructions:
1. Read this secret out loud as if it were your own secret.
2. Say how you would feel if this were your own secret.

Secret

My parents are getting a divorce.

Instructions:
1. Read this secret out loud as if it were your own secret.
2. Say how you would feel if this were your own secret.

Secret

I have had sex.

Instructions:
1. Read this secret out loud as if it were your own secret.
2. Say how you would feel if this were your own secret.

Secret

My dad is in jail.

Instructions:
1. Read this secret out loud as if it were your own secret.
2. Say how you would feel if this were your own secret.

Secret

I have gotten drunk.

Instructions:
1. Read this secret out loud as if it were your own secret.
2. Say how you would feel if this were your own secret.

Secret

I sometimes feel like killing myself.

Instructions:
1. Read this secret out loud as if it were your own secret.
2. Say how you would feel if this were your own secret.

Secret

_____

Instructions:
1. Read this secret out loud as if it were your own secret.
2. Say how you would feel if this were your own secret.

Secret

_____

Instructions:
1. Read this secret out loud as if it were your own secret.
2. Say how you would feel if this were your own secret.

Secret

_____

Instructions:
1. Read this secret out loud as if it were your own secret.
2. Say how you would feel if this were your own secret.

Secret

_____

Instructions:
1. Read this secret out loud as if it were your own secret.
2. Say how you would feel if this were your own secret.

Secret

_____

Instructions:
1. Read this secret out loud as if it were your own secret.
2. Say how you would feel if this were your own secret.

Secret

_____

Instructions:
1. Read this secret out loud as if it were your own secret.
2. Say how you would feel if this were your own secret.

Module Two: Anger Management and Emotion Regulation Skills

Session One

1. Anger Thermometer (Appendix B-2a)
   a. Make a two-sided copy for each student (front side lists triggers and body feelings, and back side lists coping thoughts and coping actions)
2. Relaxation Log (Appendix B-2b)
   a. Make a copy for each student.

Session Two

1. Cool-Head Thoughts and Actions (Appendix B-2c)
   a. Make a copy for each student.
2. My Anger Journal (Appendix B-2d)
   a. Make a copy for each student.

Session Three

1. Hot-Head Cool-Head Game Cards (Appendix B-2e)
   a. Use different-colored cards or paper for Problems, Alternatives, and Consequences.
   b. Copy statements onto cards, remembering to use both sides lined up properly (e.g., Problem with the actual problems; Alternative with Hot and Cool; Consequence with Short-term for you, Long-term for others, etc.).
   c. Cut and, if possible, laminate cards.

Anger Thermometer

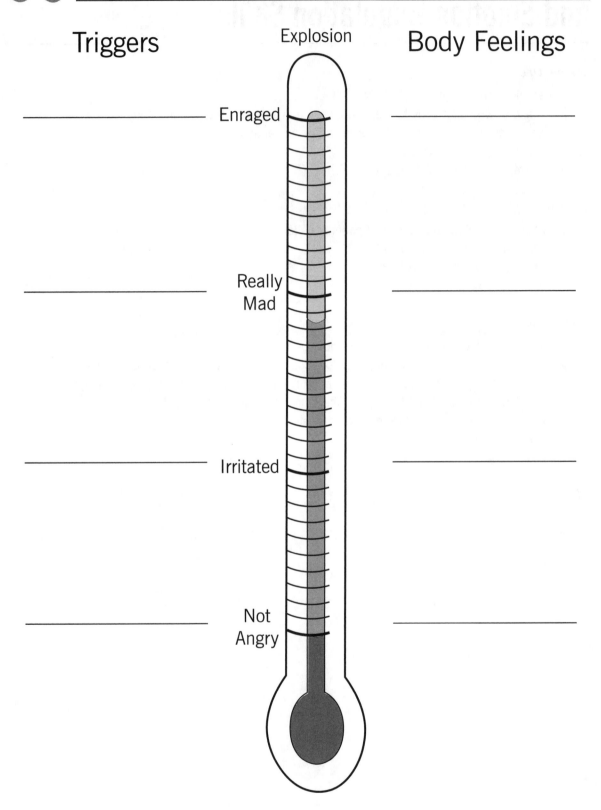

Triggers

Explosion

Body Feelings

Enraged

Really
Mad

Irritated

Not
Angry

APPENDIX B-2a. From Waterman and Walker (2009). Copyright by The Guilford Press.

Anger Thermometer

Coping Thoughts

Coping Actions

Explosion

Enraged

Really
Mad

Irritated

Not
Angry

APPENDIX B-2a. From Waterman and Walker (2009). Copyright by The Guilford Press.

Relaxation Log

Use this log when you practice the things we learned that can help you relax when you notice angry body feelings.

Use deep breathing at least twice this week and muscle relaxation at least once this week.

1. **When I Used Deep Breathing:**

   What triggered my anger was _____

   _____

   Where I felt it in my body: _____

   How angry I was: (circle how far up thermometer)   1/3   2/3   near top   at top

   Deep breathing helped (circle one)   a lot   some   not at all

   When I Used Deep Breathing:

   What triggered my anger was _____

   _____

   Where I felt it in my body: _____

   How angry I was: (circle how far up thermometer)   1/3   2/3   near top   at top

   Deep breathing helped (circle one)   a lot   some   not at all

2. **When I Used Muscle Relaxation:**

   What triggered my anger was _____

   _____

   Where I felt it in my body: _____

   How angry I was: (circle how far up thermometer)   1/3   2/3   near top   at top

   Muscle relaxation helped (circle one)   a lot   some   not at all

Cool-Head Thoughts and Actions

Cool-Head Thoughts

1. **Giving the benefit of the doubt**—alternative explanations

EXAMPLES:
- "He probably didn't mean for it to come out the way it sounded"
- "It was probably an accident"

2. **Calming self-talk**
- "Let me stop and think" (reduces acting impulsively)
- "Relax and breathe"
- "I can stay calm and bring the temperature down"

3. **Reframing the situation**

EXAMPLES:
- "This is an opportunity to really get to know him"
- "If he hadn't shut my locker, I might have forgotten that I needed my history book from in there"

Cool-Head Actions

1. **Relaxing yourself**
- Relax your muscles
- Breathe deeply and slowly
- Use your calming image

2. **Taking a time-out**
- Walk away
- Ignore the person
- Avoid going where person is

3. **Problem solving**
- Talk it out
- Look at all options and consequences of each option

4. **Seeking out help**
- Talk to a friend
- Ask a trusted teacher or parent to get involved
- Meet with a counselor or therapist

My Anger Journal

During the next week, notice two situations where you get angry.

Use cool-head thoughts and actions to deal with these situations, and write them down below.

If you used a hot-head response, write it down along with a possible cool-head thought and action.

1. What triggered my anger was _____

   _____

   Where I felt it in my body: _____

   How angry I was: (circle how far up thermometer)   1/3   2/3   near top   at top

   Cool-head responses I used: _____

   _____

2. What triggered my anger was _____

   _____

   Where I felt it in my body: _____

   How angry I was: (circle how far up thermometer)   1/3   2/3   near top   at top

   Cool-head responses I used: _____

   _____

If you used a hot-head response this week:

1. What triggered my anger was _____

   _____

   Where I felt it in my body: _____

   How angry I was: (circle how far up thermometer)   1/3   2/3   near top   at top

   Hot-headed responses I used: _____

   _____

   Cool-head thought I could have used: _____

   _____

   Cool-head action I could have used: _____

   _____

PROBLEM	**PROBLEM**
PROBLEM	**PROBLEM**
PROBLEM	**PROBLEM**
PROBLEM	**PROBLEM**
PROBLEM	**PROBLEM**
PROBLEM	**PROBLEM**
PROBLEM	**PROBLEM**
PROBLEM	**PROBLEM**

My brother or sister was bothering me	My mom or dad punished me for no reason
Another kid was picking on my friend	Another kid took something that belonged to me
My boyfriend/girlfriend went out with somebody else	Somebody cheated so that they would beat me
Another kid said something about my mother	My teacher was picking on me
Somebody made a racist comment to me	Another kid pushed me
Another kid stole money from me	I got blamed for something I did not do
My friend told someone a secret of mine	Another kid called me really bad names
My best friend went out with my girlfriend/boyfriend	My brother took money from me

ALTERNATIVE	ALTERNATIVE
ALTERNATIVE	ALTERNATIVE
ALTERNATIVE	ALTERNATIVE
ALTERNATIVE	ALTERNATIVE
ALTERNATIVE	ALTERNATIVE
ALTERNATIVE	ALTERNATIVE
ALTERNATIVE	ALTERNATIVE
ALTERNATIVE	ALTERNATIVE

✿ ✿ ✿ **HOT** ✿ ✿ ✿	✿ ✿ ✿ **HOT** ✿ ✿ ✿
✿ ✿ ✿ **HOT** ✿ ✿ ✿	✿ ✿ ✿ **HOT** ✿ ✿ ✿
✿ ✿ ✿ **HOT** ✿ ✿ ✿	✿ ✿ ✿ **HOT** ✿ ✿ ✿
✿ ✿ ✿ **HOT** ✿ ✿ ✿	✿ ✿ ✿ **HOT** ✿ ✿ ✿
❄ ❄ ❄ **COOL** ❄ ❄ ❄	❄ ❄ ❄ **COOL** ❄ ❄ ❄
❄ ❄ ❄ **COOL** ❄ ❄ ❄	❄ ❄ ❄ **COOL** ❄ ❄ ❄
❄ ❄ ❄ **COOL** ❄ ❄ ❄	❄ ❄ ❄ **COOL** ❄ ❄ ❄
❄ ❄ ❄ **COOL** ❄ ❄ ❄	❄ ❄ ❄ **COOL** ❄ ❄ ❄

APPENDIX B-2e. From Waterman and Walker (2009). Copyright by The Guilford Press.

CONSEQUENCE	CONSEQUENCE
CONSEQUENCE	CONSEQUENCE
CONSEQUENCE	CONSEQUENCE
CONSEQUENCE	CONSEQUENCE
CONSEQUENCE	CONSEQUENCE
CONSEQUENCE	CONSEQUENCE
CONSEQUENCE	CONSEQUENCE
CONSEQUENCE	CONSEQUENCE

SHORT-TERM FOR YOU	LONG-TERM FOR YOU
SHORT-TERM FOR YOU	LONG-TERM FOR YOU
SHORT-TERM FOR YOU	LONG-TERM FOR YOU
SHORT-TERM FOR YOU	LONG-TERM FOR YOU
SHORT-TERM FOR OTHERS	LONG-TERM FOR OTHERS
SHORT-TERM FOR OTHERS	LONG-TERM FOR OTHERS
SHORT-TERM FOR OTHERS	LONG-TERM FOR OTHERS
SHORT-TERM FOR OTHERS	LONG-TERM FOR OTHERS

Module Three: Ethnic Identity and Anti-Prejudice

Session One

1. Labels for "Labeling Game" (Appendix B-3)
   a. Copy one adjective onto each label with an adhesive backing.
   b. Use different labels if they are more appropriate for your particular group.
   c. Make one label for each student.
   d. Make one set of labels for each group.

Labels for "Labeling Game"

GOOD STUDENT	**BOSSY**
LAZY	**TEACHER'S PET**
FRIENDLY	**GOOD ATHLETE**
SHY	**SNOBBY**
SEXY	**HELPFUL**
ANGRY	**LONER**
PLAYER	**BIG MOUTH**

Module Four:
Educational Aspirations

Session One

1. Education and Career Ladder (Appendix B-4a)
    a. Make one copy for each student.
2. My Goals/My Strategies for Success (Appendix B-4b)
    a. Make one copy for each student (front side is "My Goals" and back side is "My Strategies for Success").
    b. Bring extra goal sheets to Sessions Two and Three since some students may not remember to bring them back.

Session Two

1. My Goals/My Strategies for Success (Appendix B-4b)
    a. Bring extras to field trip in case some students need another one.
2. College Search/Scholarship websites (Appendix B-4c)
    a. Make one copy for each student (front side is college websites and back side is scholarship websites).

Session Three

1. My Goals/My Strategies for Success (Appendix B-4b)
    a. Make one copy for each student (front and back) since some students may not remember to bring back the sheets given out in Session One.
2. Student Strategies for Success (Appendix B-4d)
    a. Make one copy for each student.

Education and Career Ladder

Name: _____

Career goal: _____

Steps past high school I need to reach my career goal: _____

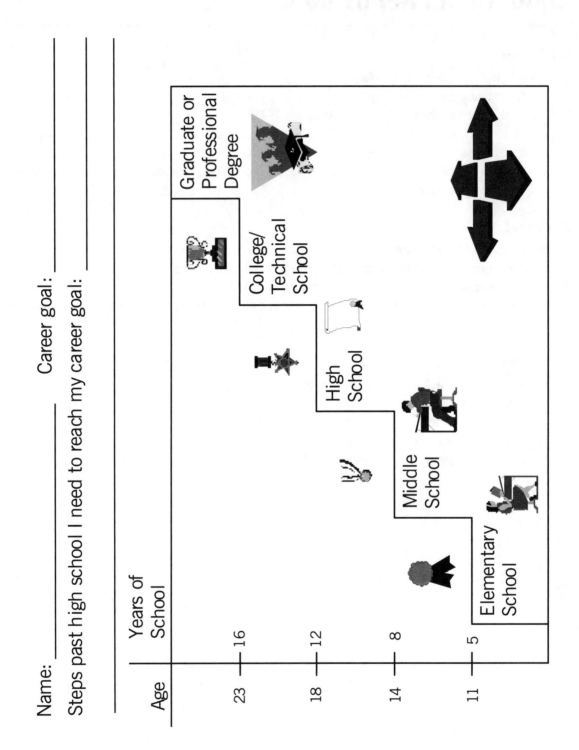

APPENDIX B-4a. From Waterman and Walker (2009). Copyright by The Guilford Press.

 **My Goals**

I will set goals for myself and work toward those goals.

My goals for this school year are:

1. _____

_____

_____

_____

2. _____

_____

_____

_____

3. _____

_____

_____

_____

4. _____

_____

_____

_____

My Strategies for Success

To achieve my goals, I will use the following strategies for success:

In class, I will:

1. _____
2. _____

To be organized, I will:

1. _____
2. _____

When doing homework, I will:

1. _____
2. _____

To reward myself for a job well done, I will:

1. _____
2. _____

_____   _____

Signature   Date

College Search Websites

The following websites have information that can help in your search for college information.

- *www.collegeboard.com*—On this very comprehensive website you will find information on planning for college, taking the tests (SAT I, SAT II, PSAT, and AP), finding the right college, getting into college, and paying for college.
- *www.review.com*—This Princeton Review site offers not only a college search opportunity, but information on better scores, better schools, aid comparison calculators, career assessment, and general advice.
- *www.usnews.com*—This site links to a best college database and has information on graduate schools, financial aid, rankings, and careers.
- *www.finaid.com*—This site provides good general information on financial aid. It also contains at least four free scholarship searches for different student groups.
- *www.fastaid.com*—A source of financial aid information and a free scholarship search database.
- *www.allaboutcollege.com*—College websites and chat rooms are available here, in addition to information on study abroad programs, test preparation, financial aid, and job search.
- *www.chronicle.com/stats/tuition*—This site will allow you to do a tuition and fee search.

Scholarship Websites

Regardless of your financial situation, there may be one or more scholarships available to you. Scholarships are given by individual colleges, organizations, companies, and community groups. If you are serious about finding money for college, you should be willing to spend some time on your scholarship search.

Remember: Never spend more than a postage stamp to get information about scholarships!

GENERAL SCHOLARSHIP WEBSITES

- *www.collegeboard.com*—This site includes a scholarship search database known as the Fund Finder with 3,300 national, state, public, and private sources. How to spot a scam is also mentioned.

- *www.fastaid.com*—The world's largest and oldest private-sector scholarship database. You will find scholarships here that you won't find anyplace else.

- *www.wiredscholar.com*—Voted Forbes' best website for college information, this site will give you knowledge on types of scholarships, requirements, tips, and scams in addition to a scholarship search.

- *www.fastweb.com*—With this database, the student registers and is assigned a mailbox on the site where information on new scholarship opportunities is posted. The database contains over 500,000 private-sector scholarships, fellowships, grants, and loans. Probably one of the best search sites available.

- *www.finaid.com*—This site will run a scholarship search in the specific areas of art, biology, computer science, engineering, journalism, and nursing.

Student Strategies for Success

IN CLASS

- Be on time to class.
- Bring all necessary supplies to class (book, pen, paper, etc.).
- Take notes in class.
- Move your seat closer to the front and/or away from friends if you become distracted easily.
- Ask for extra time on tests or quizzes if you need it (it never hurts to ask!).

ORGANIZATION

- Keep a separate binder or folder for each class; have a special place to keep homework assignments that need to be turned in.
- Keep a planner and write down all assignments and test dates.
- Clarify the assignment with the teacher after class if you are confused.

HOMEWORK

- Set aside a specific time each day to do homework.
- Find a quiet, well-lit place to do your homework.
- Pace yourself—don't leave big assignments until the last day.

OTHER HINTS

- Ask your counselor for a tutor if you need extra help.
- Reward yourself for a job well done!

Module Five: Peer Pressure, Bullying, and Gangs

Session One

1. Resisting Peer Pressure (Appendix B-5a)
   a. Make one copy for each student.

Session Two

1. "Is It OK?" (Appendix B-5b)
   a. Make one copy for each student.
2. Aggressor, Victim, Bystander (Appendix B-5c)
   a. Make one copy for each student.
3. Three Sets of Footprints for Aggressor, Victim, and Bystander (Appendix B-5d)

Resisting Peer Pressure

Situation where I was pressured:

_____

_____

_____

_____

I resisted!!!!!!
Strategies I used:

I gave in . . .
The reason is:

Situation where I was pressured:

_____

_____

_____

_____

I resisted!!!!!!
Strategies I used:

I gave in . . .
The reason is:

Name: _____

"Is It OK?"

Answer the following by circling the appropriate number (1 = you rarely do this, up to 6 = you do this often). You will not have to turn this paper in, so please answer honestly.

How often do you . . .

	Rarely		Sometimes			Often
1. Spread rumors.	1	2	3	4	5	6
2. Tell someone's secret.	1	2	3	4	5	6
3. Talk on the Internet about someone.	1	2	3	4	5	6
4. Roll your eyes when someone walks by.	1	2	3	4	5	6
5. Whisper in front of someone.	1	2	3	4	5	6
6. Pick on someone for how he/she looks.	1	2	3	4	5	6
7. Exclude someone from your group.	1	2	3	4	5	6
8. Threaten not to spend time with someone.	1	2	3	4	5	6
9. Take someone's things from him/her.	1	2	3	4	5	6
10. Intentionally ignore someone.	1	2	3	4	5	6

Aggressor, Victim, Bystander

What to Do . . .

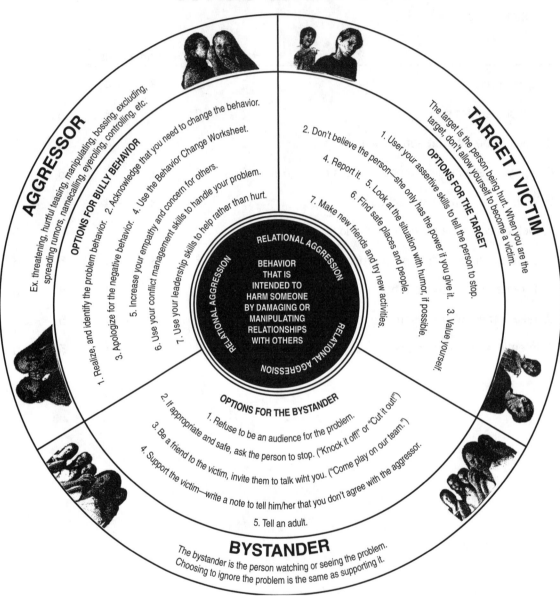

AGGRESSOR

Ex. threatening, hurtful teasing, manipulating, bossing, excluding, spreading rumors, namecalling, eyeroling, controlling, etc.

OPTIONS FOR BULLY BEHAVIOR

1. Realize, and identify the problem behavior.
2. Acknowledge that you need to change the behavior.
3. Apologize for the negative behavior.
4. Use the Behavior Change Worksheet.
5. Increase your empathy and concern for others.
6. Use your conflict management skills to handle your problem.
7. Use your leadership skills to help rather than hurt.

TARGET / VICTIM

The target is the person being hurt. When you are the target, don't allow yourself to become a victim.

OPTIONS FOR THE TARGET

1. User your assertive skills to tell the person to stop.
2. Don't believe the person—she only has the power if you give it.
3. Value yourself.
4. Report it.
5. Look at the situation with humor, if possible.
6. Find safe places and people.
7. Make new friends and try new activities.

RELATIONAL AGGRESSION

BEHAVIOR THAT IS INTENDED TO HARM SOMEONE BY DAMAGING OR MANIPULATING RELATIONSHIPS WITH OTHERS

RELATIONAL AGGRESSION

RELATIONAL AGGRESSION

OPTIONS FOR THE BYSTANDER

1. Refuse to be an audience for the problem.
2. If appropriate and safe, ask the person to stop. ("Knock it off!" or "Cut it out!")
3. Be a friend to the victim, invite them to talk wiht you. ("Come play on our team.")
4. Support the victim—write a note to tell him/her that you don't agree with the aggressor.
5. Tell an adult.

BYSTANDER

The bystander is the person watching or seeing the problem. Choosing to ignore the problem is the same as supporting it.

Three Sets of Footprints
for Aggressor, Victim, and Bystander

Aggressor

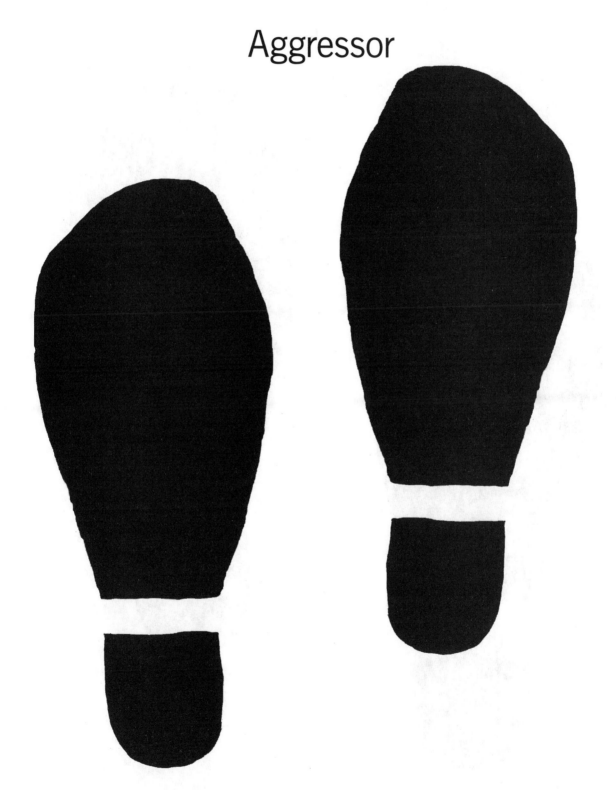

Victim

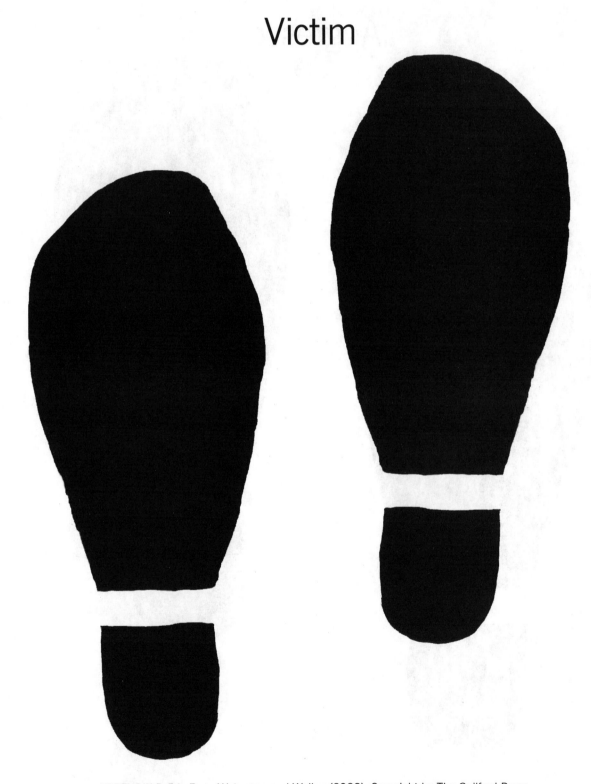

APPENDIX B-5d. From Waterman and Walker (2009). Copyright by The Guilford Press.

Bystander

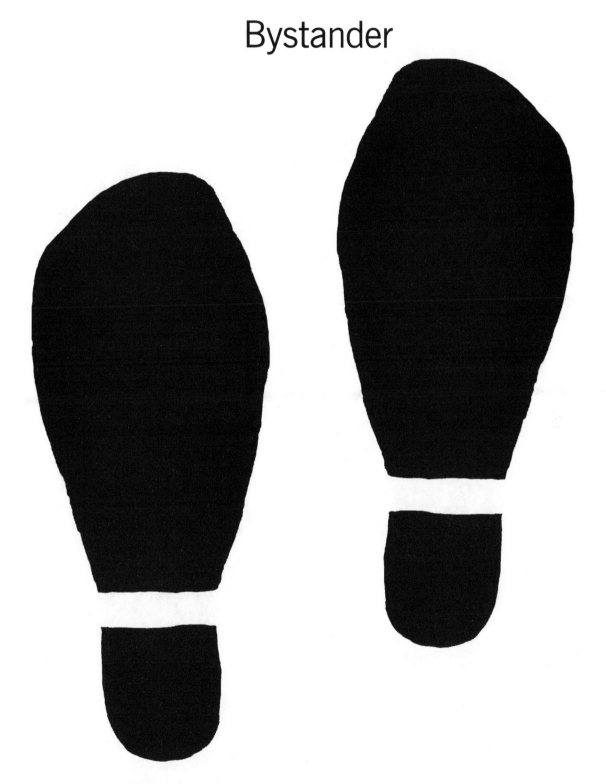

APPENDIX B-5d. From Waterman and Walker (2009). Copyright by The Guilford Press.

Module Six: Male–Female Relationships

Session Two

1. Relationship Rights Cards (Appendix B-6a)
   a. Make two copies (one for the girls and one for the boys) of both the healthy and the unhealthy relationship attributes on card stock or heavy paper.
   b. Cut up the cards so each attribute is on a separate card.
   c. Shuffle together each set of cards so that each "deck" contains cards with each healthy and each unhealthy relationship attribute.
   d. When playing the Relationship Rights game, give one shuffled deck to the boys' group and the other to the girls' group.
2. Dating Dos and Don'ts (Appendix B6-b)
   a. Make one copy for each student.

Session Three

1. Survey of Relationship Attitudes (Appendix B-6c)
   a. Make one copy for each student.
   b. Score according to the guidelines in Appendix A-6.
   c. Keep questionnaires and readminister as part of the post-test when groups are completed.

Relationship Rights Cards

Good/Healthy Relationships

CARING	INDIVIDUALITY
COMMUNICATION	LISTENING
COMPROMISE	SUPPORTIVENESS
BEING EQUAL	TRUST
EMPATHY	WIN/WIN
FAIRNESS	MUTUAL RESPECT
HONESTY	OPENNESS

Bad/Unhealthy Relationships

BLAME	MANIPULATION
CONTROL	PUT-DOWNS
DISHONESTY	SEXISM
FEAR	SHOVING/HITTING
HARASSMENT	SULKING
INSECURITY	WITHDRAWAL
JEALOUSY	WIN/LOSE

APPENDIX B-6a. From Waterman and Walker (2009). Copyright by The Guilford Press.

Dating Dos and Don'ts

1. Do not call a guy/girl more than two times in a row. He/she may get annoyed. Also, relationships should be 50/50.

2. If a guy/girl really wants to talk to you, he/she will find a way.

3. If you flirt with other guys/girls to make someone jealous, it will backfire.

4. If your boyfriend/girlfriend ignores you or flirts with others in front of you, he/she is either: (a) really rude, or (b) not that into you.

5. Do not argue or break up with your boyfriend/girlfriend via e-mail, text messaging, or in a note. Do it in person.

6. Do not have friends act as go-betweens in your relationship.

7. If you gossip about other people and their relationships—especially in e-mails or text messages—it will come back to bite you. What goes around comes around.

8. If you kiss/make out with multiple people within a short span of time, you will likely get a bad reputation. Girls may get a different reputation than boys.

9. Some BIG red flags: (a) you have to sneak around to meet up with your boyfriend/girlfriend, (b) he/she uses drugs or deals them, (c) he/she already has a kid, (d) he/she has been in jail, (e) he/she is more than 2 years older than you. These "red flags" make a romantic relationship very complicated, especially during the teen years. Avoid these relationships.

10. If you are having sex, there's a good chance one or more of the following *will* happen: (a) you will get pregnant, (b) you will get a sexually transmitted disease, and/or (c) you will get a broken heart.

Above all, respect yourself and others, and you will be respected.
Remember, you deserve the best!

Survey of Relationship Attitudes

Listed below are statements about males, females, and relationships. Read each statement and indicate whether you strongly disagree, sort of disagree, sort of agree, or strongly agree with each statement.

Please circle your gender.   MALE   FEMALE

1. In a relationship, guys need affection and companionship less than girls do.

   | Strongly Disagree | Sort of Disagree | Sort of Agree | Strongly Agree |

2. Girls who dress conservatively are less willing to have sex than girls who wear tight-fitting, low-cut clothes.

   | Strongly Disagree | Sort of Disagree | Sort of Agree | Strongly Agree |

3. The media accurately portrays the roles of males and females.

   | Strongly Disagree | Sort of Disagree | Sort of Agree | Strongly Agree |

4. It is easier for girls than for guys to talk openly about their feelings.

   | Strongly Disagree | Sort of Disagree | Sort of Agree | Strongly Agree |

5. If a guy takes a girl out on an expensive date, he can expect the girl to show him some affection in return.

   | Strongly Disagree | Sort of Disagree | Sort of Agree | Strongly Agree |

6. Equality and a win-win attitude are important qualities in a romantic relationship.

   | Strongly Disagree | Sort of Disagree | Sort of Agree | Strongly Agree |

7. Guys worry less about rejection in relationships than girls do.

   | Strongly Disagree | Sort of Disagree | Sort of Agree | Strongly Agree |

8. Males and females are portrayed in unhealthy, stereotypic ways on TV and in magazines.

   | Strongly Disagree | Sort of Disagree | Sort of Agree | Strongly Agree |

9. Guys only want one thing from girls.

   | Strongly Disagree | Sort of Disagree | Sort of Agree | Strongly Agree |

10. It is acceptable for a guy to tell his girlfriend to whom she is allowed to talk and to be very jealous if she talks to other boys.

    | Strongly Disagree | Sort of Disagree | Sort of Agree | Strongly Agree |

Module Seven: Exposure to Violence and Posttraumatic Stress Reactions

Session Two

1. Posttraumatic Stress Reactions (Appendix B-7a)
   a. Make one copy for each student (two-sided handout—Posttraumatic Stress Reactions on front, Coping Strategies on back).
2. Disks for Posttraumatic Stress Reactions (Appendix B-7b)
   a. Make 50 disks for each of the three categories.
   b. Use different-colored paper for each of the three categories; suggested colors: green for "reexperiencing," orange for "avoiding," purple for "edge"—but feel free to be creative.

Posttraumatic Stress Reactions

■ Happen after a very frightening event.

■ Very common in students who have been exposed to violence at home, at school, or in the neighborhood.

■ Can happen if you are the victim of violence or if you see the violence.

■ Are *normal* reactions to *abnormal* situations.

■ Three types of reactions:

1. *Reexperiencing the trauma.*
   a. Memories or thoughts of the trauma suddenly popping into your mind.
   b. Dreaming about what happened over and over.
   c. Feeling that the traumatic event is happening again, like flashbacks.
   d. Getting really nervous or uncomfortable if you go near where it happened.

2. *Avoiding the trauma.*
   a. Avoiding people, places, or activities that remind you of the trauma.
   b. Feeling cut off from other people or numb, where you don't feel anything.
   c. Being less interested in things you liked to do before the trauma.
   d. Thinking you won't have a career or a family or that you will die young.

3. *Feeling more on edge.*
   a. Having trouble falling asleep or staying asleep.
   b. Being irritable or getting angry really easily.
   c. Getting distracted and having trouble paying attention.
   d. Being super-aware of where danger might be or startling really easily.

Coping Strategies for Posttraumatic Stress Reactions

1. Thought stopping

2. Distraction (exercising, reading, playing a game)

3. Positive imagery

4. Relaxation (muscle relaxation, deep breathing)

5. Talking to a safe person (parent, teacher, counselor)

Reexperiencing

Reexperiencing

Reexperiencing

Reexperiencing

Reexperiencing

Reexperiencing

Reexperiencing

Reexperiencing

Reexperiencing

Reexperiencing

Reexperiencing

Reexperiencing

Reexperiencing

Reexperiencing

Reexperiencing

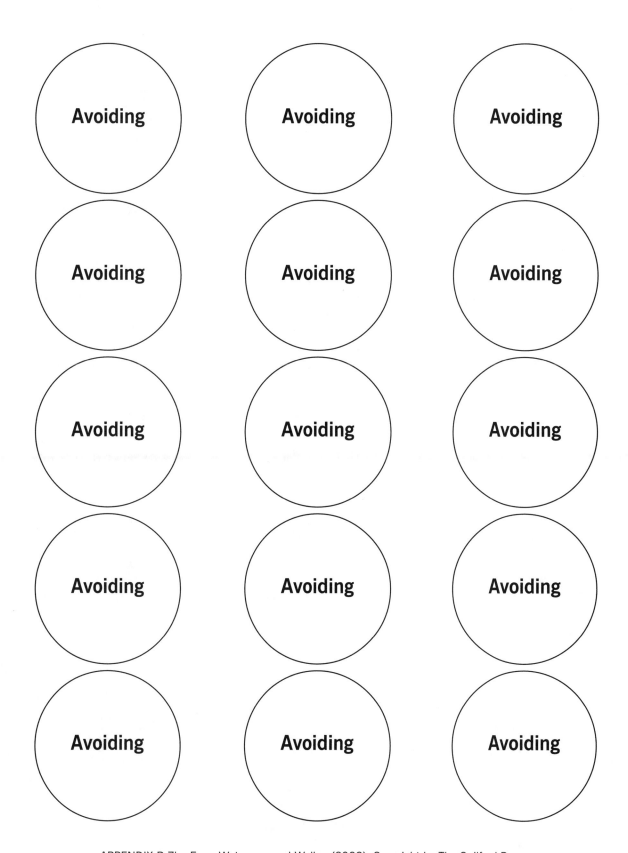

APPENDIX B-7b. From Waterman and Walker (2009). Copyright by The Guilford Press.

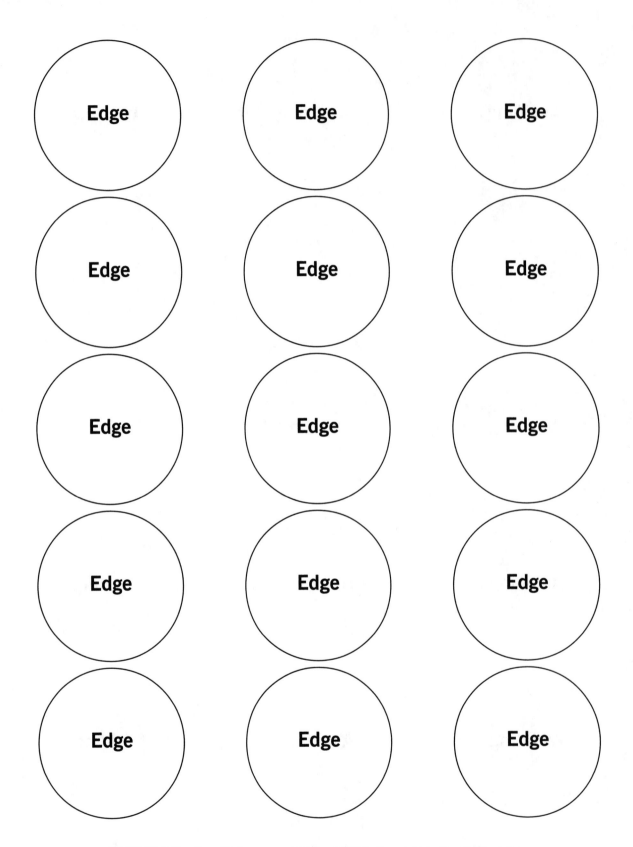

APPENDIX B-7b. From Waterman and Walker (2009). Copyright by The Guilford Press.

Termination Session: The Party

1. "What I Like about You" (Appendix B-8a)
   a. Copy on colored paper.
   b. Bring one sheet for each student.
   c. Write down what is said when group members share something they like about each member.
2. Certificate (Appendix B-8b)
   a. Bring one for each student.
   b. Fill out the information (e.g., student's name) before the beginning of the last session.
   c. If available, put gold stickers on the certificate.
   d. The certificate shown here can be modified or replaced with one developed by the group leaders.

"What I Like about You"

Name: _____

Group member	What I like about you is . . .
_____	_____
	_____
_____	_____
	_____
_____	_____
	_____
_____	_____
	_____
_____	_____
	_____
_____	_____
	_____
_____	_____
	_____
_____	_____
	_____
_____	_____
	_____
_____	_____
	_____

Certificate

Certificate of Achievement

This certificate is conferred upon:

_____

in honor of successful completion of the SPARK Program

this _____ day of _____, _____.

_____
Group leader

_____
Group leader

APPENDIX B-8b. From Waterman and Walker (2009). Copyright by The Guilford Press.

APPENDIX C

Sample Materials in Spanish for Beginning SPARK Groups

Consentimiento de Padres para Participar en SPARK

Que Son los Grupos SPARK?

Los grupos de consejería SPARK son para estudiantes que han sido identificados por un consejero escolar o algún maestro como estudiantes con el potencial de trabajar cooperativamente en un grupo y quienes podrían beneficiarse de este tipo de experiencia. Para participar en los grupos de SPARK, los estudiantes perderán un período de clase una vez a la semana por un total de 15 a 20 semanas. En las sesiones de grupo se cubrirán los siguientes temas: desarrollo de confianza, manejo del enojo, resolución de problemas, la importancia de la educación para el futuro, orgullo étnico o racial, cómo enfrentar la discriminación, cómo evitar la presión de grupo y las pandillas, relaciones entre hombres y mujeres, las relaciones familiares, y cómo enfrentar la violencia en la comunidad. Actividades específicas serán presentadas en cada sesión y se le pedirá a los estudiantes que compartan sus propios sentimientos y experiencias.

Los estudiantes serán entrevistados antes y después de participar en los grupos. La entrevista contiene preguntas sobre los sentimientos, actitudes, creencias, experiencias, tensiones y comportamientos problemáticos de los estudiantes.

Confidencialidad

Las respuestas de los estudiantes a las preguntas de la entrevista y su participación en los grupos SPARK serán confidenciales, excepto lo requerido por ley. El privilegio de confidencialidad no se extiende a información sobre abuso sexual, emocional, o físico del niño, o a negligencia de niño. Si el líder de SPARK tiene sospecha razonable o recibe tal información, es deber del líder reportarlo a las autoridades. También, si el líder de SPARK cree que un estudiante está a riesgo significativo de hacerse daño a sí mismo/a, el líder tendrá que mantener la seguridad del estudiante informando al padre o guardián y al consejero de la escuela.

Participación y Retiro

Participación en la entrevista y en los grupos de SPARK es voluntaria. Si un estudiante no participa, no habrá consecuencias negativas en la relación con la escuela o en tratamiento de clase. Puede contactar al líder de SPARK al teléfono al fondo si tiene preguntas o preocupaciones sobre la entrevista o los grupos.

Doy permiso para que mi hijo/a participe en los grupos SPARK, tal como están descritos aquí. Con firmar este formulario, doy reconocimiento de que he recibido una copia del formulario de consentimiento.

_____   _____
Firma del Padre y Fecha   **Nombre del Estudiante**

_____   _____
Líder de SPARK   **Teléfono del Líder de SPARK**

Consentimiento del Estudiante para Participar en SPARK

Sé me está pidiendo que participe en los grupos de consejería SPARK. Esto significa que faltaré a un período de clase una vez por semana por un total de 15 a 20 semanas. En las sesiones de grupo, los temas de los que se hablará incluyen: establecimiento de confianza, manejo del enojo, resolución de problemas, la importancia de la educación para el futuro, orgullo étnico o racial, cómo enfrentar la discriminación, cómo evitar la presión de los amigos(as) y las pandillas, relaciones entre hombres y mujeres, las relaciones familiares, y cómo enfrentar la violencia comunitaria. Actividades específicas son presentadas en cada sesión y se motiva y facilita que los estudiantes compartan sus propios sentimientos y experiencias.

Sé me pedirá que sea parte de una breve entrevista ahora y otra al final del semestre. Durante la entrevista, sé me pedirá que hable de aspectos de mi vida. Puedo no responder a cualquier pregunta que yo no desee responder y puedo parar la entrevista en cualquier momento. Si me siento mal al final de la entrevista, el entrevistador me dará el número de teléfono de un consejero con el que pueda platicar acerca de cualquier problema que yo pudiera tener.

Lo que diga durante la entrevista y los grupos de SPARK será confidencial. Esto quiere decir que lo que yo diga no será compartido con mis padres, maestros(as), o amigos(as). Los líderes de SPARK no le dirán a nadie lo que les diga sin mi permiso a menos de que sea algo peligroso para mí o para otra persona. Si les digo que alguien me está lastimando o me ha lastimado, el líder tendrá que decirle a las personas que son responsables de proteger a los niños y adolescentes para asegurarse que no estoy en peligro. Si les digo que estoy pensando en hacerme daño, le tendrán que decir a mis padres y al consejero de la escuela para que me mantenga fuera de peligro.

Mis padres y yo podemos llamar al líder de SPARK si tenemos alguna pregunta acerca de los grupos de consejería o de la entrevista. He leído este documento y lo entiendo.

_____
Firma del Estudiante

_____
Líder de SPARK

_____
Fecha

_____
Teléfono del Líder de SPARK

Entrevista Pre-Grupo y Post-Grupo

Nombre del Estudiante: _____   **Etnicidad:** _____   **Sexo:** _____

Administrado por: _____   **Fecha:** _____

Círcula uno: **Pre-grupo**   **Post-grupo**

Section I: Background Information

Demographics

Voy a empezar por hacerte unas preguntas generales.

1.   ¿En qué año/grado estás? _____

2.   ¿Cual es tu fecha de nacimiento? _____   ¿Así que tienes _____ años?

3.   ¿Con quién vives? (listar) _____

    ¿Hay alguien más que vive en tu casa contigo? (listar) _____

Lista de hermanos/as:	Hermano/hermana	Edad	¿Vive contigo?
	_____	_____	S / N
	_____	_____	S / N
	_____	_____	S / N

4.   ¿Así que no vives con tu (mamá, papá, mamá y papá)? ¿Por qué? (circula M para mamá, P para papá)

Divorcio	M	D	Padre/madre en la cárcel	M	D
Separación	M	D	Otro (específica) _____		
Falleció	M	D	No sé		
Nunca se casaron	M	D			

Family Stressors

Te voy a leer una lista de cosas que algunas veces le pasan a la gente de tu edad. Para cada una de estas cosas, dime si te han pasado en el último año. En caso de que sí te haya pasado algo este último año, quiero que me digas qué tan difícil fue para ti cuando esto pasó. *(Show response scale 1.)*

No	Si			
1	2	3	4
no difícil	me molesta	estresante	muy estresante

Durante el último año . . .

1. Uno de mis papás empezó a trabajar o dejó de trabajar.	N	1	2	3	4
2. Mis papás se separaron o divorciaron.	N	1	2	3	4
3. Me peleé más de lo normal con mis papás.	N	1	2	3	4
4. Mis papás se pelearon mucho más de lo normal entre ellos.	N	1	2	3	4
5. Alguien en mi familia tuvo problemas con drogas o con alcohol.	N	1	2	3	4
6. Alguien importante para mí fue a la cárcel.	N	1	2	3	4

Community Violence Exposure[†]

Que tan frecuentemente te han pasado cualquiera de las cosas siguientes en tu casa, vecindario, o en tu escuela? *(Show response scale 2.)*

0	1	2	3
Nunca	A Veces	Frecuentemente	Muy Frecuentemente

1. ¿Alguien te ha dicho *a ti* que te iba a herir o hacer daño?	0	1	2	3
2. ¿Has visto que *a otra persona* le están diciendo que le van a herir o hacer daño?	0	1	2	3
3. ¿Has sido cacheteado(a), golpeado(a), o recibiste puñetazos *tu*?	0	1	2	3
4. ¿Has *visto* a otra persona siendo cacheteada, golpeada, o recibiendo puñetazos?	0	1	2	3
5. ¿Te han dado una paliza *a ti*?	0	1	2	3
6. ¿Has *visto* a otra persona recibiendo una paliza?	0	1	2	3
7. ¿Has sido atacado(a) o apuñalado(a) con un cuchillo *tu*?	0	1	2	3
8. ¿Has visto *a otra persona* siendo atacada o apuñalada con un cuchillo?	0	1	2	3
9. ¿Te han disparado o herido *a ti* con una pistola **real**?	0	1	2	3
10. ¿Has visto que le disparen o hieran *a otra persona* con una pistola **real**?	0	1	2	3

[†]Adapted with permission from Singer (1997).

Section II: Other Information Relevant to SPARK Groups

Educational Aspirations

Ahora, te voy a hacer unas preguntas acerca de la escuela. *(Show response scale 3.)*

1	2	3	4	5
Mucho menos que otros niños	Menos que otros niños	Igual que otros niños	Más que otros niños	Mucho más que otros niños

1. ¿Comparado a otros niños en tu escuela, qué tan probable es que termines high school?_____

2. ¿Comparado a otros niños en tu escuela, qué tan probable es que vayas a la universidad? _____

3. ¿Comparado a otros niños en tu escuela, para ti, que tan importante es que te vaya bien? _____

Adjustment

Te voy a leer algunas cosas que les pasan a algunos muchachos de tu edad. Por favor dime qué tan seguido te ha pasado cada una de estas cosas. *(Show response scale 2.)*

0	1	2	3
Nunca	A Veces	Frecuentemente	Muy Frecuentemente

	0	1	2	3
1. Sentirte solo.	0	1	2	3
2. Recordar cosas que no quieres recordar.	0	1	2	3
3. Tener dificultad para concentrarte en la escuela o en casa.	0	1	2	3
4. Querer quebrar/romper cosas.	0	1	2	3
5. Querer lastimarte a ti mismo.*	0	1	2	3
6. Tener miedo.	0	1	2	3
7. Sentirte triste o infeliz.	0	1	2	3
8. No poder dejar de pensar en cosas malas que te pasaron.	0	1	2	3
9. Tener dificultad para dormir.	0	1	2	3
10. Querer gritarle a la gente.	0	1	2	3
11. Querer matarte.*	0	1	2	3
12. Tratar de no sentir nada (emociones malas).	0	1	2	3
13. Preocuparte de cosas.	0	1	2	3
14. Sentirte diferente de todos.	0	1	2	3

*Mark items 5 and 11 for follow-up at end of interview.

Anger Experience and Expression[†]

Multidimensional School Anger Inventory—Revised (MSAI-R) (Smith & Furlong, 2008)

Anger Experience Subscale *(Show response scale 4.)*

1	2	3	4
No estaría enojado para nada	Estaría un poco enojado	Estaría bastante enojado	Estaría furioso

1. No te fijaste que alguien ha puesto un chicle en tu asiento y te sientas ahí.	1	2	3	4
2. En el colegio, dos alumnos más grandes que tú quitan algo tuyo y juega contigo a "quítamelo si puedes."	1	2	3	4

APPENDIX C-3. From Waterman and Walker (2009). Copyright by The Guilford Press.

3. Le dices a tu profesor(a) que no te sientes bien, pero no te cree.   1   2   3   4

4. Alguien en tu salón se pasó de listo, así que toda la clase se tiene que quedar después de la salida.   1   2   3   4

5. Pides permiso para ir al baño y el profesor(ra) te dice "NO."   1   2   3   4

6. Vas a tu escritorio y te das cuenta que alguien ha robado algunos de tus útiles escolares.   1   2   3   4

7. Alguien en el salón le chismeó al profesor algo que tu hacías.   1   2   3   4

8. Te mandan con el director aunque otros alumnos se han portado peor que tú.   1   2   3   4

9. El preferido del profesor(ra) hace todos los mandados especiales o tiene privilegios en la clase.   1   2   3   4

10. Alguien se mete delante de ti en la fila de formación.   1   2   3   4

11. Estás tratando de hacer tu trabajo en el colegio y alguien golpea tu escritorio a propósito y te equivocas.   1   2   3   4

12. Estudias mucho para un examen y aún así te sacas baja calificación.   1   2   3   4

13. Alguien te llama con un apodo ofensivo.   1   2   3   4

Anger Expression Subscale *(Show response scale 2.)*

0	1	2	3
Nunca	A Veces	Frecuentemente	Muy Frecuentemente

¿Cuando te enojas en el colegio, qué haces?

1. Cuando estoy enojado(a), me desquito con alguien que esté a mi alrededor.   0   1   2   3

2. Si estoy enojado(a), lo converso con otra persona.   0   1   2   3

3. Cuando estoy enojado(a) (cuando me da coraje), pienso en algo diferente.   0   1   2   3

4. Cuando estoy enojado(a), odio a todo el mundo.   0   1   2   3

5. Cuando estoy enojado(a) en el colegio, comparto lo que siento con alguien.   0   1   2   3

6. Cuando me enojo, rompo cosas.   0   1   2   3

7. Antes de que explote, trato de entender por qué me pasó esto.   0   1   2   3

8. Cuando estoy molesto(a), me tranquilizo leyendo, escribiendo, pintando o con otra actividad similar.   0   1   2   3

9. Me enojo tanto que me quiero hacer daño.   0   1   2   3

10. Si algo me hace enojar, trato de encontrar algo chistoso en ello.   0   1   2   3

11. Cuando me enojo, saco mis sentimientos a través de algún tipo de actividad física, como correr, jugar, etc.   0   1   2   3

12. Si me enojo, hago berrinches.	0	1	2	3
13. Cuando estoy enojado(a) (cuando me da coraje), lo disimulo sonriendo o pretendo que no estoy enojado.	0	1	2	3
14. Golpeo algo cuando estoy enojado(a) (cuando me da coraje).	0	1	2	3
15. Cuando obtengo una mala calificación, invento una forma de vengarme del profesor.	0	1	2	3
16. Cuando estoy enojado(a) con el profesor, hago bromas en la clase para que se rían mis amigos.	0	1	2	3
17. Cuando obtengo una mala calificación en un examen, lo rompo en pedacitos.	0	1	2	3

†Reprinted with permission from the authors.

Self-Esteem

Te voy a leer algunas frases y quiero que me digas que tanto estás de acuerdo con cada declaración. *(Show response scale 5.)*

1	2	3	4
Muy de Acuerdo	De Acuerdo	Desacuerdo	Muy Desacuerdo

1. Creo que soy una persona valiosa, por lo menos igual de valiosa que los demás. _____
2. Creo que tengo bastantes cualidades buenas. _____
3. En general, tiendo a pensar que soy un fracaso. _____
4. Puedo hacer las cosas tan bien como la demás gente. _____
5. Siento que no tengo mucho de qué sentirme orgulloso. _____
6. Tengo una buena actitud hacia mí mismo. _____
7. En general, estoy satisfecho conmigo mismo. _____
8. Me gustaría respetarme más. _____
9. Me siento inútil algunas veces. _____
10. A veces pienso que no soy bueno para nada. _____

Ethnic Pride

En un minuto te voy a leer unas frases diferentes pero primero quiero hacerte una pregunta. ¿Qué palabra usarías para describir tu grupo étnico o grupo racial? _____
(If subject has trouble, say: "Martin Luther King es Negro o Afro-Americano . . ., Cesar Chávez es Latino o Hispano")

Bueno, entonces para estas frases, cada vez que diga "grupo étnico" lo que quiero decir es _____. Quiero que me digas que tan de acuerdo estás con cada frase. *(Keep response scale 5.)*

1	2	3	4
Muy de Acuerdo	De Acuerdo	Desacuerdo	Muy Desacuerdo

1. Estoy contento(a) que soy (grupo étnico indicado arriba)   _____

2. No me siento miembro(a) de mi grupo étnico/racial.   _____

3. Me siento muy orgulloso(a) de mi grupo étnico/racial y todo lo que mi grupo ha logrado.   _____

4. No me siento muy unido(a) a mi grupo étnico/racial.   _____

5. Me siento bien hacia mi cultura o raíces étnicas.   _____

Peer Attachment

Te voy a leer preguntas sobre tus relaciones con gente importante en tu vida—tus amistades cercanas. Por favor dime que cierta es cada frase para ti en estos momentos. *(Show response scale 2.)*

0	1	2	3
Nunca	A Veces	Frecuentemente	Muy Frecuentemente

1. Cuando hablamos, a mis amistades les importa mi punto de vista.   _____

2. Siento que mis amigos son buenos amigos.   _____

3. Estoy engado(a) con mis amigos.   _____

4. Confío en mis amigos.   _____

5. Mis amigos me ayudan a hablar sobre mis dificultades.   _____

6. Parece como si mis amigos estuvieran enojados conmigo sin ninguna razón.   _____

Es necesario pertenecer a una pandilla.   SI   NO

¿Alguna vez alguien te ha iniciado en una pandilla?   SI   NO

The interview part is completed. Process any distress responses to items 5 and 11 of the Adjustment Scale.

If this is a pregroup interview, say "Ya terminamos. Gracias por contestar todas estas preguntas. ¿Tienes alguna pregunta sobre cualquiera de las cosas que hablamos hoy? Los grupos van a comenzar pronto y serán muy divertidos."

For older groups of students, it may be helpful to readminister the Survey of Relationship Attitudes (Appendix B-6c) at the postgroup interview. Please see below for scoring instructions.

If this is a postgroup interview, say "Ya terminamos con esta parte de la entrevista. Solo tengo una cosa más para ti. Te voy a dar un papel con algunas preguntas sobre los grupos de SPARK. No tienes que poner tu nombre en el papel, así que puedes ser lo más honesto/a posible. Cuando termines, pon tus respuestas en este sobre y séllalo para que tus respuestas sean anónimas." *(Give the student an envelope and the last page of the interview.)*

Evaluación de los Grupos de SPARK

1	2	3	4	5
Nada	Un poquito	Algo	Bastante	Mucho

1. Usando los números en la escala de respuestas arriba, ¿cuánto te ayudó el grupo de SPARK para . . .

    a) Usar respuestas frías (cool-headed) cuando te enojas?   _____

    b) Sentirte mejor hacia ti mismo/a?   _____

    c) Expresar tus sentimientos?   _____

    d) Resistir la presión de grupo?   _____

    e) Sentir que aceptas más a la gente que es diferente a ti?   _____

    f) Comprender tus reacciones a cosas malas que te pasan?   _____

    g) Querer salir mejor en la escuela?   _____

2. ¿Cuánto te gustó el grupo de SPARK?   _____

3. ¿Cuánta ayuda te brindaron los líderes del grupo?   _____

4. En general, ¿cuánta ayuda te brindó el grupo de SPARK?   _____

5. ¿Qué sugerencias tienes para mejorar los grupos de SPARK?

    _____

    _____

    _____

¡¡Gracias por ser un miembro de SPARK!!

Escala de Respuesta 1 para la Entrevista

NO		SÍ			
		No difícil	Me molesto	Estresante	Muy estresante
N		1	2	3	4

Escala de Respuesta 2 para la Entrevista

0	1	2	3
Nunca	A veces	Frecuentemente	Muy frecuentemente

Escala de Respuesta 3 para la Entrevista

1	2	3	4	5
Mucho menos que otros niños	*Menos que otros niños*	*Igual que otros niños*	*Más que otros niños*	*Mucho más que otros niños*

APPENDIX C-4. From Waterman and Walker (2009). Copyright by The Guilford Press.

Escala de Respuesta 4 para la Entrevista

1	2	3	4
No estaría enojado para nada	Estaría un poco enojado	Estaría bastante enojado	Estaría furioso

APPENDIX C-4. From Waterman and Walker (2009). Copyright by The Guilford Press.

Escala de Respuesta 5 para la Entrevista

1	2	3	4
Muy de acuerdo	De acuerdo	Desacuerdo	Muy desacuerdo

Página de Título
para los Cuadernos del Estudiante

Grupo de SPARK

Temas que se cubrirán en el grupo:

1. Desarrollo de Confianza y Comunicación
2. Manejo del Enojo y Cómo Hacer Frente a Emociones Difíciles
3. Identidad Étnica y Cómo Hacer Frente al Racismo y Prejuicio
4. Metas Escolares y el Triunfo Académico
5. La Influencia de los Compañeros, Intimidación, y Pandillas
6. Relaciones entre Hombres y Mujeres
7. Exposición a la Violencia y el Estrés Postraumático
8. Relaciones entre la Familia

Tu Nombre: _____

Nombre del Grupo: _____

Curriculum Materials and Handouts in Spanish

Module Three: Ethnic Identity and Anti-Prejudice

Module Four: Educational Aspirations

Module Five: Peer Pressure, Bullying, and Gangs

Module Six: Male–Female Relationships

Module Seven: Exposure to Violence and Posttraumatic Stress Reactions

Termination Session: The Party

Permission to photocopy the forms in this appendix is granted to purchasers of this book for personal use only (see copyright page for details).

See Appendix B for instructions for using materials in each module.

Clasificación de Confianza

Nombre: _____ Fecha: _____

¿Cuánto confías en los otros miembros del grupo?

1	2	3	4	5
Nada	Sólo un poco	Algo	Bastante	Mucho

- -

Nombre: _____ Fecha: _____

¿Cuánto confías en los otros miembros del grupo?

1	2	3	4	5
Nada	Sólo un poco	Algo	Bastante	Mucho

- -

Nombre: _____ Fecha: _____

¿Cuánto confías en los otros miembros del grupo?

1	2	3	4	5
Nada	Sólo un poco	Algo	Bastante	Mucho

- -

Nombre: _____ Fecha: _____

¿Cuánto confías en los otros miembros del grupo?

1	2	3	4	5
Nada	Sólo un poco	Algo	Bastante	Mucho

- -

Nombre: _____ Fecha: _____

¿Cuánto confías en los otros miembros del grupo?

1	2	3	4	5
Nada	Sólo un poco	Algo	Bastante	Mucho

- -

Nombre: _____ Fecha: _____

¿Cuánto confías en los otros miembros del grupo?

1	2	3	4	5
Nada	Sólo un poco	Algo	Bastante	Mucho

- -

Contrato de Confidencialidad

Entiendo que cualquier cosa que diga o haga dentro del grupo no será divulgada por los líderes a nadie fuera del grupo, incluyendo a mis padres, amigos y maestros. Entiendo que la única excepción a esto es si revelo información sobre mí o alguna otra persona estando en peligro; entonces, los líderes del grupo tendrán que compartir esa información para mantenerme a mí o a la otra persona a salvo.

También entiendo que no puedo hablarle a nadie más sobre lo que los demás miembros dicen o hacen dentro del grupo. Esto incluye hablar con mis padres, hermanos, hermanas y amistades. Entiendo que los otros miembros del grupo confiarán en mí al compartir sus secretos, y que hablar sobre lo que ellos dicen sería traicionar su confianza. Entiendo que para que el grupo sea lo mas útil posible, debo honorar este contrato de confidencialidad.

Al firmar este contrato, acepto no hablar con nadie fuera del grupo sobre lo que otros digan o hagan en el grupo.

_____   _____

Firma   **Fecha**

Sentimientos por "Bolsa de Sentimientos"

Asustado	**Orgulloso**
Tímido	**Desilusionado**
Valiente	**Confundido**
Triste	**Feliz**
Sorprendido	**Apenado/ Abochornado**
Frustrado	**Emocionado**
Relajado	**Tenso/Estresado**
Avergonzado	**Confiado**

Posiciones de Lenguaje Corporal

No mires a los ojos
Pon los ojos en blanco
Toca tu pie sobre el piso repetidamente
Cruza las brazos fuertemente sobre tu pecho
Párrate demasiado cerca

Destrezas para Escuchar Bien

Lenguaje Corporal

1. Mira a la otra persona cuando el/ella este hablando.

2. Dirige tu cuerpo hacia la otra persona en lugar de voltear tu cuerpo.

3. Mantén una distancia respetuosa entre tu y la otra persona.

4. Mantén tu cuerpo abierto y tus manos relajadas.

5. Mantén tu cara amable o neutral.

6. Evita movimientos nerviosos con la ropa, pelo, etc.

Verbal

1. Reconoce lo que se ha dicho con decir "claro," "si," etc. o asiente con la cabeza.

2. Resume lo que escuchaste para que la otra persona sepa que estabas escuchando atentamente.

3. Usa declaraciones reflexivas que demuestran que entiendes lo que la otra persona está sintiendo.

4. No interrumpas y en su lugar escucha lo que dice la otra persona.

5. Has preguntas abiertas—empiezan con "que," "porque," "como," o "dime," y no pueden ser respondidas con un solo "si" o "no."

6. Comparte una experiencia similar que tuviste en una manera respetable.

Secretos para "Bolsa de Secretos"— Versión de Poca Confianza (Estudiantes Menores)

(Includes blanks to fill in other secrets as appropriate for a particular group.)

Secreto

Me han iniciado en una pandilla.

Instrucciones:
1. Leer el secreto como si fuera tuyo.
2. Decir cómo te sentirías si fuera tu secreto.

Secreto

He fumado marihuana.

Instrucciones:
1. Leer el secreto como si fuera tuyo.
2. Decir cómo te sentirías si fuera tu secreto.

Secreto

He robado de una tienda.

Instrucciones:
1. Leer el secreto como si fuera tuyo.
2. Decir cómo te sentirías si fuera tu secreto.

Secreto

Yo repetí un grado escolar.

Instrucciones:
1. Leer el secreto como si fuera tuyo.
2. Decir cómo te sentirías si fuera tu secreto.

Secreto

He sido detenido por la policía.

Instrucciones:
1. Leer el secreto como si fuera tuyo.
2. Decir cómo te sentirías si fuera tu secreto.

Secreto

Mis padres se están divorciando.

Instrucciones:
1. Leer el secreto como si fuera tuyo.
2. Decir cómo te sentirías si fuera tu secreto.

Secreto

Yo hago trampa en los exámenes.

Instrucciones:
1. Leer el secreto como si fuera tuyo.
2. Decir cómo te sentirías si fuera tu secreto.

Secreto

Mi papá está en la cárcel.

Instrucciones:
1. Leer el secreto como si fuera tuyo.
2. Decir cómo te sentirías si fuera tu secreto.

Secreto

He estado borracho.

Instrucciones:
1. Leer el secreto como si fuera tuyo.
2. Decir cómo te sentirías si fuera tu secreto.

Secreto

A veces quisiera matarme.

Instrucciones:
1. Leer el secreto como si fuera tuyo.
2. Decir cómo te sentirías si fuera tu secreto.

Secreto

_____

Instrucciones:
1. Leer el secreto como si fuera tuyo.
2. Decir cómo te sentirías si fuera tu secreto.

- -

Secreto

_____

Instrucciones:
1. Leer el secreto como si fuera tuyo.
2. Decir cómo te sentirías si fuera tu secreto.

- -

Secreto

_____

Instrucciones:
1. Leer el secreto como si fuera tuyo.
2. Decir cómo te sentirías si fuera tu secreto.

- -

Secreto

_____

Instrucciones:
1. Leer el secreto como si fuera tuyo.
2. Decir cómo te sentirías si fuera tu secreto.

- -

Secreto

_____

Instrucciones:
1. Leer el secreto como si fuera tuyo.
2. Decir cómo te sentirías si fuera tu secreto.

- -

Secreto

_____

Instrucciones:
1. Leer el secreto como si fuera tuyo.
2. Decir cómo te sentirías si fuera tu secreto.

- -

Secretos para "Bolsa de Secretos"— Versión de Poca Confianza (Estudiantes Mayores)

(Includes blanks to fill in other secrets as appropriate for a particular group.)

Secreto

Me han iniciado en una pandilla.

Instrucciones:
1. Leer el secreto como si fuera tuyo.
2. Decir cómo te sentirías si fuera tu secreto.

- -

Secreto

He fumado marihuana.

Instrucciones:
1. Leer el secreto como si fuera tuyo.
2. Decir cómo te sentirías si fuera tu secreto.

- -

Secreto

He robado de una tienda.

Instrucciones:
1. Leer el secreto como si fuera tuyo.
2. Decir cómo te sentirías si fuera tu secreto.

- -

Secreto

Niñas: Estuve encinta y aborté.
O
Niños: Mi novia quedó embarazada de mí y abortó.

Instrucciones:
1. Leer el secreto como si fuera tuyo.
2. Decir cómo te sentirías si fuera tu secreto.

- -

Secreto

He sido arrestado por la policía.

Instrucciones:

1. Leer el secreto como si fuera tuyo.
2. Decir cómo te sentirías si fuera tu secreto.

Secreto

Mis padres se están divorciando.

Instrucciones:

1. Leer el secreto como si fuera tuyo.
2. Decir cómo te sentirías si fuera tu secreto.

Secreto

He tenido sexo.

Instrucciones:

1. Leer el secreto como si fuera tuyo.
2. Decir cómo te sentirías si fuera tu secreto.

Secreto

Mi papá está en la cárcel.

Instrucciones:

1. Leer el secreto como si fuera tuyo.
2. Decir cómo te sentirías si fuera tu secreto.

Secreto

He estado borracho.

Instrucciones:

1. Leer el secreto como si fuera tuyo.
2. Decir cómo te sentirías si fuera tu secreto.

Secreto

A veces quisiera matarme.

Instrucciones:

1. Leer el secreto como si fuera tuyo.
2. Decir cómo te sentirías si fuera tu secreto.

Secreto

_____

Instrucciones:
1. Leer el secreto como si fuera tuyo.
2. Decir cómo te sentirías si fuera tu secreto.

Secreto

_____

Instrucciones:
1. Leer el secreto como si fuera tuyo.
2. Decir cómo te sentirías si fuera tu secreto.

Secreto

_____

Instrucciones:
1. Leer el secreto como si fuera tuyo.
2. Decir cómo te sentirías si fuera tu secreto.

Secreto

_____

Instrucciones:
1. Leer el secreto como si fuera tuyo.
2. Decir cómo te sentirías si fuera tu secreto.

Secreto

_____

Instrucciones:
1. Leer el secreto como si fuera tuyo.
2. Decir cómo te sentirías si fuera tu secreto.

Secreto

_____

Instrucciones:
1. Leer el secreto como si fuera tuyo.
2. Decir cómo te sentirías si fuera tu secreto.

Termómetro de Enojo

Causas   Explosión   Sensaciones Corporales

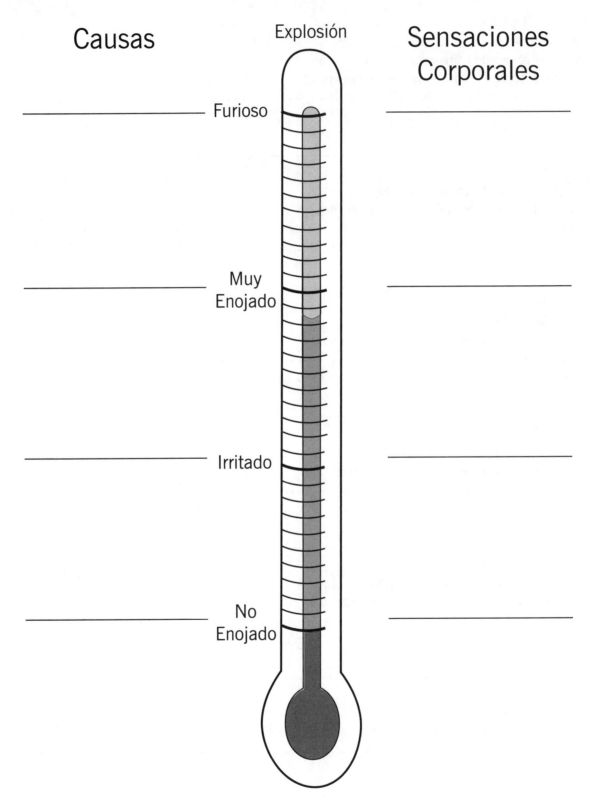

Furioso

Muy Enojado

Irritado

No Enojado

APPENDIX D-2a. From Waterman and Walker (2009). Copyright by The Guilford Press.

Termómetro de Enojo

Pensamientos
Para Bregar

Explosión

Acciones
Para Bregar

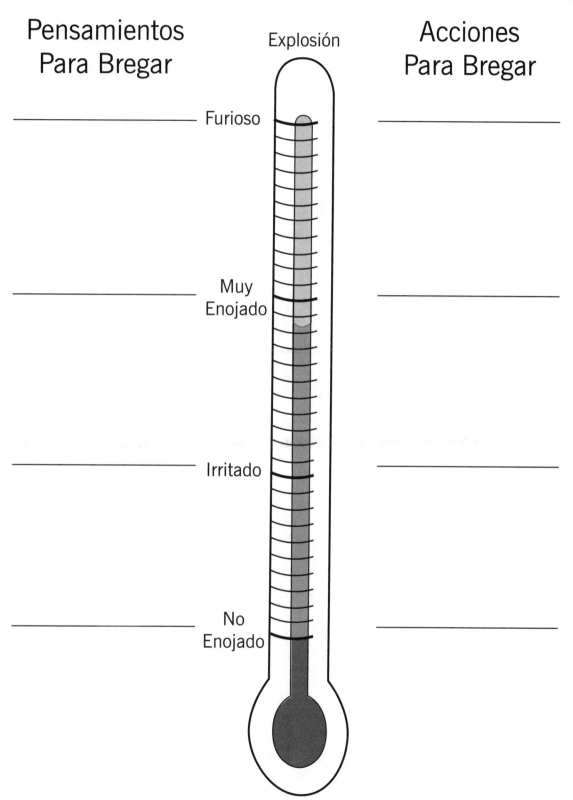

Furioso

Muy
Enojado

Irritado

No
Enojado

Diario de Relajación

Usa este diario para indicar cuando practiques las maneras que aprendimos para ayudarte cuando sientas emociones enojadas en tu cuerpo. Usa respiración profunda por lo menos dos veces esta semana y relajación de músculos por lo menos una vez esta semana.

1. **Cuando use respiración profunda:**

   Lo que me hizo enojar fue _____

   _____

   Donde lo sentí en mi cuerpo: _____

   Que enojado/a estaba: 1/3   2/3   casi hasta arriba   hasta arriba
   (indica en el termómetro)

   La respiración profunda me ayudo (circula uno)   Mucho   Algo   Para nada

   Cuando use respiración profunda:

   Lo que me hizo enojar fue _____

   _____

   Donde lo sentí en mi cuerpo: _____

   Que enojado/a estaba: 1/3   2/3   casi hasta arriba   hasta arriba
   (indica en el termómetro)

   La respiración profunda me ayudo (circula uno)   Mucho   Algo   Para nada

2. **Cuando use relajación de músculos:**

   Lo que me hizo enojar fue _____

   _____

   Donde lo sentí en mi cuerpo: _____

   Que enojado/a estaba: 1/3   2/3   casi hasta arriba   hasta arriba
   (indica en el termómetro)

   La relajación de músculos me ayudo (circula uno)   Mucho   Algo   Para nada

APPENDIX D-2b. From Waterman and Walker (2009). Copyright by The Guilford Press.

Pensamientos y Acciones Fríos

Pensamientos Fríos

1. **Dar el beneficio de la duda**—explicaciones alternativas

EJEMPLOS:
- "Probablemente no intento que lo que dijo saliera como salió"
- "Probablemente fue un accidente"

2. **Hablarse a si mismo para calmarse**
- "Déjame parar y pensar" (reduce las acciones impulsivas)
- "Relájate y respira"
- "Me puedo mantener calmado/a y bajar la temperatura"

3. **Ver la situación de otra manera**

EJEMPLOS:
- "Esta es una oportunidad para realmente conocerlo"
- "Si no hubiera cerrado la puerta de mi locker, se me hubiera olvidado que necesitaba mi libro de historia de ahí"

Acciones Frías

1. **Relájate**
- Relaja tus músculos
- Respira profundo y despacio
- Usa tu imagen calmante

2. **Toma un tiempo para calmarte**
- Aléjate
- Ignora a la persona
- Evita ir a donde este esa persona

3. **Resuelve el problema**
- Habla acerca de esto con alguien
- Considera todas las opciones y las consecuencias de estas opciones

4. **Busca ayuda**
- Habla con un amigo
- Pide que un maestro/a de confianza o tus padres te ayuden
- Habla con un consejero/a o terapeuta

Mi Diario de Enojo

Durante la siguiente semana, presta atención a dos situaciones que te hacen enojar. Usa pensamientos y acciones frías para enfrentar estas situaciones y escríbelas abajo.

Si usaste una respuesta de cabeza caliente, escríbela aquí al lado de un pensamiento y acción fría.

1. Lo que me hizo enojar fue _____

    _____

    Donde lo sentí en mi cuerpo: _____

    Que enojado/a estaba: 1/3   2/3   casi hasta arriba   hasta arriba
    (indica en el termómetro)

    Respuesta fría que use: _____

    _____

2. Lo que me hizo enojar fue _____

    _____

    Donde lo sentí en mi cuerpo: _____

    Que enojado/a estaba: 1/3   2/3   casi hasta arriba   hasta arriba
    (indica en el termómetro)

    Respuesta fría que use: _____

    _____

Si usaste una respuesta de cabeza caliente esta semana:

1. Lo que me hizo enojar fue _____

    _____

    Donde lo sentí en mi cuerpo: _____

    Que enojado/a estaba: 1/3   2/3   casi hasta arriba   hasta arriba
    (indica en el termómetro)

    Las respuestas calientes que use: _____

    Pensamiento frió que pudiera haber usado: _____

    _____

    Acción fría que pudiera haber usado: _____

    _____

Cartas para Jugar

PROBLEMA	**PROBLEMA**
PROBLEMA	**PROBLEMA**
PROBLEMA	**PROBLEMA**
PROBLEMA	**PROBLEMA**
PROBLEMA	**PROBLEMA**
PROBLEMA	**PROBLEMA**
PROBLEMA	**PROBLEMA**
PROBLEMA	**PROBLEMA**

Mi hermano/a me estaba molestando	**Mis padres me castigaron sin razón**
Otro chico estaba molestando a mi amigo/a	**Otro chico tomo algo que era mío**
Mi novio/a salió con otra persona	**Alguien hizo trampa para salir mejor que yo**
Otro chico dijo algo acerca de mi madre	**Mi maestra la tenía conmigo**
Alguien me hizo un comentario racista	**Otro chico me empujó**
Otro chico robó mi dinero	**Me culparon por algo que no hize**
Mi mejor amigo/a salió con mi novio/a	**Mi hermano me quitó mi dinero**
Mi amigo le contó a alguien un secreto mío	**Otro niño me insultó**

APPENDIX D-2e. From Waterman and Walker (2009). Copyright by The Guilford Press.

ALTERNATIVA	**ALTERNATIVA**
ALTERNATIVA	**ALTERNATIVA**
ALTERNATIVA	**ALTERNATIVA**
ALTERNATIVA	**ALTERNATIVA**
ALTERNATIVA	**ALTERNATIVA**
ALTERNATIVA	**ALTERNATIVA**
ALTERNATIVA	**ALTERNATIVA**
ALTERNATIVA	**ALTERNATIVA**

✧ ✧ ✧ **CALIENTE** ✧ ✧ ✧	✧ ✧ ✧ **CALIENTE** ✧ ✧ ✧
✧ ✧ ✧ **CALIENTE** ✧ ✧ ✧	✧ ✧ ✧ **CALIENTE** ✧ ✧ ✧
✧ ✧ ✧ **CALIENTE** ✧ ✧ ✧	✧ ✧ ✧ **CALIENTE** ✧ ✧ ✧
✧ ✧ ✧ **CALIENTE** ✧ ✧ ✧	✧ ✧ ✧ **CALIENTE** ✧ ✧ ✧
❄ ❄ ❄ **FRÍO** ❄ ❄ ❄	❄ ❄ ❄ **FRÍO** ❄ ❄ ❄
❄ ❄ ❄ **FRÍO** ❄ ❄ ❄	❄ ❄ ❄ **FRÍO** ❄ ❄ ❄
❄ ❄ ❄ **FRÍO** ❄ ❄ ❄	❄ ❄ ❄ **FRÍO** ❄ ❄ ❄
❄ ❄ ❄ **FRÍO** ❄ ❄ ❄	❄ ❄ ❄ **FRÍO** ❄ ❄ ❄

CONSECUENCIA	CONSECUENCIA
CONSECUENCIA	CONSECUENCIA
CONSECUENCIA	CONSECUENCIA
CONSECUENCIA	CONSECUENCIA
CONSECUENCIA	CONSECUENCIA
CONSECUENCIA	CONSECUENCIA
CONSECUENCIA	CONSECUENCIA
CONSECUENCIA	CONSECUENCIA

A CORTO PLAZO PARA TÍ	A LARGO PLAZO PARA TÍ
A CORTO PLAZO PARA TÍ	A LARGO PLAZO PARA TÍ
A CORTO PLAZO PARA TÍ	A LARGO PLAZO PARA TÍ
A CORTO PLAZO PARA TÍ	A LARGO PLAZO PARA TÍ
A CORTO PLAZO PARA OTROS	A LARGO PLAZO PARA OTROS
A CORTO PLAZO PARA OTROS	A LARGO PLAZO PARA OTROS
A CORTO PLAZO PARA OTROS	A LARGO PLAZO PARA OTROS
A CORTO PLAZO PARA OTROS	A LARGO PLAZO PARA OTROS

Etiquetas para el Juego de Nombrar

BUEN ESTUDIANTE	**MANDÓN**
VAGO	**MASCOTA DE LA MAESTRA**
SIMPÁTICO	**BUEN ATLETA**
TÍMIDO	**PRESUMIDO**
ATRACTIVO/A	**AMABLE/ÚTIL**
ENOJADO	**SOLITARIO**
CASANOVA	**CHISMOSO**

Escala de Educación y Carrera Profesional

Nombre: _____

Meta (carrera/profesíon): _____

Pasos para lograr mi meta: _____

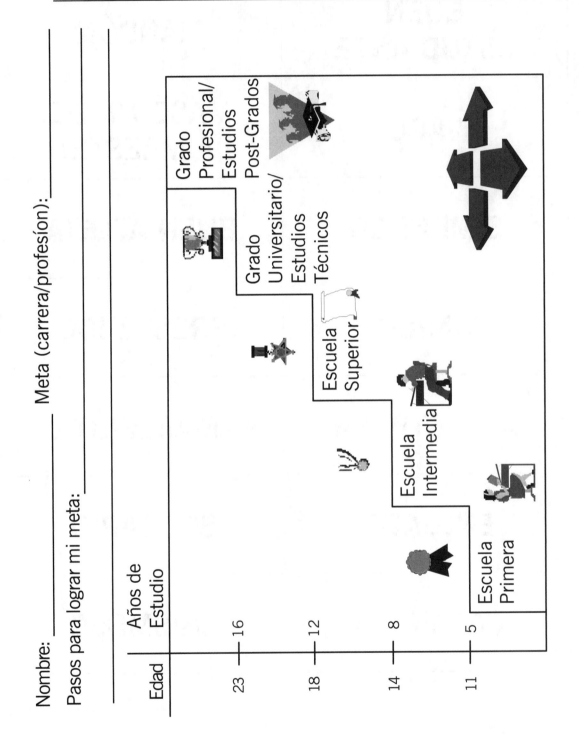

Años de Estudio

Edad	Años de Estudio	
23	16	Grado Profesional/ Estudios Post-Grados
18	12	Grado Universitario/ Estudios Técnicos
14	8	Escuela Superior
11	5	Escuela Intermedia
		Escuela Primera

APPENDIX D-4a. From Waterman and Walker (2009). Copyright by The Guilford Press.

Mis Metas

Voy a fijar metas para mi mismo/a y voy a trabajar hacia estas metas.

Mis metas para el año escolar son:

1. _____
   _____
   _____
   _____

2. _____
   _____
   _____
   _____

3. _____
   _____
   _____
   _____

4. _____
   _____
   _____
   _____

Mis Estrategias para Tener Éxito

Para lograr mis metas, usaré las siguientes estrategias para tener éxito:

En clase, voy a:

1. _____

2. _____

Para ser organizado/a, voy a:

1. _____

2. _____

Cuando hago la tarea, voy a:

1. _____

2. _____

Para premiarme por un trabajo bien hecho, voy a:

1. _____

2. _____

_____   _____

Firma   Fecha

Sitios de Web para Encontrar una Universidad

Los sitios de web que siguen contienen información para ayudarte a encontrar información sobre universidades.

- *www.collegeboard.com*—En este sitio de web muy comprensivo encontrarás información acerca de cómo planear para la universidad, tomar los exámenes (SAT I, SAT II, PSAT, y AP), encontrar la universidad correcta, cómo ser admitido a la universidad, y cómo pagar por los estudios.

- *www.review.com*—Este sito de web del Princeton Review no solo ofrece la oportunidad de buscar universidades, pero también ofrece información acerca de mejores calificaciones, mejores escuelas, calculadoras para comparar las opciones para pagar los estudios, evaluación de careras, y consejos generales.

- *www.usnews.com*—Este sitio de web tiene enlaces a una base de datos sobre las mejores universidades, ayuda financiera, clasificaciones de universidades, y careras.

- *www.finaid.com*—Este sitio de web tiene información general buena sobre ayuda financiera. También contiene por lo menos cuatro búsquedas de becas gratis para diferentes grupos de estudiantes.

- *www.fastaid.com*—Este sitio de web contiene información sobre ayuda financiera y una base de datos para becas.

- *www.allaboutcollege.com*—Contiene enlaces a sitios de web de universidades, programas para estudiar en el extranjero, preparación para exámenes de admisión, y ayuda financiera.

- *www.chronicle.com/stats/tuition*—Este sitio de web te dará la habilidad de examinar los costos de matrícula.

APPENDIX D-4c. From Waterman and Walker (2009). Copyright by The Guilford Press.

Sitios de Web para Encontrar Becas

Sin importar tu situación financiera, puede haber una o mas becas para las que calificas. Las becas son ofrecidas por universidades individuales, organizaciones, compañías, y grupos comunitarios. Si quieres encontrar dinero para atender la universidad, debes estar dispuesto tomar tiempo con tu búsqueda de becas.

Recuerda: Nunca gastes más de lo que cuesta una estampilla para obtener información acerca de becas.

SITIOS DE WEB GENERALES PARA BECAS

- *www.collegeboard.com*—Este sitio web incluye una base de datos de becas llamada "The Fund Finder" que contiene información de 3,300 organizaciones nacionales, estatales, públicas, y privadas. También menciona como reconocer una estafa.
- *www.fastaid.com*—La primera base de datos de becas privadas y la más grande del mundo. Encontrarás becas aquí que no encontrarás en ningún otro lugar.
- *www.wiredscholar.com*—Votado el mejor sitio web para información acerca de la universidad por Forbes, en este sitio aprenderás acerca de los tipos de becas, requisitos, consejos, y estafas además de poder buscar becas.
- *www.fastweb.com*—Dentro de esta base de datos, el estudiante se registra y recibe un buzón de correo en el sitio web donde anuncian las oportunidades para becase. La base de datos contiene más de 500,000 becas privadas y préstamos. Probablemente uno de los mejores sitios de Internet disponibles para encontrar becas.
- *www.finaid.com*—Este sitio de web hará una búsqueda para los intereses en el arte, biología, ciencias de computadora, ingeniería, periodismo, y enfermería.

Estrategias para Éxito Académico

EN CLASE

- Llega a clase a tiempo.
- Trae todos los materiales necesarios a clase (libro, lápiz, papel, etc.).
- Toma notas en clase.
- Mueve tu asiento así al frente y/o lejos de amigos si te distraes fácilmente.
- Pide tiempo adicional para completar pruebas o exámenes si lo necesitas (¡vale la pena preguntar!).

ORGANIZACIÓN

- Mantén un encuadernador para cada clase y identifica un lugar especial donde pondrás tareas que tienes que entregar.
- Mantén un organizador y anota todas las tareas y días de examen.
- Aclara la tarea con tu maestro/a después de clase si estás confundido/a.

TAREA

- Aparta un tiempo específico cada día para hacer tarea.
- Encuentra un lugar tranquilo y con buena luz para hacer tu tarea.
- Date tiempo y no dejes tareas mayores hasta el último momento.

OTROS CONSEJOS

- Hable con tu consejero/a y pide un tutor si necesitas más ayuda.
- ¡Prémiate por un trabajo bien hecho!

Resistiendo la Presión Entre Compañeros

Situación en la cual fui presionado/a:

_____

_____

_____

_____

Resistí!!!!!!   Me di por vencido/a . . .
Estrategias que usé: La razón fue:

_____   _____

_____   _____

_____   _____

_____   _____

_____   _____

_____   _____

_____   _____

Situación en la cual fui presionado/a:

_____

_____

_____

_____

Resistí!!!!!!   Me di por vencido/a . . .
Estrategias que usé: La razón fue:

_____   _____

_____   _____

_____   _____

_____   _____

_____   _____

_____   _____

Nombre: _____

"¿Está Bien?"

Contesta las preguntas siguientes con circular el número apropiado (1= haces esto raramente hasta 6 = haces esto frecuentemente). No tendrás que entregar esta hoja, así que por favor responde honestamente.

Cuantas veces . . .

	Raramente		A Veces		Frecuentemente	
1. Empiezas chismes o rumores	1	2	3	4	5	6
2. Compartes los secretos de otros	1	2	3	4	5	6
3. Hablas acerca de alguien por el Internet	1	2	3	4	5	6
4. Pones los ojos en blanco cuando alguien pasa	1	2	3	4	5	6
5. Murmuras en frente de alguien	1	2	3	4	5	6
6. Molestas a alguien por como se ven	1	2	3	4	5	6
7. Excluyes a alguien de tu grupo	1	2	3	4	5	6
8. Amenazas no pasar tiempo con alguien	1	2	3	4	5	6
9. Le quitas las cosas a alguien	1	2	3	4	5	6
10. Ignoras a alguien intencionalmente	1	2	3	4	5	6

Agresor, Víctima, Espectador

Que hacer ...

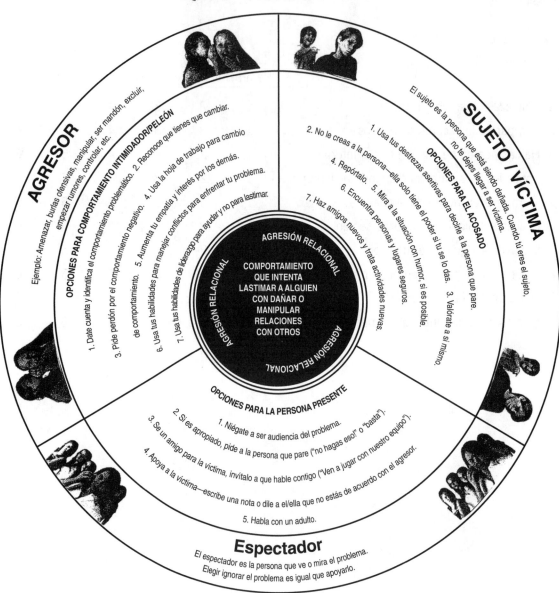

AGRESOR

Ejemplo: Amenazar, burlas ofensivas, manipular, ser mandón, excluir, empezar rumores, controlar, etc.

OPCIONES PARA COMPORTAMIENTO INTIMIDADOR/PELEÓN

1. Date cuenta y identifica el comportamiento problemático. 2. Reconoce que tienes que cambiar. 3. Pide perdón por el comportamiento negativo. 4. Usa la hoja de trabajo para cambio de comportamiento. 5. Aumenta tu empatía y interés por los demás. 6. Usa tus habilidades para manejar conflictos para enfrentar tu problema. 7. Usa tus habilidades de liderazgo para ayudar y no para lastimar.

SUJETO / VÍCTIMA

El sujeto es la persona que está siendo dañada. Cuando tú eres el sujeto, no te dejes llegar a ser víctima.

OPCIONES PARA EL ACOSADO

1. Usa tus destrezas asertivas para decirle a la persona que pare. 2. No le creas a la persona—ella solo tiene el poder si tu se lo das. 3. Valórate a si mismo. 4. Repórtalo. 5. Mira a la situación con humor, si es posible. 6. Encuentra personas y lugares seguros. 7. Haz amigos nuevos y trata actividades nuevas.

AGRESIÓN RELACIONAL

COMPORTAMIENTO QUE INTENTA LASTIMAR A ALGUIEN CON DAÑAR O MANIPULAR RELACIONES CON OTROS

AGRESIÓN RELACIONAL — AGRESIÓN RELACIONAL — AGRESIÓN RELACIONAL

OPCIONES PARA LA PERSONA PRESENTE

1. Niégate a ser audiencia del problema. 2. Si es apropiado, pide a la persona que pare ("no hagas eso!" o "basta"). 3. Se un amigo para la víctima, invítalo a que hable contigo ("Ven a jugar con nuestro equipo"). 4. Apoya a la víctima—escribe una nota o dile a el/ella que no estás de acuerdo con el agresor. 5. Habla con un adulto.

Espectador

El espectador es la persona que ve o mira el problema. Elegir ignorar el problema es igual que apoyarlo.

APPENDIX D-5c. From Senn (2007). Reprinted with permission of YouthLight, Inc. in Waterman and Walker (2009). Copyright by The Guilford Press.

Tres Sistemas de Huellas
para Agresor, Víctima, y Espectador

Agresor

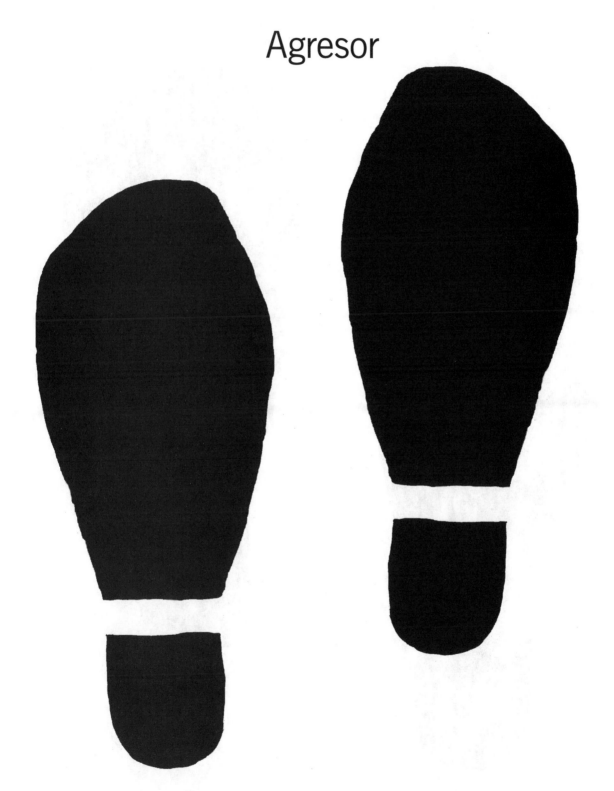

Víctima

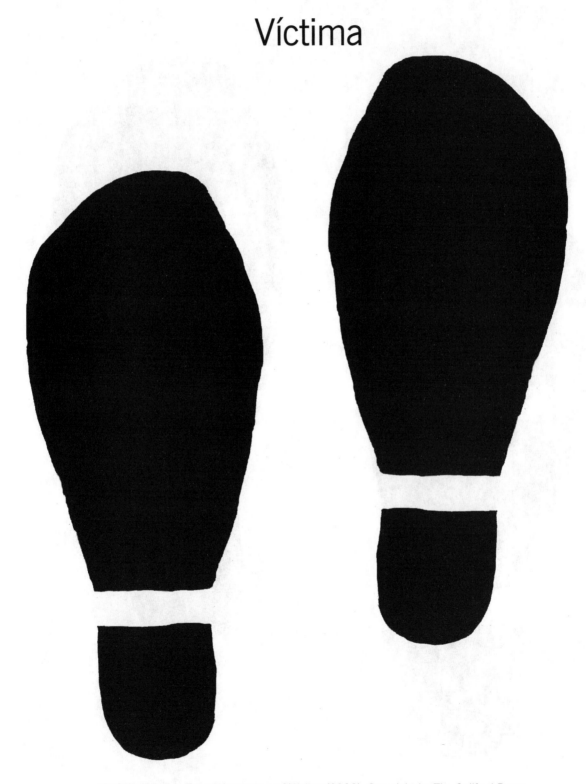

APPENDIX D-5d. From Waterman and Walker (2009). Copyright by The Guilford Press.

Espectador

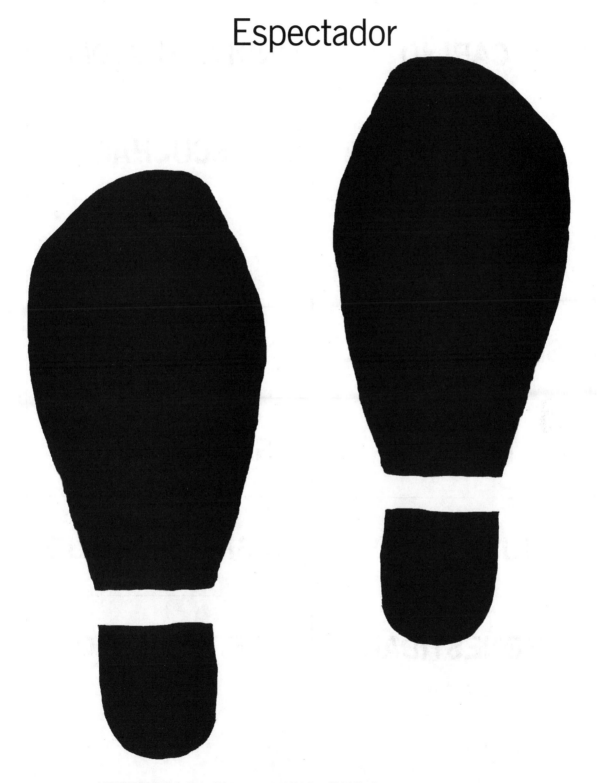

APPENDIX D-5d. From Waterman and Walker (2009). Copyright by The Guilford Press.

Cartas de Derechos de Relaciones

Relaciones Buenas/Sanas

CARIÑO	INDIVIDUALIDAD
COMUNICACIÓN	ESCUCHAR
COMPROMISO	APOYO
SER IGUAL QUE	CONFIANZA
EMPATÍA	GANAR/GANAR
JUSTICIERO	RESPETO MUTUO
HONESTIDAD	SER ABIERTO

Relaciones Malas/No Saludables

CULPAR	**MANIPULACIÓN**
CONTROL	**INSULTOS**
DESHONESTIDAD	**SEXISMO**
MIEDO	**PEGAR/EMPUJAR**
ACOSAR	**ESTAR DE MALHUMOR**
INSEGURIDAD	**RETRAERSE**
CELOS	**GANAR/PERDER**

Cosas Que Hacer y No Hacer en las Relaciones Románticas

1. No le hables a un muchacho/muchacha más de dos veces seguidas. El/ella puede molestarse. También, las relaciones deben de ser 50/50.

2. Si un muchacho o muchacha verdaderamente quiere hablar contigo, el/ella encontrará la manera para hacerlo.

3. Si coqueteas con otros muchachos/as para hacer a alguien celoso/a, las cosas van a salir mal.

4. Si tu novio/novia te ignora o coquetea con otros delante de ti, el/ella es (a) grosero/a o (b) no está interesado/a en ti.

5. No te pelees o rompas con tu novio/a por e-mail, mensaje de texto, o con una nota. Hazlo en persona.

6. No uses a tus amigos para comunicarte con tu novio/a.

7. Si tu hablas mucho o empiezas chismes acerca de otras personas y sus relaciones—especialmente por e-mail o mensajes de texto—te arrepentirás después.

8. Si tu te besas con varias personas en poco tiempo, es posible que vas a tener una mala reputación. Las mujeres pueden recibir una reputación diferente a la de los hombres.

9. Unas señales malas importantes: (a) tienes que estar de escondidas para ver a tu novio/a, (b) el/elle usa drogas o las vende, (c) el/ella ya tiene un hijo, (d) el/ella ha estado en la cárcel, (e) el/ella es más de dos años mayor que tú. Estas señales hacen las relaciones románticas muy complicadas, especialmente durante la adolescencia.

10. Si estás teniendo relaciones sexuales, es muy posible que una o más de las siguientes cosas van a pasar: (a) Vas a quedar embarazada, (b) Vas a contraer una infección transmitida sexualmente y/o, (c) Vas a terminar con el corazón roto.

Últimamente, respétate a si mismo y a otros, y serás respetado/a.
¡Recuerda, tu mereces lo mejor!

Encuesta de Actitudes Sobre las Relaciones

Al siguiente está una lista de frases acerca de hombres, mujeres, y relaciones. Lee cada frase e indica si estás muy desacuerdo, algo desacuerdo, algo de acuerdo, o muy de acuerdo con cada frase.

Por favor indica tu sexo.   HOMBRE   MUJER

1. En una relación, los hombres necesitan afección y compañía menos que las mujeres.

| Muy Desacuerdo | Algo Desacuerdo | Algo De Acuerdo | Muy De Acuerdo |

2. Las muchachas que se visten con ropa conservativa están menos dispuestas a tener relaciones sexuales que las muchachas que usan ropa más ajustada o escotada.

| Muy Desacuerdo | Algo Desacuerdo | Algo De Acuerdo | Muy De Acuerdo |

3. Los medios de publicidad representan los papeles de la mujer y el hombre con precisión.

| Muy Desacuerdo | Algo Desacuerdo | Algo De Acuerdo | Muy De Acuerdo |

4. Hablar abiertamente acerca de los sentimientos es más fácil para las mujeres que para los hombres.

| Muy Desacuerdo | Algo Desacuerdo | Algo De Acuerdo | Muy De Acuerdo |

5. Si un muchacho lleva a una muchacha a una cita que cuesta mucho, el puede esperar que la muchacha le demuestre afección a cambio.

| Muy Desacuerdo | Algo Desacuerdo | Algo De Acuerdo | Muy De Acuerdo |

6. La igualdad y un actitud de ganar-ganar (que los dos ganen) son cualidades importantes en una relación romántica.

| Muy Desacuerdo | Algo Desacuerdo | Algo De Acuerdo | Muy De Acuerdo |

7. Los muchachos se preocupan menos que las muchachas sobre la rechaza en sus relaciones.

| Muy Desacuerdo | Algo Desacuerdo | Algo De Acuerdo | Muy De Acuerdo |

8. Hombres y mujeres son caracterizados de manera no saludable y estereotípica en la TV y revistas.

| Muy Desacuerdo | Algo Desacuerdo | Algo De Acuerdo | Muy De Acuerdo |

9. Los muchachos solo quieren una cosa de las muchachas.

| Muy Desacuerdo | Algo Desacuerdo | Algo De Acuerdo | Muy De Acuerdo |

10. Está bien que un muchacho le diga a su novia con quien pueda hablar y que sea muy celoso si ella habla con otros muchachos.

| Muy Desacuerdo | Algo Desacuerdo | Algo De Acuerdo | Muy De Acuerdo |

APPENDIX D-6c. From Waterman and Walker (2009). Copyright by The Guilford Press.

Reacciones de Estrés Postraumático

- Ocurren luego de un evento que nos da mucho miedo.
- Son muy comunes entre estudiantes que han sido expuestos a violencia en el hogar, la escuela o la vecindad.
- Pueden ocurrir si eres la víctima de violencia o si vez un acto de violencia.
- Son reacciones normales a situaciones fuera de lo común.
- Tres tipos de reacciones:

1. *Reexperimentar el trauma.*

   a. Recuerdos o pensamientos acerca del trauma se aparecen de repente en tu mente.

   b. Soñar con lo que pasó una y otra vez.

   c. Sentir que el evento traumático esta pasando otra vez, como "flashbacks."

   d. Ponerte muy nervioso o incómodo si te acercas al lugar donde ocurrió.

2. *Evitar el trauma.*

   a. Evitar personas, lugares o actividades que te hacen recordar el trauma.

   b. Sentirte alejado de otras personas, como si no sintieras nada.

   c. Tener menos interés en cosas que te gustaban antes del trauma.

   d. Pensar que no vas a tener una profesión o familia o que vas a morir siendo joven.

3. *Sentirse mas agitado.*

   a. Tener problemas durmiéndote o manteniéndote dormido.

   b. Sentirte irritable o enojarte muy fácilmente.

   c. Estar distraído o tener dificultad prestando atención.

   d. Estar demasiado alerta en lugares donde pueda haber peligro, o sobresaltarse con mucha facilidad.

Estrategias para Bregar para Reacciones de Estrés Postraumático

1. Interrumpir los pensamientos

2. Distracción (ejercicio, leer, jugar un juego)

3. Imágenes positivas

4. Relajación (relajación de músculos, respiración profunda)

5. Hablar con alguien de confianza (padre, maestro, consejero)

Discos de Estrés Postraumático

Reexperimentar	Reexperimentar	Reexperimentar
Reexperimentar	Reexperimentar	Reexperimentar
Reexperimentar	Reexperimentar	Reexperimentar
Reexperimentar	Reexperimentar	Reexperimentar
Reexperimentar	Reexperimentar	Reexperimentar

APPENDIX D-7b. From Waterman and Walker (2009). Copyright by The Guilford Press.

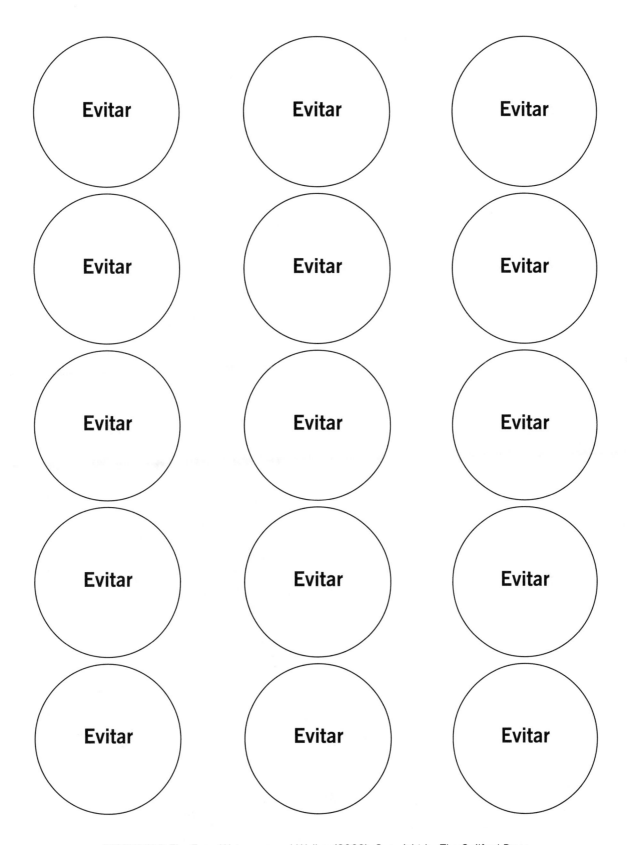

APPENDIX D-7b. From Waterman and Walker (2009). Copyright by The Guilford Press.

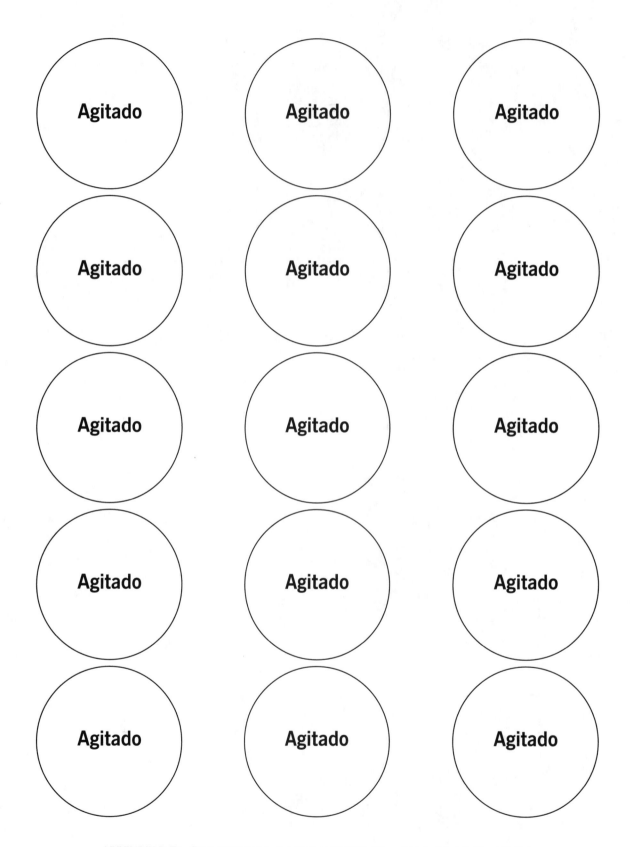

APPENDIX D-7b. From Waterman and Walker (2009). Copyright by The Guilford Press.

"Lo Que Me Gusta de Ti"

Nombre: _____

Miembro del grupo   **Lo que me gusta de ti . . .**

_____   _____

                            _____

_____   _____

                            _____

_____   _____

                            _____

_____   _____

                            _____

_____   _____

                            _____

_____   _____

                            _____

_____   _____

                            _____

_____   _____

                            _____

_____   _____

                            _____

_____   _____

                            _____

Certificado

Certificado de Reconocimiento

Este certificado se le otorga a:

_____

por haber competado con éxito el Programa SPARK

este _____ de _____, _____.

_____
Líder del Grupo

_____
Líder del Grupo

APPENDIX D-8b. From Waterman and Walker (2009). Copyright by The Guilford Press.

References

Armsden, G. C., & Greenberg, M. T. (1987). The Inventory of Parent and Peer Attachment: Individual differences and their relationship to psychological well-being in adolescence. *Journal of Youth and Adolescence, 16,* 427–453.

Briere, J. (1996). *Trauma Symptom Checklist for Children (TSCC): Professional manual.* Odessa, FL: Psychological Assessment Resources.

Goodman, G., & Esterly, G. (1988). *The talk book: The intimate science of communicating in close relationships.* Emmaus, PA: Rodale Press.

Gottman, J., Notarius, C., Gonso, J., & Markman, H. (1976). *A couples guide to communication.* Champaign, IL: Research Press.

Jaycox, L. (2004). *Cognitive behavioral intervention for trauma in schools (CBITS).* Santa Monica, CA: RAND Corporation.

Johnson, S. (2004). *Therapist's guide to clinical intervention: The 1-2-3's of treatment planning* (2nd ed.). San Diego, CA: Academic Press.

Kazdim, A. E. (1993). Adolescent mental health: Prevention and treatment programs. *American Psychologist, 48,* 127–141.

Larson, J. (2005). *Think first: Addressing aggressive behavior in secondary schools.* New York: Guilford Press.

Pedro-Carroll, J. L. (1985). *The Children of Divorce Intervention Program procedures manual.* Rochester, NY: University of Rochester Center for Community Study.

Phinney, J. S. (1992). The Multigroup Ethnic Identity Measure: A new scale for use with diverse groups. *Journal of Adolescent Research, 7,* 156–176.

Randall, K., & Bowen, A. A. (2007). *Mean girls: 101½ creative strategies and activities for working with relational aggression.* Chapin, SC: YouthLight.

Roden, M., & Abarbanel, G. (1993). *How it happens: Understanding sexual abuse and date rape.* Santa Monica, CA: Rape Treatment Center.

Rosenberg, M. (1979). *Conceiving the self.* New York: Basic Books.

Senn, D. (2007). Aggressor, victim, bystander wheel. In S. Bowman (Ed.), *Bullying in the girls' world: A school-wide approach to girl bullying (grades 3–8).* Chapin, SC: YouthLight.

Singer, M. I. (1997). *Exposure to Violence Scales: Grades 3–12.* Cleveland, OH: Case Western Reserve University.

Singer, M. I., Anglin, T., Song, L., & Lunghofer, L. (1995). Adolescent's exposure to violence and associated symptoms of psychological trauma. *Journal of the American Medical Association, 273*(6), 477–482.

Smith, D. C., & Furlong, M. J. (2008). *Multidimensional School Anger Inventory user guide.* Santa Barbara, CA: University of California, Santa Barbara. Available online at *www.education.ucsb.edu/csbyd.*

Swearingen, E. M., & Cohen, L. H. (1985). Measurement of adolescents' life events: The Junior High Life Experiences Survey. *American Journal of Community Psychology, 13,* 69–85.

Taylor, J. V. (2005). *Salvaging sisterhood.* Chapin, SC: YouthLight.

Watt, D. (1998). *I'm in charge here: Exposure to community violence, perceptions of control, and academic and aggressive outcome in inner-city youth.* Unpublished doctoral dissertation, University of California, Los Angeles.

Wiseman, R. (2002). *Queen bees and wannabes.* New York: Three Rivers Press.

Index